bLU TALKS PRESENTS

BUSINESS, LIFE AND THE UNIVERSE

Vol. 3

Compiled by

COREY POIRIER

bLU Talks Presents:
Business, Life and the Universe Vo. 3

Copyright © Corey Poirier, 2020

Cover Design by:
vcbookcovers.com

Interior (Formatting) Design by:
3daybookformatting.com

Read This First

Grab your free copy of The Book of WHY (and HOW) Audio.
Just to say thanks for downloading or purchasing this book,
I would like to give you a copy of my audio book,
The Book of WHY (and HOW), 100% free.

To grab your free copy, visit: www.thebookofwhyaudio.com

Oh, and don't forget to visit www.blutalks.com
for more information about bLU Talks.

Table of Contents

Introduction

As i sit here today, life is no less strange than it was when we released the first volume in the blu talks book series. We are still dealing with the effects of covid. People are still wearing masks every day, while others dispute the effectiveness of said masks.

A massive election that has ramifications around the world is about to take place. People in many places are still under lockdown (it feels so weird to say that in 2020).

People are looking for hope.

It is my dream that this bLU Talks book, and the bLU Talks brand, provides some of that hope.

It is also my dream that the important messages of those involved in the bLU Talks brand continues to reach more and more people.

In terms of how many people we have reached thus far, now that the brand has been launched for over a month, we have some stats and I couldn't be more grateful.

As of this writing, our YouTube page is averaging 10,000 views each week, the podcast has spent five of the seven weeks since launch on podcast charts. The last book in this series was #1 in multiple categories for weeks.

We have run four virtual events that have been viewed by over 50,000 people, based on the numbers we have been able to confirm, and have highlighted almost 50 bLU Talks speakers/authors alongside the likes of Les Brown, Michael E. Gerber, Heather Monahan, Larry Winget, and more.

We have also seen the release of eight bLU Talks speeches on YouTube and we have run four live events including bLU Talks at Harvard University featuring roughly 45 speakers, which allowed us to donate a lot of food to charity, and we were nominated for Entrepreneur of The Year (for me, but in connection with bLU Talks) plus more.

By the end of this year we'll have featured roughly 200 people across the bLU Talks platforms.

When I see these numbers it is mind boggling to me since we literally just started, and I truly feel I have you all to thank. #grateful

It gives me excitement for what the future holds for the bLU Talks brand and I hope that means more of these books which hopefully will give you distraction from the world at large while also inspiring, motivating, educating, and entertaining you.

Until then, again, I simply thank you for helping to make it all possible.

Yours in Success,

Corey Poirier

Oct. 2020

Powerless to Powerful

By Brittany Uchach

We all have moments in our life where everything feels impossible. Where the little things feel like big things and the big things feel like the weight of the world is on our shoulders. This feeling can be paralyzing and can make it terribly hard to move, especially when we fear moving the wrong way. The fear of knowing that nothing is certain and failure is always an option can make us feel powerless.

I want to take a quick second to take you back to a time where I felt powerless. Over 14 years ago I had the courage to come out to my friends and family. You know that feeling when something is literally eating you up inside and you absolutely cannot keep it in anymore? The weight of this secret of being gay was far too heavy to hang on to and I had to tell the world. In the LGBTQ world we all have different coming out stories, some are wonderful and empowering and others are a little more rough around the edges. Mine was a little rough around the edges and even though I was finally stepping into my truth, the internal battle between being who I truly was and who I thought I should be was difficult. I was terrified to be judged, not included, harassed, hurt and abandoned. There was so much fear attached to every outcome. The past 14 years have been an incredible journey for me. A journey in which I have learned to keep stepping into the best version of myself, a version that is true to me, who I am and what I

3

bring to this world. I want to share with you the things I have learned, the things that have worked, and the things that haven't. Despite the different things that make us all feel powerless, the feeling is still the same. My hope is that you read this and change that feeling of powerless to powerful!

The story you keep telling yourself is exactly who you have become and is the life you are currently leading; like Tony Robbins says, "you need to divorce your story and marry the truth".

If you are still wondering what this means, I am about to lay it on you. We all tell ourselves a different story in our head of why we are where we are, why we do what we do and where we are going in life. For example, for 15 years I told myself I was a poor, overworked personal trainer that could never own my own company, afford to buy a house, take days off and become successful. My story was that this is just how it is in this industry and there was nothing I could do, so I had to stay this way. Because this was the story I was telling myself I created the self-talk to validate it and I told myself this daily. So without any surprise this is exactly where I stayed for 15 years.

What is the story you keep telling yourself? That you're not lovable, always fail, not skilled, stuck, broke, will never be successful, that you have no other options?

Whatever you are telling yourself, you have to stop! Your self-talk, your story is where the best you starts but also ends. I know this because I held myself back for over a decade. So, what is the truth? Are you truly not enough, stuck, not lovable, successful and not capable of building a life you love and deserve?

Even if you don't believe it yet, you have to tell yourself a new story. The mind doesn't know the difference between what is real and what isn't. If you talk to yourself in a way that reflects the best version of you and puts you in the best possible light this is what will happen and what you will start to become. You have formed these bad habits over time so it will take time to make a new healthy habit of self-talk. It's exactly like a muscle, if you don't continue to keep working on it, it won't grow. So do not give up and keep building that new muscle!

Always choose action not motivation. This is where most people go wrong because motivation is crap. We are constantly waiting for the right time, or the time that we finally feel ready. Guess what?! This time will never come and if you continue to wait for it, you will be waiting forever and you will remain in the exact same spot. The answer to get unstuck is always taking ACTION!

Here are some tips on how to get moving and start taking action that doesn't result in failure.

Start slow and pick one or maybe two things to accomplish everyday so you don't start to feel overwhelmed and eventually quit making progress. If the things you have picked feel too big and overwhelming break them down into smaller chunks. For example, if exercising feels like a big task then break it off into committing to 15 minutes a day or even 15 minutes 4 times a week. Once you feel confident in that add another 15 minutes each day or where you see fit. Keep building on these new habits and actions you are bringing into your daily life because slow and steady wins the race. If you take on more than you can commit to you will always fail. This is why I never advise clients to make multiple changes at once.

"If you have an instinct to act on something, you must physically move within 5 seconds or your brain will kill it". If you have not read the book *The 5 Second Rule* by Mel Robbins, you must literally run to the store and grab it. This book is a game changer at helping you finally start taking action. The idea revolves around how we only have five seconds to talk ourselves out of doing something that we fear, feels overwhelming or is attached to a self-limiting belief. You just have to move your body. For example, you just finished work and are looking at your gym clothes in your car. You could easily talk yourself out of going to the gym or going home to complete your workout. When you feel that little voice in your head, countdown, "5, 4, 3, 2, 1" and then just move. Drive yourself to the gym or grab your gym bag from your back seat and walk right in that gym.

There are so many areas of our life that we can apply this rule to. Like I said before motivation doesn't just show up and you will not always feel like it, so count down from five and just do it. Sometimes all we have to do is start and we can keep the momentum going. If we just worked on becoming 1% better every single day instead of 100% better tomorrow, we would experience so much more happiness. Progress equals happiness in all areas of our lives. I have seen so many clients aim for 100% better right out of the gate and not be able to maintain all the changes and new habits they have taken on, that they throw their arms up in frustration only to give up and go right back to where they started. You will find that if you work at taking on small actions, building on them gradually, and keeping consistent with them you will actually make progress that is maintainable and will experience more joy and happiness than you ever have.

Stop giving your power away to people and things that don't deserve it and that drain your batteries. Take some time to really reflect on this and think about these things. These areas could be work, always saying yes even when you don't want to commit to something, breaking promises to yourself or your spouse, seeking approval from others all the time, not putting yourself first sometimes, or it could be friends or family who bring negative energy to your life.

There are two ways we give our power away. One is by allowing people and things that drain our energy from our lives, and the other is allowing people to make us "feel" a certain way. There is not a single person in the world that can make you feel anything. We have to get in the habit of owning our own thoughts and understand why they are creeping in and where they are coming from. Your partner, friends, or family cannot make you feel angry, inadequate, sad, guilty or stressed. It's a crazy thought but you have complete control over your thoughts which then directly affect the way you feel.

Emotions are good because they are a call to action. However, often what we feel isn't necessary as there is no action required. Doing an inventory of what you're feeling and then doing a reality check will filter out unnecessary negative emotions. If you find the emotion or feeling isn't necessary and isn't true then you can just let it go. If the feeling is in fact true then taking action to rectify it will dissipate any negative feelings or emotions.

Sit down and make a list of things, people, and emotions you are giving your power away to. Own your feelings because they are 100% yours and yours only. You always have the power and the choice in any situation. Start saying no to things that don't fulfill you and make you feel empty or that don't serve you.

To sum it up here is how you go from feeling powerless to powerful.

1. Start telling yourself a new story of who you are and where you are going

2. Take action instead of waiting for the motivation or the right time

3. Stop giving your power away through unnecessary emotions, people, or things that don't serve you

It's time to step into the best version of yourself. You matter, you deserve this and you can do it! Take it one action at a time, one day at a time, and stop breaking promises to yourself. I know you don't break promises you have made to other people, so get out of the habit of doing that to yourself. Make the rest of your life the best of your life.

Brittany Uchach has been in the fitness industry for over 16 years. She graduated from the Northern Alberta Institute of Technology as a personal trainer and is also a certified personal trainer through the Canadian Society of Exercise Physiology. Her mission is to help enrich people's lives through the power of movement and mindset.

She helps individuals who feel stuck and overwhelmed to transform their habits and develop a strong mindset with purpose. She creates energy and momentum for people struggling to finally start moving forward into the best version of themselves. She believes fitness and wellness is a frame of mind and it is in that framework we find happiness, thankfulness, energy, and possibilities.

The Essential Void

By Amy Neil

It's a Tuesday night, I just tucked my daughter back into her bed with a kiss and a whisper. Truthfully, I've been avoiding putting words to paper for a while now, but as I slipped into bed they arrived. When I first said yes to this journey of contributing to this book, I thought I'd be sharing something spectacular, a mind-bending story about animal communication and dog training. Something knock your socks off revolutionary about the dog-human dynamic. Yet, here we are months later, and I've stepped into my next chapter of life: a home design mentor for women, supporting them as they clear clutter and energize each room of their home, transforming it into a high vibe sanctuary for their soul.

It's been a slow, arduous, and not so beautiful process of letting go. Letting go of the business I loved so dearly, intuitive dog training, and growing into a new business with even more promise. In December 2018, that business led me straight into the dragon's lair of transformation and personal growth. It led me to the depths of my soul. It led me to the house and life of my dreams. The one I had mapped out on my vision board only months earlier. That little business took so many twists and turns in its 5 years of existence. From dog walker, to trainer, to intuitive animal communicator and healer. Underneath it all, there was a deeper heartbeat to my work with dogs. I felt a strong desire to build a healing retreat center for dogs. Never in my wildest dreams did I think I'd be telling you the story about how that all fell apart. I also didn't fully believe something better would come as I watched that dream slip away. Unbeknownst to me, my next best version was on its way in. Looking back, I now see how that business held the space for me to dream beyond my wildest imagination. It pulled all parts of me forward, into The Essential Void, whether I liked it or not.

The Essential Void is an interesting place. It's the space between where you've been and where you're headed. Everyone goes through voids, whether it's realized or not. Learning to recognize the void is a powerful life skill required to reach those dreams that feel too big or too outlandish to go after.

The Essential Void is an emotional state of being. It's a growth phase. It starts out as feeling everything you've created is wrong. Like nothing is going right and all that you can see is everything you don't like, enjoy, or desire. In its most intense form it can feel like everything is falling apart and despair can hit like a Mack truck. Especially true if letting go and releasing the old doesn't come easy. The fastest way to move though this first phase of growth and transformation is through embracing and acknowledging that you are growing. The void starts out as intense clarity around what is no longer working. Your heart is whispering "I am ready for more, let's grow." Your ego chimes in simultaneously and saying "stay here, it's safe here. The unknown is scary, stay away." Entering into the old is a time of deep, intense, unwavering trust. Your heart and higher self are calling you into the next best version of yourself, yet your ego says "no thank you". Simple awareness of this shift eases the myriad emotional responses that come as you release, grow, and expand.

The beginning of the void feels a lot like the start of a new home design project. First you look around and think "wow, I really dislike the color on the walls." You start daydreaming about new colors that you would prefer. Next your smaller self or ego chimes in and says "painting takes time, energy, and creates chaos, it's not worth the change." You are faced with a decision. The power of The Essential Void is in the clarity that the old isn't working and claiming your desire for change.

Once you fully embrace the void, addressing your smaller self is the next growth phase. The smaller self is comprised of primal, survival-based instincts, it doesn't want to grow. Growth and change are scary. It reminds us day in and day out of all the things you need to survive. When it comes to painting your home, A back and forth starts between your heart self and your small self. "Keep it the same," your small self says. "Pick a color that feels relaxing and luxurious," your heart self says. The easiest way to navigate this dialogue is by giving your small self a voice. Hear it out. Listen to what it has to say. Give that part of you a container to be heard. Journaling is a great outlet for giving your small self space to breathe and be heard. Feel into what is being kicked up. Before you know it, your heart self has more room to expand and soothe your small self. Equilibrium flows back in and, quickly, you are ready to welcome in growth and change.

The void becomes a powerful tool, when heart and small self are given their space to speak. Harnessing the power of your own sensitivity ushers in clarity around what no longer feels good for you. A path is cleared for you to flow into an open space for dreaming. This is the door to the unknown. The space is where your heart self leads the way. Standing in the doorway of the unknown you are able to claim your vision. It's a space of gratitude for all that led you here, and deep dreaming into what the next best version of you feels like. In a dream state, ask yourself what does each of your senses desire to experience? What does this dream taste, smell, feel, look, and sound like? Dream it into life. Stand in the door way of the unknown and breathe your vision into physical form.

The clarity of what no longer serves you begins to clear away. Clearing comes in many forms. Sometimes it's relationships, your body, or your physical living space that changes. The shift from there (the past version of you) to now (the next best version of you.) begins to gain momentum. This can feel really uncomfortable, if you don't know what's happening. Learning to hold on loosely is a key dynamic here. Letting go of control. Remember the power of The Essential Void is all about shifting. The real shift happens through taking action. Take radical action to clear out what no longer serves your next best version of you. Allow it to fall away.

The more you clear, the more space you make for new to flow in. As new versions of you flow, a rhythm starts to take shape. You begin to understand yourself on a deeper level. Your dreams begin to take shape. Sometimes, when you are fully in the flow of The Essential Void, it feels like hardly any effort at all. The new version of you that seemed like a dream flows in effortlessly. It is the attachment to safety that makes The Essential Void emotionally difficult.

Awareness of The Essential Void and self-care are the best ways to flow through this growth phase. Knowing, understanding, and embracing your emotional states are powerful tools. Society has taught people to ignore their emotions or to stuff them down. Have you ever eaten your anger or sucked it up? Pretending like emotions don't exist and badges of honor for the most intense suffering in life have become a fad in our culture. This is where you can lean on self-care.

One form of self-care I am focusing on here is essential oil aromatherapy. Essential oils are a powerful healing tool for the body, mind, and soul. They can support you in so many different ways. I prefer to use them for emotional support, during meditation, or journaling. Especially those times when my small self is kicking up dirt and I have freshly entered The Essential Void. Oils connect the body, mind, and soul together, creating emotional awareness. Essential oils can be used aromatically or topically. They have the power to calm, motivate, inspire, connect, improve emotional flow, and even enhance creativity. Every single essential oil is connected to specific emotions. Every emotion is linked to specific body parts. This is part of the mind-body connection. Simultaneous awareness of your emotional states and physical body states make self-care with essential oils a force to be reckoned with. Pairing body ailments, emotions, and essential oils together can provide deep amounts of emotional support. They are especially helpful if you aren't well connected to your emotional or physical bodies. Take your shoulders for example, they can symbolize carrying the weight of the world on your shoulders. Your teeth symbolize feelings of overwhelm, and your nose symbolizes running away or avoidance. If you know your shoulders aren't feeling great, this awareness can inform you of an emotional state wanting to be explored and healed. Bringing essential oils into the mix, whether you diffuse them or apply them topically can help you release whatever is holding you back as you grow into your next best version of you.

Say for example, you begin to experience throat issues. The throat symbolizes speaking your truth. Inquiring why you are feeling afraid to speak up can lead you to deeper levels of understanding yourself. Is it rejection? Are you afraid to be seen? Does speaking up feel too vulnerable? These are all emotions the small self will bring to the surface. This experience is an invitation for your heart self to heal and grow. In this case you can lean on lavender, lime, or even cinnamon essential oils to support great levels of courage and self-acceptance as you up level speaking your truth and courageous self-expression.

Of course, this is just one example of how essential oils can support your journey through The Essential Void. There are many different ways essential oils can help support the health of your mind, body, and spirit. Learning to work through the essential void is a key part of self-mastery. For me personally, it is how I supported myself in releasing my intuitive dog training business and embracing the next best version of me. Flowing through the void fearlessly is the next level of self-mastery. Essential oils and aromatherapy are great ways to care for yourself as you master The Essential Void. I learned to love the Essential Void and the journey it took me on. Learn to embrace and love the Essential Void and it will take you exactly where you desire to go too. It is the place dreams come true.

 www.nostalgiabyamyneil.com

Amy Neil is a home design and essential oil queen. She helps women who want to transform their home from cluttered and messy to refined and designed by helping them release physical, visual, and mental clutter so they can live in a home that feels like a sanctuary for their soul. One of the many ways Amy supports her clients to declutter is through the power of essential oils. She believes aromatherapy has the power to reconnect women back to their physical and emotional bodies in powerful ways. Over the course of the last decade Amy raised beef cattle, goats, chickens, planted countless gardens, and more! Those experiences solidified and reminded Amy that a home is more than a house, and it's an important place to invest time. She currently lives in Massachusetts with her husband, 2 kids, and 2 dogs. In her spare time she is reawakening her dream home and dusting off its nostalgic flair. To connect with Amy visit www.nostalgiabyamyneil.com

2020 The Year of Transformation

By Angela Morris

Nothing could have prepared me for this crazy, life altering year and I'm sure most of you reading this will feel exactly the same way. Let's go through the timeline quickly shall we: The devastating Australian wildfires that burned a record 47 million acres, displaced thousands of people and killed at least 35. Prince Harry and Meghan Markle stepped down as senior royals. On January 9th the World Health Organization announced that a deadly coronavirus had emerged in Wuhan, China. In a matter of months, the virus spread across the globe to more than 20 million people resulting in at least 750,000 deaths.

Who knew that by March of 2020 we would be in a full blown pandemic and the world as we knew it would shut the f*@k down. We lost Kobe Bryant on January 26th. The impeachment of US President Donald Trump was on February 5th. The disgraced Hollywood film maker, Harvey Weinstein was convicted on February 24th for rape and sexual assault. #MeToo movement. The Stock Market crash. The empowering and impactful Black Lives Matter (BLM) protests which erupted due to the unjustified and unnecessary murders of so many of my fellow African American kings and queens by law enforcement. Jeffery Epstein's "madame", British socialite, Ghislaine Maxwell was arrested on July 2nd for sex trafficking charges. Murder hornets arrived in the US. Champion of Gender Equality, the beloved Justice Ruth Bader Ginsburg died on September 18th at the age of 87. She was the second ever woman appointed to the high court.

How absolutely incredible is that? Take in all of that chaos, sickness, death, poverty, and suffering in a matter of nine months. I don't know about you, but reading that all at once made me realize that even in the midst of all that madness and destruction, I still managed to find the time to focus on pointless, insignificant shit that in reality doesn't even come close to any of the events that have happened and are still taking place. Are you guilty of the same thing?

When will we finally stop acting so oblivious to what is actually going on around us and open our f@$ing eyes to the decay of our beautiful planet? I am guilty as charged for this as well. I have been so fixated on such superficial shit and honestly it took this pandemic to get me to recognize it, acknowledge it, and inevitably change it.

I have never considered myself a victim. It didn't matter what life threw at me, I always figured things out. I have pulled myself out of some pretty dark and scary places, literally, and I am still here to tell the story. That, my friends, is only possible because of God's grace.

A wild child, a divorcee, a widow, once a single mom, a survivor of sexual exploitation, several other traumas, and now, a survivor of 2020. That is my life in a nutshell thus far. I worked damn hard to get to where I am today and although I am not exactly where I want to be (yet), I am proud to say that I am not where I used to be. My kids are happy, healthy and I am actually genuinely happy! So, how did I manage to pull that off during this wicked and vicious year? I am a big believer in "mindset is everything" and trust me folks, whatever you THINK and AFFIRM out loud will either build you up or tear you down.

It honestly still baffles me that I am a Mindset Coach. I am a MIndset Coach who started a business during a friggin pandemic! Looking at myself a year ago I would have never thought that this is what I would be doing and I especially never thought I'd finally get the balls to do it while the world was literally falling apart. Deep down I always knew I wanted to give back but I had no clue how. Looking at our current state of affairs, I strongly believe that this is the best time to offer myself to the world because so many people need encouragement, motivation, love, and inspiration to get through each day.

At the end of the day my friends, this life isn't forever. We weren't created to live forever so why do we spend so much fucking time being mad or stressed out? We literally worry about things that we have ZERO control over. Whatever is meant to happen will happen regardless if we spend time stressing over it so why do we continue to do it? I have spent the last several months in deep self-reflection and do you know what I realized about myself? I spent the last 25 f'n years being in a delusional state of "poor me."

I mean, how could I do anything for anyone if I didn't even have the strength to do anything for myself? You can meditate, practice yoga and chant all the f*@ing affirmations you want but unless you actually believe in what you're doing and saying, none of that will ever work. I found myself always being in a state of anger and anxiousness because my circumstances were never changing. How could my circumstances change if I was being a fraud? How did I actually expect things to change if I wasn't willing to put in any work? And let me tell you, half-ass work won't change a damn thing. Take it from me. That inconsistent half-ass shit won't bring you anything except half-ass results.

DEFINITION OF INSANITY: doing the same thing over and over and over again but expecting different results. What kind of madness is that? Well folks, that's exactly how I lived the last 25 years of my life. I wasn't prepared to fully acknowledge my own toxic bullshit and hold myself accountable for the crap decisions I had been making. So, if I wasn't going to admit that my own self-sabotage was quickly ruining my life, how would I ever have any chance of serving the purpose I knew I was created to fulfill?

Full disclosure...I struggle with inconsistency. I am consistent about being inconsistent, LOL! Until now that is. I was listening to another coach recently and she was explaining how imperative it is to be in full alignment with your thoughts because your thoughts are what produce your actions. In my excitement to gain wisdom and start a business, I took on several mastermind classes, webinars and free self-help courses, however, I became lost within it all. For as organized as I consider myself to be, I couldn't keep track of everything I was doing. The email reminders became overwhelming and I was unable to differentiate between what was actually a priority and what wasn't. I didn't realize that I wasn't obligated to say yes to everyone or sign up for everything that they were offering. I didn't have the time and I sure as shit didn't have the money! That same coach taught me about the importance of boundaries, how to set them and how to stick with them. It was one of the single most important lessons I have ever learned and I will be forever grateful to her for that.

In this modern day and age, we need to learn how to set those boundaries and follow through with a vengeance! I get it, that in itself can be incredibly difficult to do, especially if you're a people pleaser. I have spent my entire life (up until recently) trying to please everyone else and wanted so desperately for everyone to like me that I forgot who the f@*k I actually was. I lost myself completely. Let me tell you how exhausting it is to constantly live in a world where all you do is wait on someone else to validate your every move. I couldn't say no, to anyone. Not even to my kids. Parenting out of guilt and entertaining a circle of friends who really didn't have my best interests at heart. It was time to set some boundaries! If you have no boundaries in place you leave the door wide open for anyone and everyone to walk all over you. Saying NO is like second nature now!! I say no to anything and anyone, kids included, if it is draining me of my energy or interfering with commitments I have made for myself. And guess what...I do it without feeling guilty! Your true tribe will support you and love you always. They will understand you when you speak but they will also understand your silence. Not only will they understand it but they will respect it.

Now I am not gonna preach to you but it was my journey into spirituality that allowed me to get over myself and start living a life that I was truly proud of.

I know using the word God can scare people off but let's be real folks, we all believe in something. You most likely believe in some form of higher power that you feel determines the course of your life, right? Look at the devastation in our world. At some point, especially in 2020, you've prayed or done some version of praying for something or to someone, right? Whether you call it: Source, God, The Creator, The Universe, Intuition, The Divine or whatever other labels there are out there, you believe in something greater than you and that is what gives you hope.

Total transparency, I shouldn't even be here sharing this with you. When I look back at the high-risk lifestyle I lived, I should have been dead a hundred times over but here I am, writing a chapter for a bestselling book during a friggin pandemic!! WHAT!!! That is crazy but it is my reality and I owe that all to my higher power. I could have never taken the steps to change my negative attitude which then enabled me to give myself permission to ask for help which then in turn shifted my mindset. My life altered drastically for the better because I finally chose to fully surrender and let go of the stifling belief system I had been programmed to believe. I decided to choose FAITH OVER FEAR and that was the most freeing thing I had ever f@*king done. Just because you are alive it doesn't mean you are truly living. You are not here on this earth to just pay bills and die, that is not the way YOUR higher power intended you to live.

Do I have it all figured out yet? Absolutely not. I am human, I make mistakes, I curse, I allow my emotions to get the best of me sometimes and I still overthink the shit out of some things but I am not ashamed to admit that because I am and never will be perfect. I am living proof that literally anything is possible if you are willing to just let go and try something different. One of the best quotes I have ever read, "YOUR BRAIN IS YOUR BITCH," by Jen Sincero. It was like I was slapped right upside the head with the book when I saw that! How did I not look at it like that?

Again, it won't matter what you read, how many self-help seminars you attend, or how many life coaches you hire if you have not had YOUR "A-HA EPIPHANY." You need to hit your own version of rock bottom and embrace the beautiful chaos called your reality before you can move forward with an open heart and an open mind.

My past was meant to destroy my future but instead I turned my pain into my purpose. I had to uncover the blessings in each lesson and grant myself permission to heal. How could I possibly become a Life Coach and help other people if I were still that broken, skeptical, scared little girl? I had big woman dreams to fulfill and a predestined purpose to serve but I could not accomplish any of it until I looked deep within myself for the answers I so desperately needed.

We only get one life my friends, ONE. How do you want to spend that ONE f@*king life? Time goes by no matter what you do so why not challenge yourself to live blissfully happy. Take bold, deliberate, intentional action towards living your best f@*ing life and never look back! Cut off anything or anyone who disrupts your peace. Learn to love hard and forgive quickly regardless of past hurt you suffered because the only thing certain in this life is death. I apologize if that upsets some people but it is the truth. Allow your higher power, your intuition, to be your guide and unapologetically live your truth.

Stay safe and stay blessed.

 www.angelamorrismindsetcoach.com

Angela Morris is a Certified Life and Mindset Coach with a growing coaching business. She Is a mother to four amazing children and they are the reason for everything she does. Angela's purpose is to share her life story with others in hopes that it will help women realize that absolutely anything is possible, regardless of the circumstances they are facing. She wants to lead by example and empower others to tap into their leadership skills and understand their self-worth and potential.

Angela's life story has empowered her to be an advocate for sexually exploited victims, domestic abuse victims and suicide prevention. She is giving those who cannot speak a voice. Her journey to becoming a life coach who is now thriving in continuous growth and happiness has not been easy, but she has courageously endured extreme situations to understand that you will never become the best version of yourself without believing that mindset is everything.

How to Integrate
A Holistic Approach
into Ongoing Recovery
from Addiction

By Alan Simberg

My intention in this chapter is to provide you, the reader, with a basic understanding of what it means and how to integrate a holistic approach into ongoing recovery from addiction. This will be accomplished by explaining the rationale behind my therapeutic approach that focuses on four life areas that are affected by ongoing drug and alcohol use. Next the components that I have found to benefit from clinical attention will be described. I will then summarize the information presented with suggestions on how to utilize them either for yourself or as a tool in your clinical toolbox.

During my 48 years of professional experience counseling clients, I have developed a deep understanding of the factors which contribute to addiction and the strategies that have been most helpful to those in recovery. Over the course of my counseling career, I recognized that developing strategies to improve specific life areas helped different clients with their recovery effort to varying degrees. An idiom (i.e., "a chain is no stronger than its weakest link") which was first printed in Cornhill

Magazine in 1868 reflects my approach to helping clients. It made sense to me to see a single chain link as representing a specific life area that was receiving therapeutic attention and the entire chain reflected the state of recovery that each client was currently experiencing. I proceeded to apply this perspective by assessing each client's treatment needs and facilitated them to learn about four different life areas and strategies for managing each of them in a way that could complement their recovery efforts. My intention was to see if the effect on their recovery would be quicker or longer-lasting than when they did not focus on all four life areas and the accompanying recovery strategies. Although what I found is purely anecdotal, clients seemed to benefit more from this approach and their feedback to me supported my perception.

The four life areas were bio-psycho-social-spiritual (i.e., physical, psychological, social, spiritual). During clinical interviews, I assessed each client's level of functioning within each life area based on their reported level of satisfaction and the improvements they wanted to achieve. To further clarify how I applied this approach in my clinical work with clients I will now identify the focus of the specific life areas we discussed that included developing an individualized relapse prevention plan for each client as well as the skills and/or strategies related to each of the individual life areas.

The physical or biological life area relates to an individual's physical health which is affected by using harmful substances, their nutrition and quality of sleep. To help clients achieve optimal functioning in this life area we identified their healthy and unhealthy food choices as well as steps that could facilitate good quality sleep. I see this life area as providing a foundation for change in the other life areas which is based on the idea that good physical health is necessary to be able to manage the challenges we all face as effectively as possible.

The psychological life area relates to the way an individual thinks and manages challenges. To help clients achieve optimal functioning in this area we reviewed their "stinking thinking" (i.e., their past ways of thinking) as well as the current way they were thinking and helped them to identify and develop strategies that could facilitate their recovery efforts. In addition, clients were taught the cognitive behavioral technique of challenging their thoughts and exploring alternative ways to think about managing their challenges.

The social life area relates to an individual's interpersonal relationships and the quality of those interactions. As many of you may already know drug and alcohol use adversely affects relationships. And when you consider this within the context of the importance of human interaction to overall wellbeing it is essential to remember that the quality and maintenance of recovery is strongly connected not only to having fulfilling social interactions but also to making amends with those who were affected where doing so would do no harm.

The spiritual life area relates to an individual's concept of a creator or higher power and the accompanying beliefs to those ideas. It is interesting to me that people who tend to avoid and/or dislike the 12 Step approach to recovery think that any reference to God is meant to be accepted within the context of organized religion. They seem to misinterpret or misunderstand the actual meaning of the third step which clearly states, "made a decision to turn our will and our lives over to the care of God as we understood Him". What they seem to miss is the idea that they have the freedom to decide and define what God means to them.

Another reason that clients have told me that they are not interested in the spiritual component of the 12 Step approach is that they are angry with God for a variety of reasons. They have further explained that this was due to their having had a disturbing experience or that they were disappointed with organized religion in the past which seemed to be preventing them from recognizing the overall intention of the third step as reflected in the words, "as we understood Him". I have found that some clients allow themselves to consider giving the 12 Step approach another try after I introduce the idea of them possibly erroneously assigning blame to God for what they have experienced in the past.

The purpose of this chapter was to present a practical holistic approach that could facilitate and maintain an individual's ongoing recovery from addiction. The basic premise of this perspective is the sum is greater than its parts. To me this suggests that paying attention to as many contributing factors as possible to ongoing recovery would have a cumulative effect which potentially would be greater than if attention were just paid to certain parts of the plan. Therefore, assessing our own or each client's needs, facilitating them or ourselves to learn the needed strategies and monitoring progress provides the best opportunity to achieve and maintain ongoing recovery.

 https://www.alansimberg.com/

Dr. Alan Simberg has a Ph.D. in Counseling Psychology and is a Licensed Marriage and Family Therapist and a Licensed Chemical Dependency Counselor. In addition to being certified in Applied Clinical Nutrition he is a certified NET practitioner and has been certified by Mary Morrissey as a Dream Builder Coach and Life Mastery Consultant. Alan has 48+ years of professional experience helping individuals, couples, families and organizations to identify their challenges and implement solutions. He engaged in esoteric studies for 5+ years with a spiritual teacher. Alan contributed a chapter to a bestselling compilation book titled, "Share Your Message with The World".

He incorporates all that he has learned from his traditional and nontraditional trainings into a holistic approach that he has found to be highly effect when serving his clients.

Nana Korobi, Ya Oki

'Fall down seven times, get up eight'

By Becky Wells

Just like a famous Japanese proverb 'life is full of challenges', it's how we deal with these challenges that define our journey, our characters and the world around us. I'd love to take you on part of my journey. By intertwining my stories and those I've met along the way who've allowed me to share their stories. I'd like to give you hope, opportunity and the knowledge that anything is possible if you just believe.

If you met me today, you'd probably never believe how shy I used to be. I was hesitant to talk, even in a room full of my own relatives. An experience in my first career left me hiding in my shell like a turtle being stalked by a predator. In 1990, I embarked on my first job, fresh from school and excited to enter the world of adulthood.

I had plans after a couple of years to join the police force and had been a police cadet since the age of 14. Surprisingly, when I put on my cadet uniform that shyness faded and I truly believe this was the chink of light I needed, to know that somewhere in there was the real vocal me.

Anyways, back to the office...I'd been working there a few months and one thing people should probably know about me is I'm rubbish at lying, so when someone did something wrong and I was asked, I told the truth.

27

That resulted in the person in authority threatening to ruin my career before it had even begun. Hiding back in my shell I decided I would never speak out again; in fact, for ten years that included numerous promotional interviews. I kept quiet, never daring to speak out for fear of retribution. I don't think I even realised I was doing it if I'm entirely honest, it had become an ingrained habit.

I'd like to help anyone reading this chapter to learn how to find their voice and take ownership of their thoughts. Your quirkiness, your personality, your point of view, and your life experiences are the things that make you who you are. The idea of using my voice and sharing my thoughts publicly seemed impossible. I was the one who went pink, the one who read so quickly, so quietly, that nobody heard me.

Embrace the discomfort of the situation and I challenge you to take it a step further and lean into it. There's something quite incredible on the other side of discomfort. Imagine right now standing in front of a mirror of the person you wish to become. Use your powerful imagination seeing everything about that person. Their body language, their voice, the people around them. Even the people around that don't want to listen. One of the biggest pieces of advice I offered to a well-known public figure was to positively visualise the negatives too.

What do I mean?

A person that makes a negative comment to you may just be lonely and it's their way of getting attention. They may have their own challenges going on. Look at the biggest reactions generally on social media, they're often linked to negatives.

The shy person I was, realised that they were hiding behind fears, doubts and insecurities. When I stood up tall and embraced my quirkiness, I found people embraced me too. Yes, some will always judge and I know that's okay, because they're on their own journey, looking for their own tribe.

As you may have noted in the previous part of my journey, I was intent on joining the police. This was probably one of my biggest falls that sadly took several years, if not decades to recover from. A fit active athlete competing at county level and beyond, the physical aspect of the police entrance examination should have been a walk in the park for me.

I don't remember how, but I managed to rip a disc in my back, tearing it so badly that it's now beautifully held together with metal plates and wire! My whole life crashed around me as I no longer had a plan to follow. I was in a job where I was terrified to speak out. I was no longer able to join the police, because in those days that type of injury ruled me out of even applying again...a lucky escape I realise now when I look back.

The first fall in my life made me hide before I learnt to be seen again in full technicolour. This second fall paralysed me to hide behind my injuries. Without realising, I kept myself from recovering because of the fear of the unknown in the future. What if I didn't have pain, who would support me then. I had family and a medical team worrying about me. Who would I be without my pain?

One day, which was around five years after the operation. I was driving down a local country road and listening to a song on the radio, "Don't Stop Believin'" by The Journey, I think it had a profound effect on my coping mechanisms. Decades later it would have to be "This Is Me" from the Greatest Showman. What is your song?

It was like the flick of a switch. I realised then that everyone in the past who told me I was holding that band aid in place, had been telling the truth. I literally ripped it off.

It had been too easy to be fuelled by the negative. The attention I received was still attention. However, I now know that there is a fine line between healthy attention and unhealthy attention, but because it became part of who I was, I just didn't see it.

How can we overcome this?

Just like the epiphany in my car, it is to acknowledge the fact that we are seeking attention or approval from others. At that point, fear or self-doubts may kick in, but remember, the current attention is not healthy and may potentially lead to the need for more and more. A truly negative downward spiral.

Learn to focus on what makes you happy. I love being a storyteller, I use it with my work as a therapist to explain a situation. It can be challenging to accept every part of us, but that is where self-confidence begins. As we accept who we are, we find we don't need others' approval. Our own opinion should be the one that matters.

What do you love to do?
What makes you happy?

Just because you're not going down the same path as other people, doesn't mean it's the wrong path.

Words always seemed to get confused between leaving my mind and either entering the tip of pencil, pen or being tapped out the end of my fingers onto a screen. It was as if gremlins fiddled with the order of words, the meanings; they even hide my full stops from me.

I was always the one who was told I'm just not concentrating when writing, I got away with a lot because of being the athletic one at school but I'm pretty sure there are important documents from my initial job which make no sense at all.

Becoming more and more fearful of putting pen to paper, my spoken words had become louder over time as my own self confidence grew, but my writing had been fading away in the background.

Stories that needed to be told were silenced to the back of my mind rather than shared out in print.

Why would someone wish to read my words? What difference can I make?

Let me tell you what difference your words can make.

To the friend who was struggling with all that's going on in the world, those words can make a life changing difference. Learning to share a word or two has allowed friends around me to know I care when they're struggling to stand up again.

The person struggling and wondering, why bother with this world, knows someone is there. That first step, that first call or message of help. That's why I learnt to find my pen again. I want to be reading about that person's future stories, not their obituary.

I was not stupid,
I was not lazy.

Sometimes when writing I feel like I've got a football team of naughty gremlins playing a disorganised Superbowl or football match in my head, but I've learnt and I'm still learning to team manage them.

Get those neurons playing in format. Neuroplasticity is the brain's ability to grow new neurons and this only happens under certain conditions. As an example, a combination of exercise and the process needed to learn new ways of moving, causes new neurons to grow. Are you ready to get that team playing in formation?

Myself and my team of gremlins are now, at the grand old age of 47, in their second year of university, studying a BSc in Health Science. I'm extremely proud of my achievements to date and I can honestly say I've found a new voice.

I had been stumbling along in life, getting back up, brushing myself off and carrying on. What lessons did I learn along the way?

- Well, that shyness is actually one of my superpowers. It taught me an invaluable lesson, the ability to observe. As I listen to clients, to friends, or people in general. I observe their body language and their tones. It's interesting how being the quiet one gives me an insight beyond a person's words.

- The journey you are taking may not seem to make sense, it may not feel logical but surprisingly when you look back, it will all make perfect sense. I've had people comment that I've had a mixture of unrelated jobs, but when I look back at that well-worn path behind, I can see each job, each experience has taught me about people. It's taught me the power of observation beyond words.

- It also taught me the ability to be unique and use that uniqueness to inspire others by starting to explore new pathways and opportunities.

"Life should not be a journey to the grave with the intention of arriving safely in a pretty and well-preserved body, but rather to skid in broadside in a cloud of smoke, thoroughly used up, totally worn out, and loudly proclaiming "Wow! What a Ride!" as quoted by Hunter S. Thompson.

I challenge you to put on those knee and elbow pads as you jump on that metaphorical ride of your life. I want to hear your exclamations of excitement as you take the path less travelled, but a hell of a lot more adventurous!

No more what if's when you look back.
No more if only...

I've got my safety pads firmly attached, I've got a fire in my heart... well, if I'm entirely honest it's a cheeky mischievous gremlin, but don't tell anyone else that.

Yes, I'll fall down I'm sure, like I have many times in the past but as the famous Japanese proverb states, 'Fall down seven times, get up eight', I'm going to see it as a place to rest before the next adventure.

We have one life to live and I'm determined to live mine to the max. Are you ready to join me?

You can find out more about my stories at www.beckywells.com

www.beckywells.com

Becky Wells is a UK based International Hypnotherapist and Intuitive Coach.

After leaving school at 16, I embarked on my first career as a civil servant, only to find early on that bullying prevented me from ever getting promotion. After ten years I left and continued on a career path towards a field I was, and still am, extremely passionate about - health and mental wellness.

My passion has inspired me to train in several therapy techniques, which work seamlessly to help individuals, using a combination of hypnotherapy, tapping techniques and neuroscience techniques. I have been featured in several magazines over the past ten years.

I am also studying a part time BSc degree in health science; should be finished in 2024!

In my spare time, I am generally found outside with my friends, walking my two gorgeous dogs. I also enjoy the spiritual side of life, including oracle and angel cards.

My work is my passion; it's like a heartbeat within me. Helping individuals thrive and overcome gives me more energy and passion than I could ever explain.

Like the story of Cinderella, I discovered I could go to the ball and it was also alright to go in my Converse trainers and a hoodie.

Becky's website

Into the Lyme Light

By Nattacia Greene

Seven weeks ago, I looked at my biofeedback results. There were no *Borrelia* bacteria. No *Bartonella, Babesia,* or *Mycoplasma*. No trace of the tick-borne pathogens that plagued me for eight long years. I scanned the pages again in disbelief, making sure my birthday wish came true...an uncontrollable grin spread across my face. Tears welled with joy. I held my hands over my heart and closed my eyes to pray: *"Thank you Universe for this healing, for showing me the way, for creating in me a new heart and a new life. Thank you for your continued loving guidance, in living my purpose for this world."*

It feels incredible to be free from Lyme dis-ease. I'd love to move on and never speak of it again...but I feel this deep sense of responsibility to help those who are still suffering. To spread awareness for change. And to share the blessings in disguise that came with surviving a life-threatening illness.

Seven years ago, I was struggling with late-stage chronic Lyme. I was twenty-two years old, but I felt a century older. I could sleep seventeen hours and wake up exhausted. Walking from one room to the next required pauses, hands clutching the walls to keep from blacking out. My main goal everyday was to eat, despite the chronic nausea, and to take the antibiotics that were slowly killing me, yet allowing me to survive.

Time warped together. I slept propped up on pillows, hungering for air, crying in pain with involuntary tremors. Nightmares haunted my sleep. A constant tightness in my chest felt like wearing a metal corset. Chronic chills, cold sweats, hot flashes and profuse sweating kept me alternating clothes day and night.

Housekeeping, dressing, and preparing food became physical and mental difficulties. I couldn't think clearly to do tasks that had been second-nature. If my then-husband was home from a three-week stint, he'd help with personal care and errands. I was barely fit to drive. After an appointment, I'd rest two days. After a social engagement, I might rest for four. I became a social recluse.

I felt embarrassed in public, let alone with family or friends. Communication, emotional regulation, and appropriateness were severely impaired. I lost my mental filter. I was slow to find words, repeated myself, and called people by the wrong names. In some nice clothes, makeup and hair done, I appeared fine. Few could see my afflictions with arthritis, debilitating pain, and dementia.

Cognition declined. Reading, watching television, or following a film storyline became taxing. Listening to music, my long-time therapist and friend, was painful too. I could hear electricity running through anything plugged in. Some days I wore sunglasses indoors. All sensory input was intensified.

My spine felt like a hot metal rod on fire. My head felt like a pressure cooker on high with no valve for release. This was Lyme meningitis. *(For further understanding of a similar experience, <u>Brain On Fire</u> is a telling resource.)* Being conscious in my body was excruciating. I began involuntarily floating out of it. Depression was an understatement. I felt only pain, apathy, and rage. And like a useless burden to friends, family, and especially my spouse.

Canadian blood tests were negative, while specialized American testing showed exposure to Lyme. Local alternative treatments and out-of-country testing and antibiotics drained our savings. The progression slowed and I was alive, but living in agony. I sought pain-relief from local doctors, but was rejected. I felt like I was dying. I knew my name, but didn't know who I was. I didn't recognize myself in the mirror. I saw no hope for the future and didn't want one if it meant living in that hell.

Seven years ago, I sat down to write letters to explain why I ended the pain. I was content with my decision. At peace. Even excited at the thought of relief. But when I neared pen to page, I abruptly woke from that dark dense daze. Suicide would devastate many if I didn't get help.

Seven weeks later, I sat in a circle in a group therapy room in a psychiatric hospital. I pondered a quote on the wall: *"Don't put your key to happiness in somebody else's pocket."* The Serenity prayer became one I turned to often: *"God, grant me the serenity to accept the things I cannot change, courage to change the things I can, and wisdom to know the difference."*

I saw doctors daily, but they refused to help with what ailed me. I was ridiculed, humiliated, and told it was all in my head. Therapists disagreed. They watched me sit restless in silent insanity from the pain of being in my body. Finally, I was prescribed with analgesics. One medical doctor took me seriously. He contacted the university's Division of Infectious Diseases. "We don't deal with Lyme disease" they replied. It was outside their education. They weren't willing to consult international resources. I accepted what I couldn't change. So, I focused on my mental health.

In group, we examined family dynamics, childhood traumas, patterns and conditioning. We learned anger management, affirmations, and meditation. I felt dumbed down on drugs, but these dulled the hypersensitivity. I could listen to music again and let it heal me.

The art therapy was incredible: a ceramics studio, leatherworks, woodwork, a craft room, and musical instruments. I delved into playing piano, singing with guitar, and painting my heart out. These were the gifts I'd been missing; the pieces of me the dementia couldn't touch. I didn't need to know who I was to create or connect with myself and others. It took losing my mind to rediscover the artist.

Tolerable pain, new coping strategies, and a fresh perspective provided hope. I wanted to give life a chance. Before I left, my therapist gave me a set of Divine instructions: *"Look into positive psychology, Eastern philosophy and alternative medicine."*

Home afforded freedoms: cannabis for nausea and appetite, fresh fruits and vegetables, and the solace of family pets. I implemented everything relearned: a schedule, good hygiene, getting dressed, going to sleep at ten. I used music to raise my energy, help me feel, motivate and keep me company. I bought a guitar as medicine and dedicated space for creative expression. Visual reminders were displayed to support a substantial shift in mindset.

I reflected on who I became through so much pain: pessimistic, irritable, and unpleasant to be around. I journaled about who I wanted to become: Optimistic, Happy, Loving and Radiant. Every month, I visualized this healthy version of me. And every day, I did my best to emulate her.

Positive psychology, neuro-linguistic programming, Eastern philosophies *(i.e. Buddhism, Taoism)* and affirmations upgraded my mental health. Daily meditation generated self-awareness. I dropped victimhood for a victor mentality, and took responsibility for my life. I stopped focusing on limitations and practiced gratitude. Problems transformed into challenges; circumstances into opportunities for growth. The nightmares became adventure dreams. No longer would I be tortured by the dragon. I would tame it, and ride it into the sun of a new dawn.

I studied nutrition, Ayurveda, Chinese and American herbalism. I couldn't retain what I read, but I could write. I made charts for my kitchen, lists of detoxification practices, and documented everything I did. Lemons, turmeric, dandelion tea, probiotics and chlorella became staples. Stretching, gentle yoga and salt baths reduced inflammation. After three months of cutting out gluten, refined sugar, dairy and preservatives, energy improved and arthritis disappeared.

I read every ingredient I put in or on my body. Over-the-counter medications, hygiene, cleaning, and beauty products containing toxins were discarded, and replaced with natural alternatives. With less toxic load, the body was better equipped to eliminate dis-ease.

Synchronicities led me to essential oils, colloidal silver, and herbal tinctures. These have natural antibacterial, antiviral, antiparasitic, and antifungal properties. With no access to modern medicine, I treated myself for Lyme meningitis, Lyme carditis and parasites. The harsh tinctures rendered unconsciousness, but doing nothing could be fatal. Unlike pharmaceuticals, these had few side effects. As I progressively detoxed, cognition returned.

Sacred plant medicines opened my perception, sparked scientific and spiritual insights, and unhinged deep emotions to be healed. Quantum physics, sacred geometry, gemstone crystals and experiments (scientific and personal) proved the power of thought and vibration over matter.

Treatments were effective but overwhelming. I needed more support. People had prayed for me for months. It was time I renew my personal relationship with Spirit. One day, I sat down in the shower and prayed:

"God, I believe in you. I'm ready for your help. I'm sorry I stopped talking to you. I'm sorry for how I treated my body, for not loving myself. Please forgive me." I cried, forgave myself, and released past guilt and shame. I finally accepted unconditional love and assistance. *"I don't want to die. I'll do anything. God, bring me to the best medicine, the best practices and people... whatever I need to fully heal. I want to live for my purpose, whatever that might be. Please show me the way."* That simple conversation was a catalyst for more miracles.

Spiritual guidance came daily. Angels visited and spoke to me. I began mental and energy training in dreams, like Neo preparing to re-enter the Matrix...

With improved health, I worked odd jobs to finance complementary therapies: reiki, massage, acupuncture, craniosacral, past-life regression, shamanic soul retrieval, and family constellation. I felt well enough to return to a nursing degree, but forsook that dream for holistic studies.

I trusted intuition with a willingness to learn from every part of Creation: color, sound, symbol, number, mineral, plant and creature. I interpreted subconscious information from dreams to heal old wounds and grudges. And I worked on the emotional and metaphysical components of every physical ailment.

Everything is frequency and vibration. We experience the energy we project. This led to the energy medicines that ultimately brought vibrant health: custom frequency remedies, homeopathy, and Bio-Electro-Magnetic Energy Regulation. As the frequency of the body rises, dis-ease cannot exist.

In truth, Lyme allowed me to heal from two decades of ails before that tick bite. I'd been depressed since childhood; coping with isolation, people-pleasing, perfectionism, eating disorders, addiction, over-achievement, and codependency. I didn't know how to love myself, and worried excessively, manifesting my deepest fears into reality.

Lyme was my greatest teacher. She taught compassion, self-love, and the art of being present; courage, perseverance, unending faith and trust; to detoxify my mind, body, home, and relationships; prioritize play and relaxation. To live in gratitude, forgive all, and release all judgement. And she revealed the true meaning of wealth: health, love, joy, time, energy, and interconnection.

Seven years ago, I was pressed to believe I could be the woman I am today. I am twenty-nine years young. I love my life. I am happy, healthy, laugh often, love my body and treat it well. I make music, paint, meditate and follow my bliss. I jog, hike, drive again, and enjoy time with loved-ones. And most importantly, I know who I AM. I feel beyond blessed for the gifts that showed up in exactly the right place and time. I live my purpose in sharing these with all who are open to receive them.

With compassion, I founded Vibrancy Holistic Health; focusing on integrative and non-invasive energy medicine, holistic health education, and personal empowerment. We believe in root-cause healing as opposed to symptom management, and teach our clients strategies from first-hand experience. We offer remote healing sessions and PEMF microvascular therapy to support the body's natural healing systems. We hold a special place for those affected by Lyme, and anyone seeking assistance for chronic illness, trauma recovery, lifestyle transitions, and health transformations.

You are worthy of happiness and health. You can do anything if you believe it. Let faith be stronger than fear. For we live in a world of miracles.

Namaste. God bless. And love always,

Nattacia Greene
Holistic Health Practitioner
Vibrancy Holistic Health
www.vibrancyhealth.ca

www.vibrancyhealth.ca

Nattacia Greene is a Holistic Health Practitioner specialized in Energy Medicine, Public Health Education, and Personal Empowerment. With a background in Biological and Nursing Sciences, and success in overcoming multi-systemic Chronic Lyme Disease and coinfections, she founded Vibrancy Holistic Health. As a Certified Reiki Practitioner, Authorized BEMER Electroceutical Distributor, Lightworker, Intuitive Clairvoyant, Meditation Guide, and Feng-Shui Consultant, she is passionate in supporting clients through holistic healing, lifestyle transitions, and health transformations, through the gifts, resources and technology that saved her life.

Nattacia is an artist, painter, poet, musician, singer-songwriter, and composer. She enjoys exploring the natural world through hiking, rock climbing, paddle-boarding and kayaking. Her yogic lifestyle comprises of aromatherapy, shamanic journeying, stargazing, and lucid dreaming.

She is an auntie to thirteen, a loving girlfriend, a mental health advocate, and an altruist for positive change in the world. She loves volunteering, taking cross-country road trips despite a fear of driving, and continues studying the many cultures, spiritualties, sciences, psychology, and medicines of the world. Nattacia's vibrancy and zest for life are sure to spark hope and motivation for gaining optimum health and happiness.

Someone is Trying to Tell Me Something

By Brenda Juby

It was a Saturday evening. The children were in bed and I was lying on the couch exhausted with every part of my body aching. My head was spinning as I was trying to understand how this could possibly have happened again. I had just returned home from the hospital after my third car accident in ten months. I said to my sister who had come to help me and the kids, "someone is trying to tell me something and I'm not paying attention." There had to be a message behind these car accidents as I was assured by the doctors after each accident that I should have died. Yet, here I was, alive after a third car accident with only soft tissue damage and a mild concussion.

The previous year in April, my husband of fifteen years walked out on me and our marriage. I had come home from a twelve-hour shift when I noticed a suitcase packed at the front door. As I walked up the stairs into the living room, I saw my husband sitting on the couch. I asked him about the suitcase and what he said blindsided me. His words felt like a knife stabbing and twisting through my chest, ripping my heart out. My world as I knew it would never to be the same. I was left numb inside.

Two weeks after this on Mother's Day, my children and I were driving to my mother's home. I was driving through an intersection when a car proceeded out from a stop sign. I had a split second to react. That car hit my car on the passenger side and we ended up on the other side of the road, facing in the other direction. The passenger side door was indented a foot. Myself and my two children were all okay, just a little shaken up. The ambulance took us to the hospital where my mother met us. She called my ex-husband to tell him about what had happened and to ask him to come and pick us up. I remember the look on his face when he saw us. He looked scared yet he remained distant. He drove us home and after making sure we were settled, I again watched him walk out the door of our marital home.

Fast forward nine months from that first accident to February. I was going down a country highway about 80 km/h when I saw, out of the corner of my eye, a truck moving out from a stop sign and proceeding through the intersection toward me. Again, I was hit. It happened so fast yet it felt like it was all in slow motion. When my car finally stopped, my car was backwards in a ditch. I remember feeling panicked and just wanting to get out of the car. I frantically tried to open the door, but it wouldn't budge. I felt closed in and just needed to get out. The whole inside of the car was dislodged and pushed forward towards me. Somehow, I managed to get myself free and over to the passenger seat where I tried that door; it also did not open. By this time, the driver of the truck who hit me had come to see if I was okay. All I could do was scream at him "What were you doing?!"

I was extracted from the car and transported to the nearby hospital. Once at the small-town hospital, the emergency doctor looked at me and said, "Whatever you did, it saved your life." That hit me hard as I honestly did not know what I had done to come out of this accident in one piece. Again, I had to call my ex-husband to come pick me up as the car was not driveable. To this day, I remember him standing at the doorway to the hospital room just looking at me. He did not come near me, he just stood there with a blank look on his face as we talked. I never felt so alone as I did on that day

The next month, I was driving home from picking up my youngest son from hockey when I was again struck at an intersection by another car. The driver had run a red light. The day had started out as a regular Saturday filled with my children's activities. But this was a special day as I was picking up my new car that afternoon. During the morning, my children and I had been joking about the two car accidents I had and what if I have another one. We never thought that would have come true.

After they removed me from the car with the jaws-of-life, my son and I were taken to the hospital for assessment. I do not have much memory about this accident. Other than seeing my light turning green, I have glimpses of a policeman looking down on me in the car; someone covering me with a blanket as I was screaming; and then being in the ambulance with the EMS attendant asking me if "I knew where I was going". For about 30 seconds my mind was blank but then I remembered I was on my way home. I was lucky that I had no broken bones only soft tissue injuries to my neck, back, and groin and a mild concussion. I still remember the look of shock on the doctor's face when I told him that I was still in physiotherapy from my previous car accident only 3½ weeks earlier. It all seemed so surreal. My ex-husband took us home and left once my sister arrived to stay with me for the night.

I still don't know how I am alive today. I do believe that during those car accidents angels were around and keeping me safe. In the first ten months after my husband walked out, I was like a robot hiding from my reality of being separated. I was just living in the busyness of life, children, part-time work and going to university part-time. I was drowning in my pain and the varying emotions of anger, disappointment, fear, and what I thought was failure as a wife. I remember having intense fear whenever my friends tried to get me out of the house for a movie or dinner. The thought of change scared me to death and left me paralyzed. My friends joked that I had turned into a real "Martha Stewart" focusing only on my household and what needed to be done and nothing else. Every time my ex-husband would visit, I was either sad and heavy-hearted or short-tempered and yelling at him for not wanting to talk about our marriage. There were times I would just go to my bedroom and cry silently after he left. Instead of being the energetic positive woman I used to be, I now was lonely, sad, and did not know who I was without my marriage. My life had stood still for those ten months between my car accidents. There was no growth, no expansion, and no fulfillment in my life. I definitely wasn't thriving.

I did not fully understand what had happened to me until I had the third car accident. It was a gift; a mirror to show me that I had given up on life and was merely surviving day-to-day and even at times, minute-to-minute. The third accident was the final wakeup call that had me start to question what I was missing. It was time to lift the veil clouding my vision to see my situation through fresh eyes. I stopped numbing out and avoiding and started to listen to my inner voice that knew it was time to shut the door on my marriage, go on with my life, and change my story to one of possibility.

It wasn't until I saw my separation as a blessing that I saw my lessons clearly, and even much later realize I was resilient too! I had never thought about my resilience, as I only saw myself as a survivor. However, I knew I needed to stop just surviving and begin thriving.

Since this experience, I have had many moments that have provided me with a deeper understanding of resilience. I believe that as individuals we are all resilient and with the appropriate tools and resources, we are able to express ourselves, expand, and bounce back from any challenges we may face in our lives. Three keys messages I have come to learn with fostering resiliency and thriving in life are:

1) Invest in yourself and your development as a person. Go within and start to explore who you are and what feeds your soul. It is when we slow down that we have courage to listen to our inner voice and intuition. This could be taking time for you, exercising, journaling, taking moments to stop and do some deep breathing, or tapping into your spirituality e.g. praying, meditating, etc It is really hard to make change when you don't even know who you are.

Questions to Ponder?

- Who am I?
- What is my purpose?
- How do I want to be and feel?
- Why I am here?
- What do I need?
- What do I want to do?

2) Lean into the experiences you are having in your everyday life. We live in a world where we go from one moment to next without ever understanding how they are impacting or distracting us from our life purpose or joy in life. This requires us to slow down and reflect. It is when we intentionally take the time to step outside the situation that we truly understand what is going on within our self, the other person, between us and the environment around us. Don't fear your experiences but get curious. It is through curiosity you can embrace, forgive and find the love within. Let that empower you.

Questions to Ponder?

- What am I thinking about this experience?
- How am I feeling?
- How does this feel inside my body?
- What was happening in this relationship?
- What outside factors were contributing to this experience?
- What resources or supports do I have to draw upon?

3) Focus on what is working rather than on what is missing. Change your perspective and lens to see the light within your experience. We live in a deficit society where focusing on the negativity or risks that we are experiencing is the norm instead of reminding ourselves of the positive aspects or strengths that we innately have.

Create spaces for conversations about your dreams, aspirations and being. Have the courage to tap into your strengths to not only empower yourself and others but use when faced with challenges. Embrace the opportunities and challenges that you are facing in order to understand and change the landscape of what is happening in your life. Move away from just surviving toward thriving as that is what we ultimately deserve.

Questions to Ponder?
- What are my strengths/talents?
- In previous difficult situations what helped?
- What resources do I have to increase my resilience?
- What have I found to be helpful when faced with uncertainty?

Through unravelling what it means, I triumphed over the voice inside that said I was not good enough or worthy and began to cultivate a practice of self-love and understanding of who I was personally, professionally, and spiritually. In the end, I chose to see the situation through the lens of opportunity and not defeat.

The car accidents are one of the many life-changing events I have been blessed with in my journey of life. Each one, whether positive or challenging, has provided me the greatest gifts, learnings and transformations. I am still a work in progress, but with each experience I am more inspired and confident in embodying who I am and the unique gifts I bring to the world.

http://www.remoment.org/

Brenda Juby is a Registered Nurse with a Master of Nursing degree who has dedicated decades of her life to helping and serving others in the health care field. Later in her career she felt drawn to use her experience and Masters degree, to reshape and refocus on education, working with schools, communities, organizations and nursing students. Through this work, Brenda became interested in the topic of resiliency and the importance of developing personal strength.

For over 10 years Brenda has been empowering students and staff to explore their current ways of thinking to discover and deepen resiliency in both professional and personal life.

Brenda has been peer reviewed, published, and is an active facilitator.

Through Brenda's personal journey of surviving 3 major car accidents, she discovered a path to spirituality. It was through exploring alternative forms of healing, she came to understand who she was and how her experiences were enhancing her life. She now takes these powerful learnings and shares them with others to inspire, provide hope and create resiliency.

A proud wife, mother, and grandmother, Brenda aims to create a legacy and have influence on the lives around her through holistic wellbeing.

Garage Walls, Grafts, and Gratitude

By CHRIS DT GORDON

My garage wall almost killed me.

To be fair, I did throw the first punch, so it was really acting in self-defense.

Truth to tell, I accepted what happened to me soon after waking up in the hospital. What occurred, while at the time was terrifying for my family and friends, has offered me a plethora of opportunities to better myself and others around me.

What happened? Well, to grasp the magnitude of my tale, we need to step back and look at my life before the wall and I had our fateful encounter.

I grew up in a small town 10 miles north of Flint, Michigan called Clio (named after the County Line 10 train line). For as long as I could remember, I was a member of Messiah Lutheran Church in Clio. Even through college, where I attended a satellite campus of the University of Michigan in Flint and earned a bachelor's degree in Elementary Education, I (more-or-less) stayed consistent with my worship.

Towards the end of my college career, I became friends with John, a vicar at Messiah who hailed from Minnesota. Long story short, our mutual love of most things geeky strengthened our friendship, and he asked me to be in his wedding a few years later. Since he was a pastor, his fiancée Jill was a Christian schoolteacher, and they had many mutual friends in the wedding party, they decided to have a joint bachelor-bachelorette party. I happily accepted and flew out of the Twin Cities to join the festivities in early June 2002. John and Jill picked me up from the airport and brought me to the hotel where the soiree would commence.

As I reconnected with John and met his brother Mark and a few of his friends, a vision of beauty burst into our hotel room and yelled, "Let's go!"

It was his sister, Becky.

Skipping ahead past the parts where I moved to New Ulm, Minnesota later that summer, married Becky in 2005, and had three fantastic kids, I accepted a teaching position with Minnesota Virtual Academy, a public, online school as a middle school special education teacher. My previous position was 50 miles away, and it was tough enough with one small child. Once the twins were born, I started looking for something closer. Eventually, I traded 50 miles for roughly 50 steps (the distance from my bed to my office, tossing in a side trip to the bathroom or to let the dog out).

So, back to the interaction with the garage wall. While Becky and the kids were preparing to leave for school/daycare, I picked up two-year-old Seth (one of a pair of twins) and flew him to the garage, swaying him back and forth. I misjudged my distance from the garage wall and accidentally scraped the back of my right hand against it. It bled a little, but it wasn't a steady stream, so I placed Seth into the van, kissed everyone goodbye, waved them off, and went into the house. I washed my wound as well as I could, put antibiotic cream and a bandage on it, and started working with my online students as an online middle school special education teacher.

Three days later, I woke up to discover a red, lacrosse ball-sized bump on my right elbow. Becky and I had gone bowling the night before with her teaching colleagues; did I torque my elbow in a weird way trying to get that 5-10 split? Regardless of its cause, I drove myself to the walk-in clinic at the local hospital. The attending doctor replied that it could have been bursitis, and that I should keep an eye on it and come back if the situation changes.

Ten hours later, I came back.

The red bump on my elbow had spread throughout my arm, shoulder, chest, and back. I basically looked like the Incredible Hulk in mid-transformation. Additionally, I was extremely lethargic and slightly nauseous. I retained my quirky sense of humor intact, as evidenced by the picture I asked Becky to take that showed both my puny Banner arm (the left one) and the Hulk Smash arm (right).

What was less humorous was the sepsis that my body was experiencing.

The nurse couldn't obtain an accurate blood pressure reading on me. At the time, I didn't think too much of it as I was overly occupied with my ginormous right arm. Later, I researched the effects of sepsis...I'm happy I was ignorant.

Put simply, sepsis is the body's overreaction to an infection. Imagine that you ask your child to pick up a toy off the floor, and the child burns the house down; that's sepsis.

The medical staff kept me overnight; in the morning the attending doctor approached me and said that they could not do anything else for me; my problem was beyond them. She followed up by asking me where I wanted to go. Immediately I said, "Mayo (Clinic in Rochester, MN)."

Few hospitals exist where you can identify them by one or two words alone. Mayo is the Cher of health care providers; you could say "Clinic," but to most people, it's superfluous. The Rochester, MN health care giant is world-renowned for their expertise and list of high-profile patients. Saudi Arabian royalty have made their presence known in Rochester beginning in 2009 when seeking medical assistance. So, telling the doctor that I wanted to go there was a no-brainer. Plus, my in-laws Bill snd Dea lived 10 minutes from the hospital, and Bill was one of their chaplains. That way, Becky and the kids could stay someplace safe and familiar for the few days I would be there. Certainly, this would only take a few days.

Right?

They soon wheeled my gurney to an ambulance, whisked me away to the municipal airport, and strapped me tightly into the gurney which was then latched to the inside of the cabin of a Cessna-style airplane (they would've used a helicopter, but a snowstorm was quickly approaching). After 20 minutes of practically kissing the cabin wall, we landed, and I was wheeled to another ambulance and taken to St. Mary's Hospital, the largest hospital within Mayo Clinic.

Once there, things start to get fuzzy. I vaguely remember seeing Becky and Bill as I entered the hospital, and the next thing I remember is having a surreal conversation with the surgeon who would end up performing my first operation. I was seated in a wheelchair, and I felt my head listing back and forth. Apparently, the surgeon informed me that I had contracted necrotizing fasciitis (flesh-eating bacteria), and they would start removing the infected skin and underlying tissue; again, my memory of the conversation is not lucid. I do recall being rather gung-ho and "jokey" about the whole situation. This weirded out the surgeon a bit; he was used to people in my situation being scared, weepy, and more concerned for their lives, not cocky and jovial while in a drugged stupor.

That's the last thing I remember for about five days.

At the time of my first surgery, the infection had encompassed my right arm, shoulder, chest, and back. Doctors used a red marker to track its progress as they were preparing me for the procedures. The employed a similar technique to how firefighters battle a forest fire: They marked spots ahead of the trouble spots so they would be sure to completely remove the infection. When the red marker line touched the base of my neck, Becky left the room.

I was fortunate to have a world-class team of surgeons and medical professionals save my life and body parts. Becky was told before my second surgery that they were going to amputate my right arm, no question. The infection had progressed so deep into my forearm that they thought that it couldn't be saved. However, the occupational therapist in attendance noticed that I still had hand function, so they removed a 15" by 4" flap of skin from my left thigh (that included part of an artery) and attached it to the back of my hand and forearm. Since it's my thigh on my hand, I call that flap my "thand"; I might copyright that term.

Since I had a 60-square inch section of skin extracted from my left thigh (and I have large, runner/soccer player thighs), doctors could not close the wound without making physical alterations. So, they removed my vastus lateralis (the exterior thigh muscle) and attached a double knob/Jacob's ladder-type contraption to my thigh. Two knobs flanked both sides of my wound, and doctors tightened them over time using the Jacob's ladder in order to close the wound. In addition to my thand, I now also have a "tri" instead of a quad in my left leg.

When a significant portion of your torso is filleted, you need numerous skin grafts to cover that area. It's a good thing my thighs and back were ready to serve! The surgeons used a skin graft harvester (imagine a souped-up cheese slicer) to remove over two dozen slices of my sweet, sweet ivory goodness and placed them all over the infected areas, which were already covered with foundation material that helped the skin grafts take hold more securely. Fun fact about skin graft harvesting sites: they do not fully heal, so it looks like I had a horrendous waxing mishap. If I were awake during my surgeries, I would've yelled, "Kelly Clarkson!"

The next thing I remember (again, five days after I went under), I was at the bottom of a water slide, engulfed in a huge cast, immobilized by a thigh brace, and being pummeled by gallons of green water. You likely have two questions after reading that last sentence:

1) When did they start installing water slides in hospitals?

   Answer: Never. I was hallucinating while throwing up after awaking from a four-night coma.

2) Why was the water green?

> **Answer:** It was the fluid that doctors used to take CT scans of my body as I was out.

I was, to say the least, not pleased to find myself in that scenario. My brother Jeff, who had traveled from Michigan to help Becky and the kids, almost jumped back on the plane after seeing my tirade. I also scared a nurse; I should have apologized to her. Thankfully, Jeff did not leave. Instead, he called Becky and Bill to let them know I was awake. He also gave me an iPad; I've since forgiven him for the jerky things he had done to me over the years.

Over the next few weeks, I experienced several hallucinations that freaked me out on many levels (case in point: the water slide). As my numerous surgeries caused me severe, debilitating pain, doctors prescribed me painkillers to deal with the agony. One of those was Ketamine, a powerful antidepressant and painkiller; it, however, can cause severe hallucinations. I had never taken or been prescribed "hardcore" drugs before, so I was not ready for what I would face. Some of the more vivid mindfreaks include:

- The room flipping upside down
- Seeing bugs and open windows inside my ICU room...in March
- Hearing the "Macarena" ad nauseum (Note: ICU rooms do not come with radios.)
- Imagining that Becky had brought me a bag full of comic books and a Tesseract-shaped hologram projector that displayed several famous Marvel Cinematic Universe scenes
- Seeing a picture of the Disney movie *Mulan* in a ceiling tile directly above me (it even included the line "The greatest honor is having you as a daughter" written on a scroll)

I consider myself a reasonably intelligent and even-keeled person (weird and awkward, but still even-keeled). So, when I experienced those hallucinations, it REALLY messed with me. I thankfully did not suffer any post-traumatic stress disorder, but those instances have really stuck with me, even though I know they weren't real.

That said, I'm still convinced there was a leaky swimming pool above my ICU room.

The rest of my two-month hospital stay (yeah, a little longer than a few days) improved as the weeks passed. As I strengthened, my recovery procedures also evolved. For instance, shortly after losing my catheter (I won't go into that), I started walking. My first jaunt was from my hospital bed to the nearest nurses' station; after that 30-foot trip (that's counting from my bed), I was wiped! A week before I fell ill, I had run a Pi Day race (3.14 miles) in 19:29. That isn't a shabby time, so to go from that to needing a nap after shuffling 10 yards could've been a devastating blow to my ego. However, I kept something firmly in mind that protected my fragile self-image...but more on that later. I kept up the walks, advancing farther from my bed each time until I could walk the length of the two-block hallway unaided. Then I added stairs to the mix and continued to progress.

I also experienced 15 trips to nearby Methodist Hospital via ambulance where I participated in 90-minute doses of pure oxygen in a hyperbaric oxygen chamber. They would wheel me into the center, take my vitals, place me in a leather recliner within the bus-sized chamber, slip a Family Dollar Mr. Freeze cosplay helmet over my head, and let me nap for a pair of 45-minute stints, taking a five-minute break to return the complimentary cranberry juice I downed before I started the procedure.

Additionally, I lost the enormous cast that cocooned my right arm, trading it in for a pulley system and sponges. My muscles atrophied from lack of use, so I needed to rebuild them. I wasn't a bulky guy by any means before the incident, but my forced sedation caused my right arm to look almost surreal. Tanya, my wonderful physical therapist, would come into my room every other day or so to make sure I was working out the right way. Initially, she helped me sit down on the floor of my room with my back against my bathroom door and fastened the pulley system to the top of it (the door, not my back). At first, my poor deltoids struggled with the weight of my stick-like arms; but with persistence (and ALL of the protein shakes), my strength quickly returned. Cara, Bridget, and Stephanie (a trio of fantastic hand specialists) helped me regain grip strength and dexterity with the use of sponges, foam grippers, and hand squeezers. Stephanie was also the one who basically saved my arm in that second surgery, so I really need to hand it to her.

At this point in my story, many people wonder how I could have stayed so positive during this entire ordeal. I made that conscious decision a couple days after I awoke from my medically induced coma. Becky sat down next to my hospital bed and explained how so many people stepped up to help us out. From reflecting on my faith, to family and friends visiting us and watching over our house, to colleagues buying toys for the kids, to complete strangers donating hundreds of dollars to a GoFundMe account established by a high school friend of Becky's, I was overwhelmed by the love and generosity that we were shown.

At that moment, I decided to adopt what I now call The Attitude of Gratitude (remember what I mentioned earlier?). I knew that I would have bad days, but I would not become pessimistic or overly negative. Doing so, in my opinion, would be a slap in the face to everyone who helped us out.

That mindset kept me positive and optimistic for the duration of my stay at Mayo and helped me make several friends among the staff, especially Dr. Karim Bakri and the nurses (including Kris, who actually bought me a DVD of my favorite movie at a weekend garage sale). It allowed me to thoroughly enjoy my time with visitors, including the numerous lunch and evening visits with Bill and Dea, a date night with Becky, a weekend social call from my best friend Dave and his wife Beth (who flew in from Montana), and a second visit from Jeff, who brought HIS Becky and their daughter, Hope. It also fueled me with a burning desire to nor merely return to form, but to surpass my previous bests.

Since my discharge in May 2015, I've:

- Set or tied four personal running records
- Won four races and finished in the top 10% of virtually every race I've run
- Run in three Ragnar long distance relay running events, including an Ultra (where I ran 33.5 miles in about 24 hours)
- Set a goal of qualifying for the Boston Marathon before 2030 (Note: I do NOT run marathons well.)
- Earned my recommended Black Belt in Tae Kwon Do
- Secured my Autism Spectrum Disorder teaching license

In January 2020 I also decided to pursue public speaking. I had performed a few speaking engagements before that time, mostly for high school health classes to show off my Deadpoolesque physique to future medical students. When January 1st rolled around, though, I felt driven to share my story and message to a much larger audience. After a couple months of soul searching, I decided that middle and high school students would be my target audience. Like me in the hospital, they are facing tribulations that will test them physically and mentally. However, they lack my life experience and may need a solid foundation on which to anchor themselves when times get tough. By seeing that they have so much more going for them than they first realize, they too can more than rise above their struggles; they can forge their futures and become the leaders we need them to be. I've also started a podcast called Scar Bearers that I've used to sharpen my speaking skills amidst the pandemic and offer other survivors a platform on which they can share their own tales of trial and triumph.

Life is crazy. One week you're outrunning kids less than half your age; the next, you're almost dying while experiencing an origin story worthy of a comic book superhero. We don't really know what tomorrow has in store for us. The best we can do is to be thankful for all we have, acknowledging those whom we appreciate, give others a chance to be thankful, pass on perfection, and go for greatness!

We can also score a legitimate beer prescription, but that's a story for another time.

https://Linktr.ee/chrisdtgordon

chrisdtgordon@gmail.com

You can also search for
"Chris DT Gordon."

Chris DT Gordon is a faithful husband, father of three, online middle school special education teacher, professional speaker, runner, Tae Kwon Do student, and pop culture geek. He is also a survivor of necrotizing fasciitis (flesh-eating bacteria) who uses his story and message to inspire others to adopt The Attitude of Gratitude and positively affect their lives.

Brought to My Knees

By Chris Ferguson

On March 23rd, 2012, I had just gotten out of bed and was in the process of getting ready for work when I started feeling an extreme heaviness across my chest. I had no idea what it was but I just didn't feel right. I called work and said that I wasn't coming to work and I was going to contact my doctor's office as soon as it opened. I told my boss I would let him know the findings.

The pressure kept getting stronger and stronger as the time passed before I could contact my doctor's office. I called my husband who was still living in South Florida because he had 25 more months until he could retire. He would commute to Tennessee about every six to eight weeks depending on my schedule at work. We kept talking until almost 8:00 AM when I could call the doctor's office.

At 8:00 AM, I called the answering service and they connected me with the backline to the office. I explained my symptoms to the nurse, who knew my history and I did not have a history of any heart issues but due to the type of work and driving distance I do every day to get to work she was thinking it could be stress or a heart attack. She recommended I get a friend to drive me to a specific hospital in a town 50 minutes away. She then said if the pain gets worse, call an ambulance. Of course, I didn't even consider calling an ambulance and there was no one locally to me I could call to drive me.

I started looking for all the things that I needed including my car keys, my driver's license, and my medical cards. I then left the house and started heading towards the hospital. I noticed I needed gas and I didn't have my gas card with me since I only brought what I thought was necessary for the hospital at the time. I turned my vehicle around and drove home. The whole time the anxiety was increasing from not knowing what was going on with me physically. I wasn't far, but I live rurally so it took about 15 minutes to get home. I grabbed my gas card and headed towards the gas station to fill up my vehicle so I didn't have any other issues keeping from making this drive.

I called my husband from my OnStar phone in the vehicle. We kept talking about how I was feeling and if I was okay the entire way to the hospital.

I arrived at the hospital ER and explained to the nurse I was having an extreme heaviness in my chest. I then went through the admissions process to be seen by the physician. They hooked me up to the blood pressure cuff and checked my oxygen level. A lab person came with an EKG machine to check my heart rhythm. The lab personnel came into my cubical multiple times doing different things like taking blood, checking my heart rate, and my blood pressure.

After several tests and approximately four hours later, the Doctor came in to see me and give me the results.

She started out saying, "Ms. Ferguson, your heart is fine but we need to admit you into the hospital". I was extremely puzzled. I asked her if she was absolutely sure my heart wasn't the issue. The chest pains were so extreme by this time I was becoming unsure of everything around me. The next words out of her mouth were mind-blowing for me. She said, "You have two pulmonary embolisms, one in each lung." I looked at her and I was confused and I asked her what an embolism was? She replied, "You have blood clots in your lungs."

At this point, I felt like Charlie Brown in one of his cartoons where he is at school and the teacher is now talking and I do not understand a single word being said. I checked out in my ability to comprehend, listen, or acknowledge anything or anyone. I went into a state of shock. I do not remember being taken from the ER to my hospital room. I do not remember calling my husband and telling him the news. I didn't have the capacity to comprehend my next step in life.

I remember laying in the hospital bed scared to close my eyes, would I wake up? Then the thoughts became even more real, what about the next moment, minutes, hours? I became very vulnerable of the unknown. In my life, I am not intimidated by much, but this put me on my knees in fear. I couldn't even put it in perspective until the thought came to me, you need to prepare for your death. I then thought, how do you do that? My mind started racing. Who can think further than this moment after you have been diagnosed with pulmonary embolisms in each lung?

I stayed in the hospital for a week because my body was not leveling out with the Warfarin I had been prescribed. The doctors are making my blood thin so I do not develop any more clots but I still had to get the blood clots in my lungs dissolved in a slower process. I was out of work for seven weeks to get my blood levels where they needed to be. I had daily check-ups at my doctor's office to monitor my blood level.

Being home every day was really rough for me since I have been working since I was 12 years old. The biggest issue for me was the acceptance side of being vulnerable. The thoughts of life are precious and the next minute is not promised. I started thinking of the simple things I could do from this moment to the next to not allow myself to dismiss, take for granted, or without being present in the moment for myself, my husband, my children, and grandchildren.

I started taking better care of myself physically, started watching my diet, and in interacting with people. Even though I am in good shape, I eat healthy, I started noticing the little details I had overlooked in the past. I started to rely on my intuition more, enforcing my boundaries more, and seeing the whole picture of each incident, person, or situation.

I have always been of service to people in my career, but this incident was taking me to a whole new level of love for life, love of others, and love for myself on a spiritual level. I have volunteered most of my life to children's organizations to help those who do not have that support, guidance, and wisdom in their lives to become their best selves.

 www.chrisferguson360.com

Chris Ferguson has been in the Law Enforcement / Corporate Security industry for over 40 years. She graduated from University of Phoenix with a bachelor's degree in Criminal Justice Administration. She had also graduated from both Correctional and Police Academies through the course of her Law Enforcement career. She is also certified as a life coach, Advanced Ho'oponopono Practitioner, Intuitive Investigator, and Medium. Her mission is to help guide others through the knowledge of how to change the mindset in their lives.

Chris helps people become authentic and positive in their lives professionally, personally, and individually. This creates the ability to enhance the opportunities in their life in becoming their best version of themselves in all relationships, the first relationship is the most important one and to start with self-awareness in your life. This will set all other relationships in life.

Authentically Bullied

By Chris Wilson

To this day, I'm always reminded by my aunt that I was born during the 1984 Olympics. Although I can't really remember what games were played and or took home the gold, I can always depend on my Aunt Louise to tell other people that I'm good luck because I was born on August 1, 1984, year of the Olympics in Los Angeles.

I was born in Whittier, California to John Earl Wilson and Brenda Flores Wilson, two hard working parents. I like to think that they were so happy with me that they made only one of me. Honorably, I can still claim the title as the only child. Raised Catholic, my mom gave me a biblical name. First starting with Christopher, which meant Christ. Then came my middle name, Michael. This was given to me exclusively by my mother. Saint Michael the Archangel, who is not technically a saint in the Catholic religion, but rather an angel who is the leader of all angels and of the army of God. You might recognize his picture as he is often portrayed as stepping over the devil with his sword raised high in the air. His name was given to me so that he can always protect me. And Wilson, well, I'm sure you can figure that one out.

I never really had a big family, but I feel that they were just enough for me. My dad was your typical by the book guy. He was the one who would open a box of something that needed assembling and read the instructions first. He believed that there was always a process for everything no matter what.

My dad was born in Bay Minette, Alabama in 1940. Growing up as an African American man, my dad experienced racism on a regular basis. Some of the stories he told me made me cringe because I could not believe one person could treat another person so degradingly simply because of the color of their skin. He moved to California in search of a better life and opportunity at the age of 18. For many years, he worked at Western Electric. He made it to a supervisory level where he met my mom. Before suffering a stroke that forced him to retire, my dad woke up at 4:30am every morning with no complaints driving his 1975 cherry red Corvette Stingray listening to the tunes of Smokey Robinson. He was always a very committed yet stylish guy.

My mom, on the other hand, is probably the hardest working person you will ever know. She was a mother of many creative talents. For much of my life, she was always involved in some sort of blue-collar job. Whatever it was, she always put in 100 percent of effort into it. That's just who she was. She was the type of person who put others before herself. She was born and raised in East Los Angeles. She'd kill me if I spoke about her age. So, I won't. Her mother was a housekeeper and lived until 100 years old and her dad was a walnut picker, turned jeweler, before going on dialysis.

Growing up, I never really had a lot of friends. In fact, to this day I still don't. I always could manage to count how many best friends I had with one hand. I suppose we all have our own definition of what friends are. I had three best friends that I could consider were my "ride or die." Today, they are still in my life and while they have their own lives, we are still as close as ever. I originally met Mark, James, and Domata both in elementary school and middle school. Those years were the hardest of my life. One of those traumatic moments that I never was open to talking about until recently was when I was bullied.

I attended Hillview Middle School in Whittier. Our mascot was a husky. I guess you can say I really wore my school colors proudly because I was very much into school. However, one of my school periods that I dreaded going to was Mr. Pritchard's Social Studies class. It was not because of what was being taught. Instead, it was who was in it. His name was Randy and he sat directly behind me in Mr. Pritchard's class. We were both seated somewhat in the middle left of the room. Randy sat directly behind me. He wasted no time in making his presence known to the class with his loudness and outbursts. It was always a good day for me when he was absent or in detention. For the days he would be in class, he would aggressively tap me on my shoulder and whisper disturbing remarks to make me turn around. At times, I eventually did. Otherwise he would not stop what he was doing until I did. Then came the kicking of my book basket under my desk. We all had one in class. What was the annoying part was when Randy would kick it and it would send waves of penetration. He would do this consistently until he either got tired or I turned around. Very seldom would I say anything to Mr. Pritchard. I think it was because I was more scared of what would happen outside the classroom than inside. Randy did not know what the words, 'leave me alone' meant. It got to a point where I eventually dreaded going to school. He bullied me during nutrition, lunch, before and after school, and frankly anywhere where he would see me. He would make fun of me in front of others about my hair. I had an afro at the time. I would be later given the nickname Fro, which I accepted, however until then I had to endure years of teasing and bullying.

My parents were hardworking people who did not make a lot of money. Every morning before leaving school, they would put four to six dollars in my mom's pink jewelry box for me. That was my lunch money for the day. However, my hands were not the only ones who touched those dollar bills. Eventually the bullying got so bad, I had to pay Randy nearly every day to leave me alone. It was so embarrassing that it got to a point where I had to ask my parents for double the money. I never told them the truth. Instead, I made up stories like they were raising prices at school or I lost some of my money. To this day, I cannot believe I looked my mom and dad in the eye and told them bold-faced lies nearly every day.

In eighth grade of middle school, Randy eventually dropped out because his grades were not so great, and he missed too many school days. That was music to my ears because it meant that I wouldn't be bullied any more, and I was free from telling my parents any more lies as to why my clothes were always dirty.

Today, I look back and sometimes wonder what ever happened to Randy. Yes, I was robbed of my two years of middle school and I will never get them back. However, I also know that we all have stories as to why we do what we do and why we feel what we feel. Today I am encouraged to speak openly about bullying because I know firsthand how it can affect a child's life. I'm also a big believer that a bully is only as powerful as allowed to be. I forgave Randy a long time ago because I knew what he did to me was deeper and bigger than he and I. Most of all, I forgave Randy for myself and to move on.

I was immensely proud to have been born in the mid-1980s. Largely because I was fortunate to grow up and listen to 90s music in High School. I loved every type of music genre that was out there except for country. Today, not so much. One of the artists I was really into was Craig David. He was a British Pop and R&B singer. I stumbled upon one of his hit songs scrolling through the radio one day and fell in love with him soon after. It was my sophomore year when I really got wind of him. I eventually bought his album.

One morning during class, my best friend Mark came up to me and said, "Fro, did anyone ever tell you that you look like Craig David?" I was flattered by Mark connecting me to Craig David in that way. Keep in mind that all throughout high school I had low self-esteem and no confidence. I remember going home that afternoon and looking myself in the mirror comparing myself to the British artist. One of his signature features was his facial hair. Craig David had clean and slim sideburns connecting to his goatee and mustache. As soon as I walked in from school, I went straight to my mother's bathroom. I searched for her mascara. I took the edge of it after lightly dipping it into the black tube and carefully drew a line connecting my sideburns to my goatee. After applying the mascara, I took my thumb and lightly smudged it to create a shadow and not make it too fake. I remember spending nearly an hour in the bathroom going back and forth comparing whether it looked good or not. I woke up the following morning and enthusiastically walked into the bathroom to apply the makeup. When I stepped foot onto campus that morning with the newly applied mascara, I confidently walked around. I managed to receive a few looks from girls but not as many as I hoped. I kept applying the mascara on for the next week. Toward the end of it, one of my close classmates approached me in awe and confusion while looking at my face. She said, "Fro, do you have mascara on your face?" I was embarrassed as I answered her. "Yes, I do." She replied, "Why?" I did not really have a straight answer other than "I wanted to look and feel like Craig David."

At the time I did not realize I was trying to be someone I was not. All I cared about was wanting to be liked and noticed, even if it meant putting makeup on my face. To this day, I look back and reflect that I was not being my authentic self. Despite my flaws and insecurity, I was not being my true self. I was doing my best to fool everybody with fake makeup simply because I wanted to feel and look like someone I was not. I admit it was an amazing feeling when I first heard the compliment from my friend and then receiving the same from others after that. It is one of my most intimate and open stories I am proud to share today. Back then, and even two years ago, I was very embarrassed to tell that story.

Sometimes it is difficult being authentic because of the many distractions the world presents. And sometimes the things that make us amazingly beautiful and unique are the very things bullies attempt to make us feel bad about. However, with all my trials and flaws, I accept who I am and love who I am not. I am emotionally and mentally stronger that I ever was because of my past. Most of all, I am a regular kid living in a small town focused on inspiring people one story at a time.

Christopher Wilson was born to two working class parents in Whittier, California who believed in hard work and the value of a dollar. His father went on to become one of the first African American supervisors at AT&T while his mother marched alongside social justice movements for better wages, healthcare, and working conditions.

His grandmother, who lived until the age of 100 years old, was his role model, inspiration, and the reason why he got involved in public service at the of 16.

🌐 **https://wilsonforthefuture.com/**

✉️ **mr.wilson562@gmail.com**

🐦 **@mr_wilson562**

📷 **@mr_wilson562**

Chris believes in being authentic to yourself, comfortable in uncomfortable situations, and making mistakes.

His upbringing from elementary school to high school presented a lot of challenges both in and out of the classroom. Nonetheless, Chris is who he is today because of the sacrifices his parents made and the choices Chris made for himself.

Today, Chris has the great fortune to be in a position to encourage and motivate young leaders with his story and life experiences. He is a believer that as we climb, we should lift.

Chris is a public servant, community activist, public speaker, and was labeled a "Hidden Gem in the South Bay" by VoyageLA Magazine in early 2020. Most of all, Chris is an African American and Latino man who lives in a small town focused on inspiring people one story at a time.

The Burdens We Carry

By Crystal Berscht

The heat of the mid-morning sun became unbearable under the suffocating weight of my backpack. Clenched teeth could no longer fight against the gnawing pain that shot through my foot and sent daggers into my hips and low back. My once steady walk was now a staggered limp, while subtle groans of frustrated defeat seeped from every pore, forcing me to stop. My screams of neglected rage were consumed in an angry cloud of dust as I repeatedly stomped my trekking poles into the hardpacked ground of the Camino De Santiago.

For days the cramping pain worsened, but I pushed on. I ignored my body's pleas to slow down, to pay attention, to see the lesson unfolding in front of me. The constant discomfort of every movement hid the suppressed fury of an ancient narrative begging to be heard. I was unaware that the surge of fearful old stories was pushing me into the habit of passive survival.

Two weeks prior, a warm sense of inspired hope surrounded me with the rush of fresh mountain air as we stepped off the bus in the quaint, cobblestoned village of Saint Jean Pied de Porte. My optimistic excitement hid the fragility still lingering from the cascade of confused and scattered lessons that unfolded in the preceding months. It started with a pointed question: "What do you think is fantastic about you?" The unresolved pain of my youth was exposed, as the walls of protection I had built around myself started to crumble.

As we approached the lush misty mountain side of the Pyrenees, I relaxed my pace, scanning from side to side before swiftly scooping up a rock a little bigger than my hand. My quest for this journey was clear: discover what was fantastic about me. I held the stone tight whispering, "it's time to let go of the pain. It's time to heal. It's time to move on." Closing my eyes for a moment, I imagined the stagnant energy of suffering releasing its grip on my body and entering this stone of burden, before I slipped it into my backpack.

The clang of hidden cowbells near and far was the only sound that broke through the dense fog. My mind drifted to the fragmented memories of my high school sweetheart and the tortured poems that once spilled from my heart, revealing a mess of unrelenting sorrow mistaken for love. I was eager to please, even though his hurtful charm strung me along at arm's length. The trail of promises captivated me, even after I knew they would be broken or forgotten.

My thoughts cleared with the lifting fog as we made our final descent of the day. Though my body ached with fatigue, I felt light with gratitude knowing those days were behind me. That night I stared at the bunkbed overhead, lost in an orchestra of snores, too tired to sleep. I thought back to the previous summer when I struggled to fill the blank pages of my "I love me journal" – my first attempt to improve my relationship with myself. Every evening I'd impatiently stare at the wall, before jotting down a quality I thought others might like or appreciated about me – "I am adventurous." The harder I tried, the harsher my inner critic relished, as salty tears left more imprints than ink.

Steep slopes turned to quilted hills and valleys. With every step forward I ached with exhaustion, but my spirit felt energized. Fellow pilgrims came and went, sharing inspiring and emotional fueled stories of the day before or the challenges of life. For the first time, I talked less and listened more. I became spellbound by the generous honesty and trust of strangers who felt like close friends in a matter of hours. But no matter the depth or openness of others, I only grazed the surface of my own tales, saving my deeply hidden stories for the private company of my travel companion.

My life felt like a hopeless mess not worthy of divulging. Shame often hung heavy when words of blame or complaint mindlessly escaped me. I'd beat myself up, believing I pushed others away with my negativity and the emotions that easily arose, convincing my mind of an unforgivable weaknesses. I felt lost and confused despite my honest attempts to improve the transpiring hurt that brewed within.

Less than a year before, I clenched a soggy tissue while sitting across from a gentle soul who practiced mindfulness-based counselling. Through impulsive sniffles, I released my earliest guarded memories of endless moves, of always being the awkward new kid, and of the pressures of my childhood responsibilities. I skirted around the abandonment of a man I considered my father and the lack of presence from my mother, who was forced to work long hours to feed four hungry mouths. I rejoiced at the healing of a few short months, gleefully ignorant to the developing storm growing deep within.

The vibrant green of rolling hills faded into endless fields of golden wheat, delicately speckled with red poppies as we embarked on the Meseta. My happy-go-lucky mood flattened with the landscape, while a familiar but nameless unease settled around me. Restful nights turned to restlessness, as though I was slipping back into the burnout that consumed me only months before in my other life as nurse.

It hadn't been the vivid stress-induced dreams, sleepless nights, or shattering headaches that triggered me to the signs that my seams were ripping apart. Rather, the empty stare reflecting at me in the bathroom mirror said it all. My puffy face was wet with tears and water, as I tried to cool the redness of uncontrolled cries that flushed over me. Embarrassed by the unrestrained angry outburst that unfolded moments before. The turning lava within erupted after I was innocently reminded of a forgotten meeting I needed to attend. In a heated flash, I swore and threw my headphones across the tiny office.

I fretted about my inability to cope with the external pressures of work and life, acknowledging my need to learn healthy strategies to manage my volatile mood. Instead, the workplace psychologist cut our meeting short and handed me a piece of white paper. I nervously bit into my cheek peering at the handwritten note: "recommend 4-6 weeks medical leave to relieve adjustment disorder."

I started to grow weary of the dark shadow of a fellow pilgrim who joined us day and night, eager to appease my every pain. The walls closed in around me as I began to feel trapped, withdrawing into the intensifying spasms spewing from my hips and feet. I didn't notice the romantic passes thrown my way until one hot evening while watching an approaching thunder storm with my back pressed into a stone wall. The cool relief of the wall relaxed my senses and opened my awareness to the love-struck twinkle gazing at me from the corner of my eyes.

Things move fast on the Camino, but it was in this moment I awoke to the voice within, warning me of old patterns that were no longer supporting my growth. The hidden co-dependency I developed during the long abusive relationship with my high school sweetheart, disregarded the subtle insecurities, the jealous looks when I talked to others, and the angst when I was gone longer then expected. Panic and fear devoured me, turning my tired relaxed demeanor to stone. Once again, I could feel the red-hot lava burn through my chest as I shut down and obsessed about how I could keep myself safe.

Black clouds from the previous night's storm lingered around me during the next morning's walk. The cramping in my foot intensified with every step, radiating throughout my body. Feeble attempts to simmer the impeding pressure growing within, causing more frustration as pleasantries and words of encouragement from this unwelcome admirer, narrowed my focus and constricted my lungs. I didn't want to be saved but I didn't know how to say that. Instead, I politely asked him and my travel companion to walk ahead. "I'll catch up," I smiled, waving them on.

Shallow forced breaths escaped through my nose like an angry bull waiting to be released. My shuffling feet slowly pushed on, even when the knife stabbed at me. The more I tried to control my breathing, the more forceful the steam built up. Desperate for relief, I narrowly threw my trekking poles into the lazy river while my uncontrolled arms flailed to remove the weight on my back. Cries of hysteria quickly turned to yelling on the surprisingly quiet road. If anyone did pass by, I didn't notice. I threw my backpack to the ground and repeatedly kicked; violent emotions burst with each connection.

After the storm settled, I caught up with the small group waiting ahead. A new determination moved me forward to the next town. My travel partner and I graciously accepted the cab my admirer hailed for us. We said goodbye, leaving behind a soon-to-be broken promise to meet up again. I protected myself in the only way I knew how: I ran.

Relief filled my constricted lungs and reminded me of my purpose for this journey. If I didn't make myself a priority, I'd only expose myself to the needy grips of co-dependence and a life of conditional romance. I had no idea what I wanted in my life, confusion and indecision were commonplace, but my eyes were starting to open to what I didn't want.

Moving out of the stagnant heat and into the crisp mountain air brought a comfortable sense of home. Dawn was just starting to break the darkness of night when we arrived at the pile of stone burdens in Cruz de Fierro. A bitter chill aided my alertness as we gazed at the vibrant glow peaking over the jagged horizon. Taking a moment to breathe in the frigid morning breeze, I placed my stone among the others and continued, one step at a time.

I started to feel the weightless optimism and encouragement stirring within. Fleeting conversations with fellow walkers became intensely intimate and to the point. "Why are you walking?" was a question more important than asking someone what their name was. Kindness and compassion flowed within, revealing a safety net for the vulnerability that danced on the rays of sunshine. My perspective had shifted, and the heavy burden of life felt a little lighter and, with that, the pain in my foot subsided.

My greatest discovery that led to forgiveness of self was revealed by the beauty in life that came once I accepted my greatest sorrows. I embraced each story with love and took to heart the words gifted to me by strangers: "you underestimate yourself" and "you should open yourself up more." Like the petals of a rose emerging from the warmth of a spring sun, I started to see the radiance blossoming within.

 beautyinlife.ca

 **crystal.berscht@beautyinlife.ca**

Crystal is a Registered Nurse, meditation teacher, Reiki healer, and blogger. She is passionate about holistic healing, self-discovery, and gardening. After navigating her way through chronic stress, burnout, and childhood trauma, she has found that connecting with herself has been the real remedy to her success.

Crystal lives in Edmonton Alberta, with her husband, two cats, and dog – who loves to teach her about patience. She is enthusiastic about growing her healing toolkit and is studying to be a herbalist. When she isn't creating more work for herself and her husband, she's dancing and enjoying the outdoors.

Crystal is the owner and author of Beauty in Life (beautyinlife.ca) and hosts workshops to help others on their healing journey to self. Crystal may be contacted via email at crystal.berscht@beautyinlife.ca

C*nt Life

By Geraldine "Ger" Carriere

"Your body, mind, spirit, and emotional state are a form of your business-the state in which these things lie, are exactly correlating where your business will be."

When you hear C*nt Life, what do you feel? Where do you feel it in your body? How do you know you feel this way? People tend to get turned off, triggered, and disgusted by the word cunt. What I say to this, is good!!! You should feel something.

People place a lot of power on words but don't necessarily understand why, or know how to ask what else is possible. This is exactly why I've coined this phrase. Just as the word cunt holds power, I use it strategically to evoke emotion in you. C*nt life is a term I coined to give light to a hardened version of a woman; she is a woman who talks back, stands strong in her conviction, loves herself deeply and puts herself first! She is Wild.

C*nt Life was inspired from "Thug Life", a phrase made popular by the American rap artist Tupac Shakur. It is an acronym standing for 'The Hate U Give Little Infants Fucks Everyone'. The message was a warning that if we continue to bring up children in a negative environment, surrounded by racism, violence, and oppression then the cycle of Thug Life will just continue. C*nt Life is exactly this, I am not seeing the connection - Do you even need to have the above part in? Even if you say "C*nt Life has the same underlying message in that- in society if a woman fights back, defies, doesn't back down, then she is considered a bitch, a whore, and/or a C*NT". Here is my suggestion, from beginning...

When you hear C*nt Life, what do you feel? Where do you feel it in your body? How do you know you feel this way? People tend to get turned off, triggered and disgusted by the word c*nt. What I say to this is good!!! You should feel something.

People place a lot of power on words but don't necessarily understand why, or know how to ask what else is possible. This is exactly why I've coined this phrase "C*nt Life"; I use it strategically to evoke emotion in you and to challenge you to embrace and empower yourself with it.

The word c*nt holds power, but it has a negative connotation to it. In society when a woman fights back, defies, doesn't back down, she is considered a bitch, a whore, and/or a C*NT. All because she won't comply with what is considered as an acceptable female role of mother, housewife, trophy, or accessory.

C*nt Life represents a woman taking back her power– standing in her power; she is a woman who talks back, stands strong in her conviction, loves herself deeply and puts herself first! She does not allow herself to be property, be gained off of, be sexualized, or be a doormat. Equally she owns her sexuality and is stronger because of it. She is Wild.

Once a woman understands this, she can identify and understand that the cunt, which is the female reproductive space, is instead a woman's source, in fact the world's life force; And this part is what everyone wants! It's juicy, sexy, and delicious. When she is reminded of this fact, that this part of her IS her power, she can use it to her advantage and growth.

Should she need proof of this? She must know that the cunt is her power source and is what makes the world go round. After all, Men have capitalized on it for years, and still do today. Men have actually had wars over it, it's where life starts and is exactly what is needed for our survival.

From a Girl to Woman

There are certain rites of passage that all girls must go through in order to become a woman. Teachings like the birds and the bees, berry picking, fire keeping, cooking and caring for the self, things like braiding your hair, are examples of this. The intent, reasoning, and knowledge behind these teachings are very integral to our foundation to becoming a woman. The process of learning these teachings will lead her to an understanding of her roles and future responsibilities. And more specifically what to anticipate when a girl comes to be gifted her moontime (menstruation), which will lead to an understanding of why she is a life giver. This rite of passage is defined as the exact moment we are considered a woman and a life giver.

Being an Indigenous Woman

Women must realize that She is in fact a gift. Legend says that if you want to look at God, Look at a woman. As she is the only creature on this planet who can do what she does. She is the veil between this life and the spirit world. She is the closest thing to what God is, which is a creator. Creator makes things out of nothing. She breathes life into things. That is what is meant by a woman becoming a life-giver.

Fire and the Womb

Iskwew comes from the Cree word Iskotew which means fire. What this represents is that, a woman's reproductive space is the oven of life. Igniting, warming, and breathing life into those around her. The main role of a woman is to be in the flow of life, consistently creative and to be in a nurturing state. Which would look like a young girl dancing through the grass, humming, smiling sweetly, and carrying a carefree demeanor. If she is not in alignment with this in all aspects of her life, she is not living in accordance to her natural state.

The womb is so much more powerful than we understand. This is why Dali painted an image of Mary Magdalene with a spear through it. Yet no image like that, no dark magic ritual, no constant collection of cells from prodding smears, no birth control poison, no disinformation, no religious torture and murder of wise women...none of it can remove her power. Few seem to realise the extent of the war against the womb that has taken place for thousands of years. One example of this is St. Peters rejecting Magdalena and turned her into a prostitute.

To modern feminism which turns women into men and takes away their feminine powers or liberalism which turns the sacred act of sex into something to hand out too easily. To pregnancy control and birthing methods which actually disempower women because they destroy her body while taking away the natural rhythms and her ability to have an empowered alignment of controlling her own cycles/orgasmic birth in harmony with natural ways. The war on wombs has affected every woman and every man and every child in every culture for thousands of years. No one is separate from this, everyone is affected.

It is time to reclaim her power.

It is time to reclaim the power of natural birth, natural birth control, sacred sex, and the amazing ability of the womb to heal. The womb, every womb, whether you have had it removed or not, is the direct vortex to the primordial divine cosmic mother.

She is the Giver of All Life

Did you know that the biggest secret held from so many, is that the holy grail is your womb... YOUR WOMB! This is the knowledge that the ancients held, the womb that is the holy grail and woman was the priestess. She represents this knowledge. The sacred jars and vessels of priestesses seen throughout art from renaissance Italian to ancient Egyptian, represent this knowledge.

And it goes deeper than this. For the womb holds the light that gives both men and women light awakening in the pineal gland (third eye). When Mary Magdalene gave Yeshua anointment from her jar, it means that He received light awakening in his 3rd eye from their love making, from secretions from her womb with his sacred secretions, opening the glands in their 3rd eyes. This is a part of tantric teachings. No wonder sex was made cheap, no wonder the womb was made unholy. For that is the key to empowerment or disempowerment, liberation or slavery.

Your liberation, your sovereignty, your light awakening is within you. You may enter your womb in meditation, see her as a temple and a place, a beautiful crystal within her on her altar. You may imagine you clean her and fill her with Light. This is your sacred power.

Water is life. Ninety percent of your body is water,

In a sea full of fish
Be water instead
The very essence of smooth
The one that can't be played

Lighting and quenching
A life giver
The molecule that changes everything
The one that breaks down all

The fixer of all things
That which, we are made of
The one that flows
The Phoenix

Never be jealous of the fish
As they need you to swim
For your element is humility
The very essence that we all live

Power of the Moon on Water

The Moon's Effect on Ocean Tides. The gravitational pull of the Moon and the Sun makes the water in the oceans bulge, causing a continuous change between high and low tide. The oceans bulge…while both the Moon and the Sun influence the ocean tides, the Moon plays the biggest role. The strongest element is water, it can break down anything and can destroy everything in its path.

Moon Time-A ceremony

While the moon's magnetic effect is not creating a physical movement of water in our bodies (according to science), it could be bringing heightened emotions to the surface. The full moon can feel like a bit of a disruptive time, resulting in more erratic behaviour, tension, or tiredness. Moon time is ceremony, a death and rebirth—which should be celebrated. It is a time of solitude and a time of energy conservation for the self to regenerate what is being carried through her. With this teaching, women should refuse to no longer be considered, viewed, on this special time to be anything but beautiful, transformational, and healing.

When a woman is going through this time, if she is not being soft like water and flowing, this will result in her acting out in anger, bitterness, and feeling numb. The reason for this is that she is feeling forced to be or do something that she is not intended to or wants to be doing during this special time. She is at war within herself.

This is why women have to really delve deeply inside themselves, release, heal, and then integrate her feminine abilities so that she can be set free.

How did we get here?

When women are taught to be like men, progress-driven, control-oriented, and always acting in a productive manner, this goes against our very nature. Which is like throwing the planet off its axis, the balance is out of alignment. Which can be seen in the world today. Where the healers are being controlled, overworked, and burnt out. The current patriarchal world view is of the understanding that the more you can contribute, be agreeable, and obey the rules, the farther you will get in life.

Just as you can be a product of your environment, women are also a byproduct of these patriarchal societal systems. Women are given so many mixed messages about who they are, how they should act and how they should feel. We're told to, "be soft and gentle, but never cry in boardrooms", "be a virgin and a vixen." Even in the bible Mary was Jesus' mother nothing else, she didn't have a voice, a mood, or sexuality. Women have lost so much of who we are and have to be reminded of what was ancestrally given to us.

We have to relearn how to breathe, how to walk and talk again. Ultimately, how to FEEL again.

We are beautiful life givers, trying to heal in a broken system. There's a reason why we wore moccasins because it kept us connected to the land which talked to and guided us. If you see an indigenous person sitting on the ground it is to feel our Mother Earth's heartbeat. The constant beat of her heart which would give you a feeling of being home, carried and makes everything whole again.

Do you know what was the first sound you have ever heard was?
It was your mother's heartbeat
This is what music is
A home
It defies time and space and breaks barriers
Makes you feel things
Like comfort, belongingness and peace
Her constant stable beat
Connecting us again and comforting our spirits
As if to say, it is safe to nestle into her slumber
To lay safely wrapped in her womb

We can never feel anything else like it
Music is my medicine!
It wakes parts of me, I've forgotten about, neglected and repressed
Returning me to the little girl who had big dreams to be free
She is me, and I am her.
It brings me back to me again
Music is medicine

Healing

This is why I started my business, Wild Woman Personal & Professional Development. To give a voice and create a community of Matriarchs. By nature, women are intended to be nurturers. Being soft and vulnerable was always my weakness.

Toxic masculinity was easier, it was my defense. I was a master at that. Not feeling and running. This war within me is what I had to overcome. To truly master myself, this is what was needed and what I hope to pass on in Wild Woman. Wild Woman is about mastering the self, deciphering the trauma, releasing the rage, and turning it into something beautiful. It is about having fearless focus, and purpose.

Being a Wild Woman is to be in service of others without sacrificing yourself and learning how to do something productive with what's been given to you. It is using that discomfort as ammunition to push you forward in life. Knowing that you didn't go through all this shit just go through it. What you experienced was in fact intentional and trust that it wasn't for nothing. So that you can teach others to learn the lessons you have learned so that they may not to go through it either or to at least shorten their suffering in all of it. That is what being wild is to me. It is simply existing.

Balance Between Sexes

In a world designed to harden the heart and loving the self is a rebellious act. Softness is a luxury. As long as you are sweet and accommodating, we as women are taught that you are lovable. When you are a woman with high standards, high value and poise you are considered a Bitch! Stuck up! And a Cunt! And by becoming like men, we have adopted a competitive nature, not only to do things better than men. But to emasculate them while doing it.

Men...
When handling a woman,
A storm may pass through
(meaning she is angry, bitter, and overly emotional)
know that when this is happening,
she is at war with herself.
And she must be reminded to return to a softer version of herself,
who she was before,
where she is trusting,
surrendered and at peace.

This was started in the American civil war and cemented in with the industrial revolution, where women had to do their own and men's roles too. Men went to war and left women to uphold being a housewife and working at the same time. When the men returned, PTSD was prevalent and women learned to cope by adopting masculine traits to protect themselves and their children by means of survival. Generationally learned coping mechanisms, to present day behaviours, women have found themselves in a space of needing men a lot less and in a very different way than what was traditionally expected.

Emotionally, along with mentally, spiritually, and physically, women long to be with men in a more intimate and nurturing partnership. By women doing everyone's job, men have adopted a more immature, withdrawn, and selfish demeanor, and have lost their historical sense of regal pride, protective nature, and courtship values to being with a woman. They have lost the healthy masculine roles they normally would have occupied which has resulted in a lessened perception. A series of unlearning by men is in order to restore balance.

Because of this, women have become so desensitized, as a result being suspicious that a man will harm her rather than help her, and never learn true pleasure sexually.

Matriarchy Rising

Indigenous Matriarchy is not about pushing men out of the way or humiliating them.

Women and men are on the same level. We support each other. We make decisions together. We all succeed on the same human level. There is always respect. Indigenous women are not feminists and probably never will be. We are created to uphold balance.

In doing so, we've destroyed any form of connection, intimacy, and kinship with ourselves, men, and those around us. Trying to become this machine we thought would help gain us respect, honour, acceptance, and a sense of belonging in the world. In order for women to return to themselves they must take back the power of the pussy, womb space, cunt, vagina, labia, or whatever it is you like to call it, because whether you realize it or not, everyone wants it!!!

It is the main motivator in life. And when a woman realizes this, she is in her power. This is her purpose and her responsibility. She must know that not only is it sexy, juicy, life-giving, and satiating. Like biting into a peach, the juices flow all around your mouth, making your mouth water... satisfying the senses and never apologizing for her mess. It is her rightful place and it is vital.

Women mustn't deny themselves the magic of this experience. To truly live through this space, loving, flowing, smiling and the bliss that this creates. Harmony is created. There will be harmonious partnerships in all aspects of the world whether it is in organizations, government, households, or schools all of these different things... is when a woman truly stands in her essence.

> *"The elders say the women will lead the healing among the nations. We need to especially pray for our women and ask the Creator to bless them and give them strength. Inside them are powers of Love, and strength given by Moon (Meztli) and Earth. When everyone else gives up, it is women who sing songs of strength, she is the backbone of the people. So, to our women we say. sing your songs of strength. pray for your special powers. Keep our people strong, be respectful, gentle and modest. Great one. Bless our women. Make them strong today"*

-Dennis Banks Documentary- Author Unknown

Woman in Business

> *"Some women choose to follow men, and some women choose to follow their dreams. If you're wondering which way to go, remember that your career will never wake up and tell you that it doesn't love you anymore."*

- Lady Gaga

When it comes to women in business, matriarchy is at the forefront of this. This is exactly why we have been silenced. Our voices were never intended to be heard. Historically Indigenous men went to women to make big decisions on behalf of the tribe because they knew they could know or consider what women know. Woman need to take up more space and be louder.

Run businesses and...never ask for permission to do so.

Freedom is not having money but having the ability to recreate, transform, and reinvent yourself. Security doesn't come from the money in your bank account. It comes from the ability to create income anytime you want. Learn how to start a business where you are selling products and services that are residual and duplicatable. Therefore working smarter not harder.

Don't buy into the notion that there is only one way to do something. Don't even buy into a certificate or accreditation as it is a form of a patriarchal system made up to keep you in a rat race that doesn't even value who you are.

Throughout history it has been man's job to provide...

No, throughout history men have actively prevented the independence of women who have actively prevented our mobility, our rights to education, and deliverable income. They have abused our reproductive capabilities and passed us around like property. They have used religion to rationalize their hatred of us and put us in places of subordination. Now, you can all be quiet about men being providers. Like it was benevolent gestures in an attempt to rationalize sexism.

What is it about men & high heels...
It's as if they're intimidated by the strength and success
that are attached to a woman wearing them...
The cackle of the heels hitting the ground is the sound of her
strength n beauty pulsating the earth signifying her existence...
Did it ever occur to them that women are creatures
of acknowledgment and praise...
We crave those things, as we want to feel noticed and desired...
A woman who wears heels is comfortable in her own body
and is proclaiming herself to the world...
As if to say, this is me,
Take me as I am.

www.wildwomanwithin.me

Geraldine "Ger" Carriere

Author. Business Owner. International Speaker. Certified Life Coach. Performer. Stylist.

Geraldine is from the Métis settlement of Cumberland House, Saskatchewan, Canada and is of Cree descent. As well as being trained in Sociology, Entrepreneurship, Social Work, and Indian Communications Arts, she is a Fashionista, Recording Artist and creative spirit. She has hosted INCA Inspired TV, the First Nations Summer Games webcast and Reported and Produced for CBC News. She is also the winner, of the Esquao Award in Performing Arts and Telus StoryHive recipient for her debut music video "Undeservingly". Her self titled debut album can be found on all music streaming platforms.

Combining her skills from the Business world, to the Creative world, lead Geraldine to create and become the Founder & CEO of Wild Woman; a Personal & Professional development company which provides Life & Business Coaching through a variety of services. Geraldine has devoted her life to empowering others in discovering their authentic self and sense of belonging through healing and self-mastery.

She is the co-founder of the Indigenous Woman's Business Panel featuring and showcasing artists, musicians, designers and entrepreneurs.

If not in a boardroom, you can find Ger in thrift stores around the globe looking for her next treasure.

Listen to the Whispers or... Get the 2x4!

By Debora J. Hollick

Odd title? Perhaps.

For those not familiar with the phrase, and wondering what a 2x4 is, let us just say, simply put, it is a very large stick used for building. Metaphorically speaking, in this case, building character and trust in what the whispers are all about, and how you can recognize them, trust them, and use them as ultimate guidance and wisdom moving forward.

How many times can your recall having heard a little voice or felt a twinge or some sort of off feeling, telling you to do something, but you didn't pay attention? There are many names given for them...nudges, twinges, a sense, intuition. We all receive them. The question is do we "hear" them, recognize them, understand them, and use them? And if not, why not?

I call them the *whispers.*

I have had several instances in my life, more than I care to admit quite frankly, where, I definitely heard a whisper and didn't pay attention. Sometimes it became very loud and still I didn't listen. Why? When I think about it now, it doesn't make sense. Life could have been so much easier for me.

I can go back many years when I chose to date someone who I knew, absolutely knew, was not good for me, yet I did it anyway. Perhaps many of us have had that experience, maybe even married and had children with them?

I remember a time not so long ago, when I had someone working with me in my business, and I kept getting this odd feeling that something just was not right. Couldn't put my finger on it. This was at a time where I had been running one of my businesses on my own for many years. I was tired of doing it all and wanted someone to help me train so that I could focus on growing the business. This person had worked with me for several years, had the skills and was eager to help me grow my business...or so she said. In the beginning, the thought of it felt okay, although I had a bit of hesitation. **I should have listened.**

As time progressed, I found that I would hire and do the initial trainings and then when I turned the person over to their supervisor, they would quit within a couple of weeks! Before this process, when I did the training and continued to work with my people, they stayed for many, many years, including her! I was puzzled. Something felt off and it kept happening. Still, did I listen? NO!

At first, the whispers were just fleeting thoughts. As time went on and I didn't heed the information, they became stronger, becoming heavy feelings in the pit of my stomach. Three years went by. Yes, you read that right – three years! Over and over again, I kept hearing whispers, getting a bit louder each time, to the point where I began receiving actual, audible transmissions that translated into words. *"Fire her!"* *"She is sabotaging your business."* Still, I didn't listen and even though the indications were clear and now that I look back upon it, unmistakable, I felt sorry for her and overrode, much to my chagrin, my intuition; the messages and guidance the Universe was so lovingly and clearly giving me. Some might think that perhaps I'm not too bright.

I just couldn't bring myself to believe that anyone would want to do that to me. There was no reason that made sense. I guess it was too painful to fathom or understand at the time so, what did I do? I made excuses for the behaviour, situations, and events that were taking place right before my own eyes. Looking back, it seems it could have been so easy, had I just listened, trusted, and took the necessary action – truly, one could say it would have been inspired action.

Finally, I was faced with a situation that was on the brink of being catastrophic for business and for me, personally. This took me to the point where I had no choice but to finally make a decision, due to a complete and utter betrayal based only upon lies and innuendos, that almost ruined my business. At that point, **there it was my 2x4!!!**

Cringingly, as I reminisce over the way too many times, I've endured the wrath of my own failings, I remember more business and personal instances that have cost me dearly, in many ways...financially, lack of self-esteem and confidence, to name just a few. While not to inundate you with tales of woe, as I'm quite sure you are understanding and maybe even relating to what I am saying, there is one more I would like to share that was dire.

There are many details and circumstances surrounding this instance and to go into them here would be much too long and dramatic, so I will cut to the chase. I was scheduled for surgery. It was major surgery but not uncommon. In the days leading up to the date, I was under pressure and in an extreme stress situation. I received the message that I shouldn't go through with the surgery at that time but again, I overrode it, justifying that it was the next day, the surgical team is prepared, yada, yada. Even my Dad told me, and I remember his words, clearly, *"don't have this surgery tomorrow. It won't be good like the last one."* WOW! The Universe actually, verbally gave me the message again and it was definite. Decision time.

I would like to say I cancelled the procedure, but no, sadly I did not. Long story short, I ended up with an infection, a Super Bug, I believe they said, that almost cost me my life. Luckily, it only caused me to be in the hospital an additional twenty-three days, having to have a machine attached to me for three months to draw out the infection, and on strong medication for seven months.

So why do we do this to ourselves? And I believe, we do it to ourselves.

These 2x4's leave bruises, cuts, and sometimes even scars. They hurt, deeply, but they do not have to be irreparable. Do not despair. Scars are indicative of the battles we have won! We have come through, weathered the storm.

Now, what do we do with the wisdom gained?

Whispers can come in many forms. Could be ideas, inspiration, aspiration. You know what I mean, sometimes those "Spidey senses", when you get that feeling. Perhaps it's that feeling of doubt, don't do it or go there instead. You name it, we are being guided. All of us. No one more special than the other. Some have just had enough experiences and learned.

We receive guidance not always as warnings. Most often, it is something like, come this way...

just contrast. Remember, they are for you even when they seem strange.

So, how do we hear the whispers before suffering negative consequences?

Pay Attention to the Whisper – Before the Shout – Before the 2x4!

While I was making notes for this chapter, I heard "hold onto your glass." Glad I did. I was writing notes in the dark on my phone, and where I was about to set it down on the small table beside me, would have caused it to be slightly over the edge. By listening, I avoided water and chards of crystal all over the place.

When you find yourself starting to recognize the whispers, here are a few things that might help you:

- Stay calm and focus on what or how you are feeling right at that moment.

- Be in the moment and allow yourself to feel, before taking any action.

- Have fun with the process and acknowledge and celebrate when you recognize your realizations.

- Sometimes we take action too quickly because we "should" and then Oops. *(funny...Oops popped in here as I was typing notes on my phone. No conscious thought was there before about that word but because I've learned to listen, here it is.)*

- Be aware that it is about the simple things more often than the big things when we really attune to our feelings and listening skills. Things like get butter but you are in a different aisle in the Grocery Store, so you decide to get it later – only to get home to discover you didn't!

- This is not a new discovery or rocket science, but still challenging and that is good.

- Tuning in applies to business and life, in its totality.

- When you get the nudge and say, I need to write that down, an idea or something to remember, a dream...only to plan on doing it later and then forgetting, next time do it.

- **Notice how when you say to yourself, "don't forget", you often do, but when you say "remember", you do?**

- It is a different vibration, yes to the positive.

It is so much fun to see how much more smoothly life becomes the more we listen to the whispers.

Just like while I was writing notes for this chapter. It was 4:15 A.M. on a holiday. I was awakened with words and ideas bursting forth. Another whisper...get up and write them down. Still tired and half asleep, old patterns surfaced. Oh, I'll remember, I found myself thinking. A louder whisper...Oh no you won't. And up I got. Been to that movie too many times. Don't like the ending! I'm getting better at this. Can you relate?

So, when you develop your hearing skills does this mean you will never again not listen? If my experience has taught me anything, the answer to that is more than likely, no it does not.

Remember that contrast I mentioned...we cannot make decisions without it. It can be as easy and simple as do I want tea or coffee? And if I do, what cup do I want to want to choose this morning?

So, what if we choose to not listen or pay attention? Yes, we may well have a less desirable time of it for a bit, but do we have to look at it as negative? Not at all. Some of the best stuff comes through while we are navigating the twists and turns.

Perhaps you may be late and frustrated because you should have left earlier only to learn of some events or circumstances that would have been catastrophic had you been on time and in the middle of it. How many times have you heard of someone saying something like this? I know I have. In fact, I've experienced it.

The list is endless. Even something as minor as not checking a comment before posting on Facebook. Could be embarrassing maybe but can be quickly edited. This I know, it happens to me regularly.

None the less, it is your choice how you want to create your life.

We are the sum-total of our experiences, the good and the bad. All I have gone through has helped me become the me I am, who is now becoming brave enough and able to share the knowledge gleaned in many areas. Just maybe, by doing so, someone else will be served and benefit.

I like to think that it is Spirit at work, always, at its best making us better, stronger, happier, and more resilient.

About indulging in things that aren't good for me...oh, don't get me started...I'm still working on this one!!!

By the way...that bathroom in your dream...definitely, not a whisper. It is an alarm. Wake up, get up. Hurry!

🌐 **www.smashthroughmentor.com**
🌐 **www.insightfulsolutions.com**
✉ **Debora@smashthroughmentor.com**
💼 **LinkedIn**
𝐟 **FB**

Debora J. Hollick, known as The Smash Through Mentor, helps mature women, both individually and as a group, to "smash through" barriers that are keeping them from their full potential.

As an experienced Intuitive Consultant, Debora offers her many years of sales, marketing, and coaching experience; along with a proven, successful track record in business and in coaching. She has a rural background and brings a diverse perspective to the table. She appreciates the opportunity to serve and help others achieve success.

Debora has been given a wonderful gift, in that the right words and ideas seem to come to her for what people she works with at just the right time. Though not always what they want to hear, she mentors them and tells them what is needed to be heard in order to benefit them.

She's also been told that she holds "Sacred Vision", receiving messages from the Angels and The Divine to help them find their voice and be heard by those who, *may not be able to hear them. Her work is to help restore hope and empowerment to people where they feel there is none. When people work with her and participate in her programs, workshops or events, they say it feels like **while they are receiving a warm, energetic hug – they are also receiving a gentle kick in the pants!***

"Idea Explosion" is one of Debora's favorite consultation activities. Debora credits her success to her passion for helping people, but is quick to admit that she too, has been helped along the way by many and is a true believer that "all of us are smarter than any one of us." That is part of the premise of her being The Smash Through Mentor.

Debora enjoys reading, singing, brainstorming, spending time with family and friends, writing, and appreciating all life has to offer.

*Call it Karma, Good luck, or a Spiritual Intervention...however you want to describe it, you can't help but believe that Debora J. Hollick, The Smash Through Mentor, is destined to help people discover a better version of themselves! Hollick describes her success as "being paid to help people do what they do best ~ become their very best evolving selves and to **LIVE LIFE IN W.O.W!** ©"*

And Still I Rise...

FOR MY MOM
BY DIMITRIA L. COOK

One evening, as I leave an event hosted by friends, I cross paths with a woman named Jennifer. This is our first and only meeting. She runs up to me as I walk towards the door. She stops me and says, "Wait, I need to tell you something." As she proceeds, her words are staccato and she has difficulty verbalizing her thoughts. "I'm sorry. I'm sorry, I'm sorry. You don't know me." Her tears are a mesmerizing waterfall. "Can you come back in?" I oblige her. She sits while I stand in front of her. Next, she says, "You are here to heal the human race. I don't know why I am saying this to you, but I have to tell you this." She continues, "You are here to heal the human race." Our eyes lock on each other and I am unable to move. "I hope you don't mind, but I need to touch you." As she is sobbing, she reaches out and places her hand on my right arm and bows her head. A warm sensation of energy radiates through my body. "You are here to do great things and the world needs you."

The world needs me and I need my mother. I will always need my mother. I am flesh of her flesh. Yet, I am my own woman. Still, I long for my mother's approval and support as I develop as a woman. Her unconditional love is always there, yet our relationship is amiss. I am a hamster on a wheel, repeating my steps over and over yearning for a better relationship. I'm not a perfect daughter. I have many flaws and it is these flaws that make me imperfectly perfect and perfectly imperfect. I dare to make a shift in our tug of war relationship. Before things get better, they get worse. At one point, my mother says, "Get over your teenage angst. I thought you had thicker skin than that." Teenager? I'm a grown woman, many years past my teens. Nonetheless, her words cut to the bone and there is no communication between us for months.

I don't recall who blinks first. What I know is that from the depths of despair, we both emerge better women. Now, we laugh more together. Our conversations are more enjoyable. We have a respect for one another that didn't exist in the past. Yes, we still have some unpleasant disagreements. As adults, we work through them. I have come to learn, understand, and accept that with each disagreement, I gain invaluable insight into my mother and myself. It was important for me to walk away from our power struggle. I now allow her to be my mother. I love her for the beautiful woman she is on the inside and outside. I will always be the daughter and my mom will always be my mother.

Every day I rise to a new lesson in life. Some of these lessons come in the form of building my inner strength through adversity. As a sophomore in high school, I am spit on and physically assaulted by a man more than twice my age. He grabs me, throws me around, pins me with his hands and body, then violently punches me repeatedly. Again, he spits on me. I continue to struggle to get free from this mad man. My screams are ignored by those around us and no one comes to my rescue. I am his boxing speed bag. Finally, the punches stop. This is innocence lost. I am a child and he is supposed to be an adult.

For my assault, this man is prosecuted and serves a minimal jail sentence. My physical wounds heal, yet I carry an emotional scar within me. This mark reminds me that I possess the strength of a goddess. I must continue to find the inner strength to fight back through all adversity. On this day, my eyes open wide to the nastiness of racism, sexism, and physical abuse. Unfortunately, the hate doesn't stop after this encounter.

As an undergraduate, I endure another act of hate. A calm night with a cool breeze entices my dorm mate and me on an evening walk. It's a gentle night as we chat and laugh. Then the calmness of the night is soon filled with terror. We hear and see a speeding car. A young man leans out of the window and throws something at us. He throws another object. These objects are thrown with such force, that I hear whizzing as they barely miss my head. Why is this "boy" throwing things at us?" He laughs, taunting us with each throw. Under the cloak of darkness, the car speeds away. We look at each other in disbelief, bordering on shock. We search for the objects thrown at us and find several golf balls. Golf balls. He threw golf balls at my head from a speeding car!

Years later in my early 20s, an ex-boyfriend spits on me. In my mid-twenties, as I am stopped at a light and sitting in my car, a man throws an apple at me from a moving truck. Once again, I rise through all of the hate. I rise because I possess an inner strength that keeps propelling me forward. And still I rise, because I am a survivor.

As a survivor, I have experienced physical and emotional pain. However, I have unwavering integrity. Call me names, hurl insults at me, or throw objects at me. Yet, never question my integrity. When someone who inherently does not know me or questions my integrity with no basis, this is someone who is deficient in pride. This is someone who lacks character and morality. I have known such people in the work place.

One of my female supervisors, in the past, likes to spit venom at me, all in the name of, "I support women." I counter with, real women do not degrade other women. Real women lift their sisters up when they are low. Real women support one another because they know how difficult it is to achieve success on any level in a male centered environment. She says to me, "If you cross me, I will make your life a living Hell." Her obsession with me gives her tunnel vision. She decides her mission is to destroy me. Through all her back stabbing and her witch hunt, I never falter in my integrity. My integrity is unshakeable and is never up for debate.

It is my integrity that fuels my success. Someone may have a "successful" career, yet they are "failing" in their marriage/relationships. One may have success in building a base of friends who are supportive, caring, and loving, although finances and disposable income are lacking. So, what is success? Growing up, I attend a private high school that affords me the opportunity to mix and mingle with the children of "successful" people. Some are sports team owners, presidents of top accounting firms, legal firms, and other businesses. In addition, they are politicians, doctors, engineers, etc. To me, they are the wealthy elite. This never phases me because I intrinsically see people for the person they present themselves to be from the inside out.

My life wasn't always surrounded by the "successful" elite. When I was a baby, my parents moved to their current neighborhood. The neighborhood thrives with businesses. Families live in beautiful homes with green grass lawns. Children play in the streets without hesitation. There are bicycles left on the front lawns and many of us girls play with jump ropes. We play softball in the streets and rock teacher on our front porches. Although our neighborhood is a far cry from Mayberry, none the less, this a community of families who know each other. My parents work full-time jobs. They make sure we have a roof over our heads, clothes on our backs, and food on the table. There are times when my dad gets laid off from his job. Times are tough when the layoffs occur. Sometimes the lights or hot water are turned off. We are a blue-collar family going over speed bumps while trying to live the "American Dream" on the South Side of Chicago.

I leave my neighborhood and head west to go to college. I graduate with a Bachelor of Arts degree, Bachelor of Science degree, and eventually a Master of Fine Arts degree. I am an educator, writer, and author. Although sometimes, I often feel like a failure in my life. Even though I try not to measure my life and accomplishments by keeping up with the Joneses, our societal norms are a constant reminder that success is measured in dollars and ownership, rather than based in happiness and fulfillment. Success is different for everyone. I must constantly remind myself that I am successful. How do I measure my success? My success is measured through my relationships with family and friends. My inner strength gives me success.

As an educated African-American female, my perception of success and power come from within. My real power is how I handle myself in challenging situations and through grateful times. My power comes when I acknowledge the fact that I can only change myself and my reactions to situations. I can only control the choices I make, as there is always a choice to make. I am the power of one. My thoughts and my actions affect others, which creates a chain reaction of circumstances and outcomes. This does not give me power over another. I do have the power to choose love over hate, hope over despair, inner peace over riotous chaos. I know I only have power when I accept and understand that power doesn't exist. Power is a perception controlled by the id, rationalized by the ego and thwarted by the super-ego. Those of us who believe we have power over others are the ones who have power over none.

I grew up with the phrase, "knowledge is power." So I took the time to reminisce about what my mother has taught me. I wrote this for my mom and gave it to her for her birthday.

My mind is my greatest gift; my education is freedom from the onslaught of deference, and home breeds character, comfort, and clarity to self. The one thing no one can ever take from me is my education and the knowledge I have surmounted from it, but the best knowledge includes the life lessons you have taught me along the way on my journey from childhood, to teen, and into adulthood.

The ignorance of a child is its most powerful asset. The awakening of a teen conceals contempt. Adulthood brings wonderment, excitement, and finally placidity in knowing and understanding that the beginning is the end and the end is the beginning in every lifecycle.

We as women are the most powerful beings on this earth. We: create; are the smarter of the sexes and the dominant force; are wind gales; hurricanes; tornados; the blossoming sunflower in a field of daffodils; and the aquamarine gems of the sky and ocean. This is only part of the knowledge you have taught me. You have taught me to always be true to myself, to be a woman dependent on myself and independent of a man's misgivings and falsities. My strength is your strength. Your strength is what powers my love, appreciation of life, and fortitude. Knowledge is power. Thank you for sharing yours with me, as it will live on forever in my heart, my soul, my encompassing being. I Love You!

I know that happiness can't be measured and it is different for every person. I continue to thrive in my happiness. I am taught, if you build it, they will come. This is a lesson that I learned first-hand while on vacation in Cabo San Lucas, Mexico. People all around me are laughing, smiling, and having conversations while sipping on fruity and exotic drinks. I turn to one of my traveling companions and say, "Someone should start a conga line." My friend looks at me and says, "You should." I say, "Oh no. Not me." Then something comes over me. An inner voice says, "Just do it." I rise from my chair, turn toward my friend, and say, "Okay, I'll do it."

My friend places his hands on my shoulders and we start to dance. His girlfriend joins us. Then we become four, five, six. This is the beginning of my conga line. I am oblivious to what is happening behind me. I dance around tables and near the edges of swimming pools. I keep dancing and dancing and dancing. My friend bends down and whispers in my ear, "Dimitria, turn around." I turn around and what I see is unbelievable. There are at least 100 people dancing in my conga line. My friend then says, "You did this!" My only response, "Wow." I have no idea my simple act of making a decision to dance would start a movement. We all have it inside of us to positively change the world.

I am a transformational speaker who wakes every morning to #sayhername. For I am Sandra Bland. I am Atatiana Jefferson. I am Breonna Taylor. "

And still I rise..."

 www.DimitriaCook.com

Dimitria L. Cook is an empowerment writing coach, international speaker, and the author of "21 Reflections of the Inner Soul," and "Parents' Playbook: Tips, Tweets, & Other Common Sense Advice." She is passionate about empowering women to align with their inner soul and bring to life their story in their own words. Dimitria has been a featured guest on the Share Your Stories podcast, featured in the inaugural publication of "Bodacious Black Women Over 50," and a guest speaker at the Mom's Against Racism (MAR) International Race Matters: Allyship, History, & Equity conference. Connect with Dimitria by subscribing to her newsletter, Inner Soul of a Warrior Goddess, at www.DimitriaCook.com. Dimitria also enjoys writing plays, poems, short stories, visiting museums, and eating sushi.

Mom Was Right-Always Wear Clean Underwear

By Frankie Picasso

They said I flew through the air but I don't remember the flight.

I don't remember how my body crashed through the smoky grey acrylic of my custom windshield, the one I had to wait weeks for it to arrive, the one that was 'just right'.

I don't remember my hips becoming an instrument of blunt force, or how the shape of my body was left behind like a cartoon character cutout.

I don't remember my head striking the car's hood and catapulting into the night air, sending me upwards towards the waiting stars,

I don't remember being a human missile and flying in a sea of blackness, my senses momentarily deprived of their abilities to discern

I don't remember if I could have stopped or moved or changed the course of events.

I don't remember anything until my landing disturbed the sleeping gravel and sent a mixture of dirt, sand, and debris exploding into a swirling cloud of dust around me.

Then I remembered EVERYTHING!

The landing was marked by a dull thud, my breath expelled in a rush, the whoosh released into the thick, cloying night air. The ground I lay on was hard but still warmed from the hot summer sun of the day, and the deep pinks and mauves of the evening's sunset were rapidly being replaced by a deep twilight blue sky, twinkling stars and the soft glow of the moon.

I had just slid into the home plate of life, and as I did, I entered a hyper-state of reality where I became conscious of minutiae. In this surreal environment, I watched as the scene around me played out in slow motion, frame by agonizing frame. Then, for just a heartbeat or two, time seemed to stand still and nothing moved or dared to breathe. No sound was heard, as the Universe held its collective breath, waiting in anticipation for how the ump would be calling this play. Was she IN or OUT?

When I finally let out my breath, we were back in real time and the world around me exploded into a litany of pain as sensitive nerve endings flashed and sparked in their distress, a million cells calling out for help, racing to repair, control and stabilize their host in the ensuing madness. My body registered that I had just been tossed about like a rag doll, seemingly weightless, but the landing confirmed that that I was no rag doll, I was a broken doll

I did a quick check to see if my bike had made it through ok, but a cursory glance at Mercury (yes, she had a name) suggested she was a write off. I didn't have time to mourn for her just then, my body was crying out with an urgency of its own and I had to assess my own damage.

As a Community Emergency Response Volunteer, I knew that I was going into shock. I found myself thinking that sometimes it's just better not to know so much. I committed myself to staying alert until the ambulance arrived and removed my rings and my leather jacket. My forehead was sweating and my companions were keeping watch over me. One was keeping the driver away from me as the other held my head and hand.

The Fire Department and Police arrived about 10 minutes later, but for some reason the Ambulance seemed to be taking forever. The boys came over to look at me, but no one dared touch me. They would wait for the paramedics to arrive. We were out in the middle of the country, farmland surrounded us, and the smell of hay, clover and manure spilled into the night. The city lights were far away, and I kept wondering what hospital would they take me to and whether I would still be alive when I got there.

I sent off silent prayers to the powers that be to help me survive the night. I wanted to make sure my kids were safe and protected. I knew they weren't ready to lose their mother and I sure as heck wasn't ready to leave them.

Exactly eleven days prior, I had visited a divorce attorney and had obtained a Legal Separation agreement from my then husband. I had been asking him to leave for months, the marriage long over. He kept making excuses why he couldn't move out just yet, and I was no longer wanting to grant extensions. It was uncomfortable and unbearable for all of us, so I took the proverbial bull by the horns and forced the issue. I was now legally separated and very worried about what might happen to my kids without me there to protect them. My ex was an alcoholic and abusive both physically and verbally and I was finished with being afraid and belittled by him. We all were. This was my second husband and the stepfather to my children.

As we waited for help to arrive, I remember lying on the ground feeling like my body was falling away from itself, important joints no longer attached. I envisioned myself as a chicken whose thigh had been eviscerated from the pelvic bone. My legs were pulsing rapidly with a thousand nerve endings screaming in unison. It's hard to imagine the agony I was in, but I kept seeing a blinding blue/white flash, with each excruciating minute. This is the colour of pain.

When the ambulance finally arrived and the attendants put me onto a slider board for transport, I reminded the paramedics to make sure they brought my leg with me. You must understand that I have a super high pain tolerance but this was the first time in my life I actually screamed. I couldn't believe my own ears. I was the woman who had given birth to twins, naturally, no epidural, nothing, and then got up off the table and walked away.

When we finally arrived at the hospital, the nurses promptly began cutting my clothing away. I had made a point of undoing my custom leather chaps so that they could pull them out from under me, but NO, they had to cut them. They also cut off my brand new $70 bra. Well at least I had great underwear on.

They brought a portable X-ray machine into the emergency room. My mouth felt so dry at this point, I thought that a cotton plant had taken up residence. I begged the nurses for water, ice chips anything, I couldn't swallow anymore I was so dry, but they wouldn't give me anything to drink, surgery was imminent. They did offer me a liquid that was supposed to put me out for a minute so they could stabilize my legs. I was afraid to take the drug but in the end I took it anyway, because at this point, I considered it liquid, therefore a drink!

I awakened a few minutes later, wrapped up like a mummy and found myself being wheeled back into another ambulance. The orderlies told me I was going for another ambulance ride and that I was expected for surgery at one of the top Trauma Centers in the City of Toronto.

The drug they had given me before they wrapped me up kept me drowsy and I don't remember too much of the ride, but when I was finally cognizant again, I was in a recovery room, and had just come through my surgery.

I woke up to see my husband sitting across from me, staring at me. The nurses came in to tell me that the surgery was over and that I was hooked up to a self-monitoring morphine pump. They made me give myself 3 shots in succession, and then left happy that I would be content for a while. I settled back and waited for the agony in my body to subside to a dull roar, waiting until I could breathe again.

I had sustained an open fracture of the left femur, tibia and fibula, the bones had protruded through the skin and I had been bleeding profusely. My right femur was also broken at mid-thigh, perhaps from going through my windshield. Both of my femurs, tibia, and fibula had been repaired, the right femur now had a rod that ran through it from my knee to my hip joint, and my left had a giant plate and screws to secure it through the knee. My hip and pelvis would have to wait a few more weeks before they would attempt surgery again. I had just been in surgery for over 8 hours and I had lost a lot of blood. My left hip and pelvis were smashed, the acetabulum, shattered and blown out by the impact of landing. I had staples that ran over my body like railroad tracks. I had no idea if I would walk again.

My husband looked at me as I went in and out of consciousness. He asked me what I was planning to do now with my kids?

He said that there was no way that I could look after myself or my children, pay the mortgage, or even be able to go back to work for what seemed like a very long time. He offered to magnanimously forgive me any transgressions that I had made and that when I was released, he would allow me to come home. I thought to myself, 'forgive me'? Forgive me for WHAT? I hadn't done anything to forgive except marry the wrong man and finally get strong enough to rectify a bad situation.

I looked at him then, right in the eye. I had just survived a traumatic night and I didn't know what the future would hold, but I knew it didn't include me staying married to him.

"You know what? The ONLY thing I didn't hit or break last night was my head. The Separation stands! You are still moving out."

It was a defining moment for me. Even in my darkest hour, when it would have been so easy to capitulate, to have someone to lean on, to help me go through this nightmare, I knew that it would still be better to go it alone, and that I was strong enough to handle anything that was going to come my way. I was Unstoppable!

I spent six months in the hospital and then years filled with surgery, litigation, and pain.

The day of my accident, the one object that brought me the most joy in my life, my bike, also brought me the most pain, physically, emotionally, and spiritually.

I lost everything I believed defined me as ME, during my hospital stay. I had been a drummer in a band, until I learned the band came and picked up all their gear from my basement and replaced me without even an acknowledgement. I had been eight days shy of leaving for Shanghai with the Canadian Master Dragon boat Team, my place secured after rigorous training. I found out that my job was reorganized and my position became defunct. I had to fight for my freedom from my husband through a haze of morphine and pain. He finally released me, seems all that was necessary was money.

In the hospital I went through what is often referred to as the dark night of the soul. It's not literally one night but months of hell, rediscovering one's sense of self.

I am often asked how I got through this by myself. Three days after I got home from the hospital, my beloved dog died. One week later, the rod in my right femur broke, and I had to walk on a broken leg for a year, until my surgeon could get time in an operating theatre to replace it. That surgery took 6 hours where he broke 3 instruments and had to leave some of their parts inside me.

I ended up having to hire and fire a few legal firms, the first few just weren't interested in fighting for me. I found the right lawyer finally who was a true blessing. He knew from the beginning that he would fight for a Catastrophic determination and get it. Hear me when I say, no one wants to be considered catastrophic, least of all me, but when I went to traffic court for the man who hit me, the judge gave him a $26.00 dollar fine for basically just pleading guilty. He thanked him for not lying. Wow. Now THAT felt like a kick in my gut. My life had been turned upside down and would forever be impacted by pain, surgery, and only God knew what else was to come!

Whenever you are involved in any kind of legal battle, the insurance companies want to make sure you aren't lying, so I was subjected to a series of ongoing determinations. One of those included lying on a table, as two doctors entered the exam room, and without even a "hello", promptly took out their tape measures and started to measure each of my scars to record their length. I imagined myself a slab of beef on that table. With tears streaming down my face, it felt like I was about to be butchered, certainly humiliated, and who cares how long my scars are? Does the length determine the monetary value? As awful as that experience was, what came next was even worse when one of the doctors explained to me that I shouldn't try dating in the future. My commodity as a woman had been depleted by at least 30 percent. I was like OMG, who are these people? Believe it or not, he wasn't the first doctor to say something along those same lines. What gives these so-called health professionals the right to be so cruel and why would they want to be?

With all the loss, all the pain and uncertainty about my future, I am often asked who or what gave me the courage to fight for my life, especially given all the pain I was in.

I needed to be become my own "Super Hero". I had kids who needed me to be their mom, and a life I wanted back.

I am forever grateful to my dad for always making me get back on the horse after I fell. Fear would not take away my faith, confidence, and belief in knowing that I KNEW how to give birth to ideas and turn them reality. I might come back different, but I would be back in ways I might not even imagine.

Maxwell Maltz, who authored Psycho Cybernetics states "

"What is the worst that can possibly happen if I fail?" Remind yourself that "Life is long" and seek the perspective of 20/20 hindsight in advance. For the most part, today's crisis winds up being but one little "blip" on a long life history. For today, there's an immediate second act tomorrow. For this week, there's a second act beginning next Monday. For even the authentic tragedy, there's a second act waiting to be scripted and played out over time."

I am proud of what I accomplished since Aug. 11, 2002. I became a Master Coach Trainer, founder of The Good Radio Network, Author of 4 books with a 5th on the way, an artist, Metaphysical Hypnotherapist, and maybe most important of all, *The Believer*, who 'rents' my faith and belief to those who aren't quite secure in their own, but just until they are ready to take it back, and own it for themselves.

http://www.unstoppablefrankiepicasso.com/

 https://fineartamerica.com/profiles/frankie-picasso

 https://www.thegoodradionetwork.com/

Frankie Picasso is a Canadian SocialPreneur, Talk Show Host, and Champion for Change who has been transforming lives and influencing culture for the past 30 years.

Professionally, she is a Certified Life, Business and Master Coach Trainer, Author, Artist, Activist and Radio/TV Host, who just happens to specialize in the Impossible!

Frankie founded The Good Radio Network, a socially conscious radio platform as a vehicle for social impact and change. As a professional Artist, Frankie's paintings have been featured in the International Book of Contemporary Artists Volume 6 and can be found on Fine Art America, http://fineartamerica.com/profiles/frankie-picasso.html. Sale of her artwork and custom orders goes to pay for both Cleft Palate Surgery for children through Mercy Ships Canada, Saving Animals in Shelters and other Humanitarian efforts in need at the time.

Frankie's book Midlife Mojo won her recognition and the Finalist WINNER award as one of the "50 Great Writers you should be Reading in 2015!" and her last book,' For Want of 40 Pounds' was a Number1 Best Seller in 3 countries at the same time. Today, she has 4 books to her credit with her 5th being her inclusion in the BLU Anthology Series.

She is honoured to be a member of a group of high-level influencers and thought leaders who are out to cause positive change in the world.

Frankie is notably the first Female Kickboxing Promoter in the World and Manager of a 12 time Champion.

A long time animal advocate, Frankie is passionate about SAVING Animals worldwide through many organizations including the WWF, Endangered Species REVENGE, Storybook Primates, The Donkey Sanctuary and more. She hopes everyone will join her in raising AWARENESS for the compassionate treatment of all wildlife and Humans.

Frankie is a member of the Canadian Association of Journalists, a member of the International Coach Federation, and Founder of both The Good Radio & The Good Media Network and the proud Grandmother of eight with Shhh...the 9th on the way!

She lives in Cambridge, Ontario with her Golden Retriever Bongo and husband Dan.

A Story of Perseverance

By Gloria Kapeller

As I sit to write this chapter for this book, this is a new experience for me. I have written two books but know that my voice will carry farther than I could have imagined. I never thought that I would be the voice for so many that have suffered in silence. I speak for so many that have found themselves in similar situations and didn't or haven't found their voice yet. I hope that my story will inspire those that need to be heard, and that they find the courage to have that voice and to know that we each have the strength to overcome what has happened to us.

My story is a story of perseverance and overcoming sexual abuse, some of the things that I learned, and what I have done to overcome some of the truly horrendous things that happened to me as a child and into my teen years growing up.

I was born into one family but was taken away by a government who thought that being Indigenous and raised that way was wrong, they thought that being raised in a 'white' family was better. I am part of history as people have come to refer as The Sixties Scoop. I was taken by Social Services and put into a community and family that I sometimes referred to as "going from the frying pan into the fire". The sexual abuse began immediately with the 2 younger sons of the adopted family (I wasn't legally adopted until I was in grade 2) I gained an incredible 40 lbs that first year that I was there. I was 6 years old—in fact my birthday was the day before we arrived. My sister and myself were number 9 and 10 in a large family to begin with.

It took many years to finally escape, yes escape, and finally not to have the fear of being raped all the time. At 16 I thought that I was pregnant, the older married brother wore a condom but it broke. Thank God I didn't get pregnant and didn't have to deal with the repercussions of that—I was told that if I was, I would be going to Edmonton and it would be dealt with. I was 19 years old when I finally got the nerve to leave. I spent the next few years doing a fair amount of drinking just to forget. I met the father of my boys around this time and when I got pregnant I stopped drinking—I was 21. It took a few more years to learn that this had also happened to my younger sister. I always thought that I was protecting her from what was happening to me.

Around the age of 30, just after my youngest son was born, I got to a breaking point that I knew I had to deal with some of the abuse, in order not to start the drinking again—my boys were the most important thing to me, and I would protect them at all costs. I was pretty adept at hiding how I was feeling, but knew I needed some help. But when it became too uncomfortable, I stopped going to see the councillor, but at that point it was enough to take some of the pressure off.

It wasn't until I met my husband that I really opened up and told him what had happened to me—yes, I even did leave some of the details out with him. I never went 'home' alone and always had someone with me. I wanted my boys to feel like they were part of a family and this was the only one that I knew. I just in the last five years had the three 'brothers' charged. I finally had the courage to stand up for the 6-year-old me that had no voice back then. A childhood friend that I had just recently found on Facebook, asked me in our first conversation that we had 'Were you abused?' She then told me that her sister had actually witnessed me being raped and that it had traumatized her as well. She actually came to court and said that she had witnessed it happening. But even with that evidence, and other facts, the three were never convicted on their charges. One thing that a survivor of abuse needs is the fact that they are believed when they come forward. We went through the courts, but one thing that is very clear is that the system stands up for the perpetrators, and not the victims. After 50 years believe me, I wasn't lying. I feel that this is one of the reasons why so many do not have the courage to come forward and tell what happened to them. This so has to change, but there is no statute of limitations on sexual assault complaints.

I have had the courage to stand up for everyone who has gone through the same ordeal, and yes, I would do it again.

I have had to do a great deal of healing, and healing the wounded inner child. I have had to learn to cope with feeling of guilt, (why did I let this happen) learning to forgive myself first, then others who hurt me, knowing that forgiveness is a huge part of being able to deal with the past. I used to be scared at what people would think of me when I was going to share my story. As I have gotten older (and wiser) I know that my story will have an impact in the fact that it is okay to have your story heard and that you are not alone, and yes people will believe you. The truth needs to be told, and light needs to be shone into the darkness of this sexual abuse story so that no other child has to endure what I did–It Is OK to tell.

My book I wrote is called Behind The Eyes: A Story of Perseverance available on Amazon.ca and Amazon.com

I also have taken a lot of healing modalities–Theta Healing, Reiki, Access Consciousness, using my essential oils, to name a few to learn how to heal myself.

I always felt that I went through what I did in my childhood to make me a stronger person who could handle life's challenges. I really believe that we choose lessons that our souls needs to learn. My youngest son, Byron, had a stroke at the age of 7. Not only was I being prepared for that role as I had gotten a job as a teacher's assistant (after I graduated from college in Red Deer) when Byron was just 3 months old at Parkland School–a school specializing in working with Special Needs children. I worked there and when Byron had his stroke at 7 years old, not only did I have a 'family', but people who truly understood what I was going through. I truly felt that I have been Divinely guided throughout my life, meeting my husband, Jon, having someone who truly has stood by me through all of the trials of being a dad to Byron, and being a support to me dealing with the abuse.

I just wrote my son Byron's story—our journey through his stroke:

Walking Through The Storm Weathering Life After A Stroke available on Amazon.ca and Amazon.com

My wish is that even if I help one person to have a voice and to heal, I will have succeeded. The abuse stopped with me.

glow_kapeller@hotmail.com

Gloria Dawn Kapeller specializes in coaching people to heal from the past. She is a Reiki Master, Theta Healer and Access Conciousness Practioner. She currently lives in Stettler, Alberta Canada with her husband Jon and 2 sons, and works as a Healthcare Aide for Alberta Health Services. She is a best selling author of two books: Behind The Eyes: A Story of Perseverance, a story about her life, and Walking Through The Storm Weathering Life After A Stroke , a story about her son Byron, who had a stroke at the age of 7 and their journey together dealing with life's ups and down and and life challenges and lessons.

Silver Lining

By Jenna Pilot

I was 29 years old, sitting in a salon in Winnipeg, Canada; eyes bruised, big cut on my nose, mouth pulsating with pain. What was once long, thick hair was now cut short to my scalp. The receptionist looked up and gasped but managed to say "how can we help you?", I replied: "I need my hair to be fixed with long hair extensions."

Extensions, really Jenna?

I would not allow my outer image to reflect the internal disaster. I almost lost my life the night before and hair was my #1 priority (completely messed up, I know!).

I was greeted by the hairstylist, who was in shock, I am sure of the beaten look I was presenting. The stylist compassionately said, "I don't know how this is going to look, your hair is way too short for extensions", I replied, "I don't care, I just need my long hair back".

While in the chair, facing the mirror, I was frozen, in shock, and asking myself, "How the hell did you get here?" Between this repeating thought, flashbacks of the night before danced through my head. To when the anger and yelling started, to when he came at me with scissors, to when I was on the ground screaming, to when his hands were wrapped around my neck, to then waking up the next morning. I was completely naked in my bed, not knowing what had happened and him walking into the house threatening me and my family if I went to the police.

I was numb...
I was lost...
I was scared...

Now let's hit *PAUSE* before I continue, I encourage you all to take a big belly breath to release any negative energy or triggers that may have developed.

So, Inhale LOVE and PEACE and EXHALE negativity and shit.

How DID I GET HERE??

My numbness started before this violent episode, which is the reason I found myself in this situation, to begin with. This experience, this relationship, is what I attracted. I know that this may sound harsh but I believe that to my core. I wasn't healthy, when I met this man, I had no clue who I was, where I "fit" or who I wanted to be. I constantly had thoughts such as "I am not good enough", "what is wrong with me" and "I am unlovable". I constantly sought for external LOVE instead of strengthening my internal LOVE.

The biggest question I received after leaving this abusive relationship is why? Why did you stay? Why can't you get over him? Why, why???? Why was impossible to answer at the time but after years of healing, I found the why.

Little Jenna

I grew up in a small city in Saskatchewan, I had a privileged life, always had food on the table, nice clothes, opportunities to travel, so yes, I was well taken care of. However, having a privileged upbringing does not prevent negative life experiences that create limiting beliefs, nor does it prevent trauma from occurring.

My first traumatic experience was when I was in middle school and the subject of bullying. I was bullied to the point of having to leave schools, "they" didn't accept me as one of them. I was bullied for being overweight and tormented at times. This was my first scar, the beliefs of being ugly, fat, not good enough, not worthy, not accepted, it all started here.

In high school, I started coping with these belief systems negatively. I just wanted to belong, I just wanted to be loved and I would do anything to feel that way. I also started manifesting unhealthy relationships that continued to decrease my self-worth.

In my early twenties, the dance continued and I started becoming an overachiever and a people-pleaser so I could mask my self-hate. I went to university and received my Bachelor of Social Work because, of course, I thought by helping others be better, I will be in the end, better.

The next step in this dance was in my late twenties, I acted like I had it all together, good job, nice place, friends, but inside I was screaming. I felt flawed as a woman, I felt ugly, not good enough, and I didn't know where I belonged.

Quick disclaimer, this is only a brief snapshot of my life experiences and on the why, follow, or connect with me to hear the much longer version.

Meeting Mr. Right and Wrong

I had never left home or been away from my family, I feared the unknown but felt pushed to leave and try something new. In other views, I was being stupid and ridiculous but something inside me just told me I had to do it. I wanted a new opportunity, a new start, where I could be anything I wanted and maybe even find someone to LOVE me the way I wanted. The truth is, writing this seven years later, I know now, I was running from me, from the life I had, from the person I was.

When I first moved to Winnipeg, the excitement of living in a new place, with new opportunities, lasted for about two months. I started to pick up old habits and destructive thinking, I was beyond lonely and my feelings of unworthiness started creeping up again. I knew that it would take time to get adjusted to my new life but the grossness I thought I left, just followed me there. That is when I met my Mr. Right and Wrong, the most passionate yet evil person I have known. When we first started dating my gut was **SCREAMING** at me, something is not right with this guy, stop, leave, GET AWAY. Too Bad they don't teach young women to listen to their GUT.

At first, just like every other abusive relationship, he was sweet, romantic, so into me, always complimenting me and going out of his way to show that I was important to him and that I was wanted by him, this, of course, drew me in as I needed that love and validation. As I am sure you are expecting me to say, that pure bliss changed very quickly and red flags started coming from every corner. He started to become demanding, freaking out, yelling, screaming, cutting me down, obsessing over where I was, all the types of behaviors that scream abuser and well, narcissist. I knew I needed to get out of this but I continued to get sucked back in with kind words and fake apologies, every time I went back, he got worse.

It progressed to pushing, destroying my things, threatening, and sexual abuse (demanding sex or else receive his wrath). But after each episode I continued to go back to him, I even got a place with him. This shows, or I hope this shows, how unhealthy I was as a person to continually choose to go back to this. Then only after a month of living together, things progressed and he became physically abusive until the final attack discussed above that almost took my life.

Spiritually HUNGRY

After the attack, I was more lost than before but now I was also traumatized. I ran back home the day after the attack, I was scared and had no clue how to keep myself safe. My family and friends greeted me with open arms, cried with me, supported me, and really tried to let me know I was safe. But, no matter what anyone did I was lost and I was constantly living in **FEAR**.

I isolated myself and cried.

I tried to go to traditional counseling, I attended a surviving abuse group with other women, they all helped a little but not enough. I continued to search for my answers on how to heal, then of course like the universe always does, it started to show me options to heal.

A friend of mine suggested going to see a medium for guidance and healing, DONE. My appointment day came and I instantly connected with her. She provided me a comfortable place to sit and asked for my full name and birthday. Then the next thing she said was an absolute game-changer for me. The medium instantly looked up at me and stated she was connecting with an older lady who had passed and that she was shorter with blonde/white hair. I got excited and stated that it was my grandma that passed. The medium then said something that still gives me goosebumps to this day, "I am supposed to tell you that your grandma was there with you that night, that she was so scared for you and that she will always be watching and protecting you". I was in shock, any doubt of belief I had at that moment was gone, I finally had a sense of ease, a sense of pure love. The medium then continued to tell me that it was time to heal, that I have a big purpose on this planet but I need to do the work first.

My spiritual hunger grew and I made a commitment to change!

Thank you, Grandma for saving me, I know you are watching out for me, I see your 808 all the time, I miss you and I love you!

YOGA as my Savior

Prior to moving to Winnipeg, I started taking Yoga classes and really fell in love. My bestie and I had been discussing going to get certified in yoga but had no plans to do so. Then the universe again handed another opportunity to heal. My bestie found an amazing retreat in Mexico, where we would be living in a tent, showering outside, eating vegan, doing yoga, meditation, breathwork, mantra singing, and a vision quest for over three weeks. Now I really wish I had more time to discuss how LIFE changing this was for both of us but that will be the next chapter or book.

I will say that YOGA was my savior, it healed so much of me, I went there like a wounded being and I left as the Shining Goddess.

Finding the SILVER LINING

After coming home from Mexico, I felt like a NEW person, I felt lighter, happier, healthier, and more aligned with who I was and what I was going to do next. I didn't stay home for long as I felt the urge and calling to move to Edmonton. I didn't know what I was going to do in Edmonton but like never before I just trusted that it was actually the **RIGHT** move. I packed my few belongings (left everything in Winnipeg) and hit the road to Edmonton to live at a friend's place for a while.

I have been in Edmonton for 6 ½ years now and GUESS WHAT?!?

It was absolutely what I was supposed to do.

EVERY. SINGLE. THING. Has worked out for me since I have been here.

Moving to Winnipeg and meeting Mr. Wrong/Right was my Silver Lining. It was the most difficult time in my life which turned into the most beautiful time. Because of this experience, I actually healed and found myself again. Now I say to him, I forgive you and I thank you.

Both forgiveness and gratitude are for me not for him. I am grateful for this experience as it changed my life, it brought me back to **WHO I AM** and who I am supposed to be.

There is always a silver lining if **YOU** allow yourself to reflect on a negative situation. Bad things are going to happen in life YES, there is no running away from that. What matters is what you do with it, do you let it consume you, or do you let it guide and support you to a much more abundant, beautiful life.

The choice is always YOURS and I will always choose the latter.

Becoming a SELF-LOVE Ignitor

The best is yet to come!!!!

Through my own healing, I learned so much about myself, I became invested and a little obsessed with learning more about healing, shame, and how to love myself again. The more I experienced significant shifts and healing, the more I knew my calling was to share this with other women who were ready to become more spiritual, more in love with themselves, and more aligned with their authentic self. I took a huge leap a year ago and started my own business called Everything Women, my why on starting this business is everything I wrote in this chapter.

Everything Women is for **FIERY, FUN,** and **FEARLESS** Women to *Reconnect to LOVE, Elevate your Lifestyle and Live Consciously.* I am so passionate about empowering courageous, spirituality hungry from disconnect and shame to RADIANT, Energetic, Queens.

Through the years of pain, I thought I was nothing of a woman, through years of learning and healing I have completely ignited myself and scream out loud every opportunity I get to "I AM EVERYTHING WOMEN!!!"

You are Everything Women too, you just might not know it yet.

I want to say a HUGE THANK YOU to anyone reading this today, I hope you were able to take something away that may help you on your path.

Sending you all LOVE and Light.

Iameverythingwomen

groups/iameverythingwomen

@iameverythingwomen

Jenna@everythingwomen.ca

Jenna is a passionate and bold personality whose purpose is to empower women in all forms, mind, body and spirit. Jenna is the founder of Everything Women, where fun, fiery, fearless women reconnect to love, elevate lifestyle and live consciously. Jenna has been a registered social worker for 15 years, a certified life coach, speaker, writer, self-love ignitor, yoga instructor, trainer and is currently obtaining her certification as a Shame practitioner. Jenna believes that shame impacts every single person but Women see, feel and hear the most of it. Jenna spent many years of her life feeling like she didn't belong and wasn't good enough. After years of training and self-development, she has learned that she is EVERYTHING WOMEN and always was. Jenna is now driven to ensure all WOMEN, know, believe, and feel like they are EVERYTHING WOMEN.

FB: Everything Women:
https://www.facebook.com/Iameverythingwomen

Everything Women FREE group:
https://www.facebook.com/groups/iameverythingwomen

The 7 Benefits of Chaos to Help You Succeed

©2020 DR. KAREN HARDY, RIMS-CRMP

We are living in a time where norms are being challenged. I call it a VUCA world. A world filled with Volatility, Uncertainty, Complexity and Ambiguity (VUCA). This VUCA world brings about opportunities for change and to either be a part of orchestrating what it looks like versus being on the receiving end of it. In life and in business you never know how something is going to turn out. It is never a straight line between where we are and where we want to end up. I recall a saying older generations would refer to often, in that, "the shortest distance between any two points is a straight line." This is the mantra that we often use as a guidepost to determine who we want to be, where we want to go, and how we want to live. The Who. The Where. The How. Just follow the straight line and you will be ok...*unless.*

A Case in Point

I have a friend. She was born and raised in Memphis, Tennessee, the home of Elvis Presley. She grew up around the corner from Elvis Presley Boulevard. Her A to B plan was to move up to the big city, Washington, D.C. by the time she was 25 years old and she wanted to occupy a public service job. So, she did everything she could to make this a reality, to make this happen. She did all the right things. She changed her major from computer science to political science. And then she joined a campaign to help this candidate run for political office. He promised her this big, lucrative job in Washington, D.C. if he won the election and she was ready to go. It was awesome.

But most of the time, what we want and how we get there can be a maze of twists and turns. And if the latter is true, then I propose that we embrace chaos often; more so than we think.

What is Chaos?

Chaos is disorder, it is confusion. Scientifically, it is unformed matter, it has no shape or form. The best way to describe it physically is the example of a tornado. Now, for eight or nine years, I had the privilege of working in concert with meteorologists at the U.S. National Weather Service, which collects and disseminates information about weather to the public. One of the things I learned about tornadoes is that not one or two of them are the same. In fact, tornadoes can be different. Some have a destruction path of 500 feet and others have a destruction path of just seven feet.

Some tornadoes are intimidating and afar off as dark funnel clouds, and others are even weaker and invisible to the eye. But the most important thing to understand is that, when there is a tornado, it is time to either evacuate or abandon. In fact, the World Economic Forum, through their Global Risk Report, cited that, of all the global risk in the world, one of the risks with the greatest likelihood have been severe weather events. And during this severe weather event first responders sound the alarm. You are then encouraged to evacuate an area or abandon it. First Responders tell you that you cannot collect anything. It is time to leave everything you know behind. Leave your home, leave your houses, leave all your personal assets, all your dreams, your realities, your expectations. You are to leave all those things behind to get to a safer place.

Sounding the Alarm is an Opportunity

For some people, sounding an alarm and hearing the time to evacuate, is not a sign to evacuate or abandon but an indicator to pursue. And that is what storm chasers do. Storm chases are one of the riskiest activities you can possibly engage in. But for some reason, *storm chasers have this tenacity and desire and eagerness to follow the storm, to chase the chaos.* Why is that? It is because they know that unless they embrace the chaos, they cannot capture the data that is generated by the storm. This data is then used by scientists to help determine how to safely secure ourselves from disastrous weather in the future. So, they pursue the chaos.

In my career I saw plenty of chaos. My A to B plan, the straight line; had not worked. At one point in my life, I thought that maybe I discovered a new phenomenon, because every time I got a new job, the person who hired me would leave. Maybe I had a personality complex? For example, when I got the job at a research institute as the risk manager, the supervisor retired. When I got that new job as director at a government agency, my supervisor left. When I got the book deal, the publisher of risk management textbook, the acquisitions editor left the company. And then when I had my film premiere for a documentary for Veterans with PTSD, the woman that supported the film screening found a new job.

So I began to think: is it me? Could it be me? I then discovered something I called "just in time chaos." It came just in time. Someone else heard the alarms, they heard the sirens in their own lives. And they had to attend to the chaos in their own life. And they had to abandon everything they knew. Their career, their position, their organization, to pursue something else. And then I became a benefactor.

Here is the biggest lesson of all:

"If you don't abandon where you are, then you must pursue where you want to go."

-Dr. Karen Hardy

The 7 Benefits of Chaos

Some of the most successful companies today were founded during times of chaos, such as a recession. This includes companies like Netflix, founded in 1997 which nearly crumbled during the dot-com bubble in the early 2000s. Today, Netflix is worth nearly $34 billion. Airbnb was founded in 2008 during the great recession, Trader Joe's was founded during a sluggish economy in the late 1950s and MTV made its debut in a sluggish economy in the early '80s. In addition to being resilient, taking a risk and having a relationship with risk-taking is key to leveraging the opportunities that chaos can present.

Want to learn more about how high achievers relate to risk taking? Check out my Flip This Risk® podcast at

- Anchor.fm/FlipThisRiskPodcast
- https://www.FlipThisRisk.TV

Here are the 7 benefits of chaos that everyone should consider during times of uncertainty:

1) The presence of chaos means the absence of Structure.

2) The benefits of chaos means the absence of Standards (there are no standards)

3) The benefits of chaos means the elimination of Competition.

4) The benefits of chaos means what's normal becomes questionable.

5) The benefits of chaos is a great time to redefine your life and go into territories you don't know.

6) The benefits of chaos mean claiming your universal real estate. This is a definitive time to define what your new normal would be. And finally,

7) By the time the storm clears things will settle and you realize that you have established new opportunities for yourself that you never

knew before. You can now put a stake in the ground, in the land that's opportunity, that is wide open. It is time to acquire assets and opportunities previously occupied by others but is now available to you.

What Ever Happened to That Friend...?

I ran into my friend from Memphis, Tennessee. She never did reach that dream of hers, that A to B plan of moving to Washington, D.C. and occupying a government job by the age of 25... But she did by age 50! Becoming a civil rights activist. She had the opportunity to be one of the main speakers at the 50th Anniversary of the March in Washington all because of her random experiences with chaos. You, too, need to embrace chaos. Let that be your guiding force for who you want to be, where do you want to go, and how you want to live.

 https://www.DrKarenHardySpeaks.com

 courses.FlipThisRiskAcademy.com

 Anchor.fm/FlipThisRiskPodcast

About Dr. Karen Hardy

Dr. Karen Hardy is a scholar-practitioner, educator, best-selling and award-winning author as well as co-producer of a 5-time Emmy Award winning documentary film "A New Leash on Life: The K9s for Warriors Story." She advises organizations and leaders on the strategies of risk management. You can access her services and products at the links below:

Speaking engagements:
https://www.DrKarenHardySpeaks.com

Free Risk Management Course for Small Business:
courses.FlipThisRiskAcademy.com

Flip This Risk® Podcast:
Anchor.fm/FlipThisRiskPodcast

The School Librarian Told Me I Read Too Much

By Lana McAra

When I was in Fifth Grade, I used my study period to go to the library. That was my first year in middle school, and my new school had a massive beautiful library. Looking around at all the books, free and available to me, I felt like I had won the lottery. I decided to systematically mine those riches.

Every day I checked out two books. I read them, returned them the next day, and checked out two more. I worked my way through 56 Nancy Drew books, 58 Hardy Boys and kept going. When I finished one shelf, I'd move to the next one.

We lived far out in the country, so I was the first one to get on the bus in the morning and the last one off in the afternoon. Every day, I had two full hours of blessed reading time. When I reached home, the first book was almost finished. I'd start the second book that evening and finish it on the morning ride to school. Those were some of the best days of my entire life.

That lasted until around New Year's.

One day, I brought my two books to the checkout desk and the head librarian—a thin woman with deep creases over her top lip—came out of the back and headed my way. My heart squeezed when I realized she was staring right at me. *What had I done wrong?*

"What had I done wrong?"

"You're taking out too many books," she said in a strident voice. "Are you reading all of those books?"

Unbearably shy, I nodded. I clenched my teeth and tried to stop my lip from quivering.

She scratched a pen across my file card. "I'm making a note for the checkout ladies. No more than five books a week."

I left the library gasping for air and fighting tears. After all, I was eleven years old and too big to cry. *How could she? I wasn't doing anything wrong.*

I can still feel the tightness in my throat and chest, the absolute grief. For the next few months, I moped around the house in the evenings. I stared out the bus window on those endless rides. If my grades had been suffering, she might have had a valid point, but I was a straight A student. I couldn't understand why she did that to me. And—to be honest—I still can't.

"I couldn't understand why she did that to me."

Only five books per week. That brings a smile to me now. For the rest of the year, I took full advantage of my five books, and the universe started sending me more—boxes of books from a neighbor cleaning out her garage, friends who handed off books when they were finished with them. I kept on reading.

In 1996, a traditional publishing house released my first book, *Megan's Choice,* under my pseudonym Rosey Dow. It was a reader's favorite that year, and later became the first of a bundled series that sold 250,000 copies. In 2001, I won the national Christy Award for my historical novel, *Reaping the Whirlwind.* To date, I've written more than thirty titles. I earn a living as a ghostwriter, with total book sales of around a million.

I started my 10,000 hours of mastery in that middle school library.

But this isn't about reading. It's about an adult telling a child they do something too much. Has someone ever scolded you for doing something too much? Maybe they said you talk too much, or you're a show off, or you daydream too much. Maybe they said you're too focused on martial arts or drawing or movies.

"This is about an adult telling a child they do something too much."

Cartoonist Dav Pilkey was a total misfit in the classroom setting. He was so disruptive, his teacher put his desk in the hall each day. He'd spend the time making cartoon books of a character he called "Captain Underpants." His teacher ripped up his art and told him he shouldn't spend his time making silly books.

Pilkey went on to win the Caldecott Honor Award. His books have sold more than 80 million copies, and Netflix features his cartoons. He worked on his 10,000 hours of mastery in that hallway.

Pilkey didn't take his teacher's advice but, sadly, most of us do. We take in the words of an authority figure and create a belief that we are somehow defective. We put a lid on the best parts of ourselves based on someone's else's thoughtless words. We shut down what makes us feel alive.

"We shut down what makes us feel alive."

In working with clients in my personal development practice, I often see people who have shut down their natural passions to the point that we have to keep digging and digging to find the first trace of the spark inside them. Within that spark is the joy of doing something they absolutely love. That something makes time go away, and the world becomes background noise. Sometimes, the absorption is so deep that almost we almost forget to breathe.

That natural spark creates the greats in this world: the Thomas Edison's whose teachers said he asked too many questions. The Stephen Spielberg's who wanted to do nothing else but play with a movie camera, and the Soichiro Honda's who at age fifteen left home to work in a shop that repaired small engines. Later, he attached those engines to bicycles and called his invention a motorcycle. None of these people started out looking for a big bank account. They did what they did because it made them feel alive.

"They did what they did because it made them feel alive."

If you've ever felt dissatisfaction that brought up the question, *Is this all there is to life?* maybe it's time to slow down and start your own quest to find your own spark. Think back to elementary school.

What did your parents have to pry you away from in order to eat dinner?
What did you save up for at that age?
How did you spend your summer breaks?

The thing that felt easy and effortless, the thing that made the world go away—that's your passion.

Whenever I bring up this topic, the most frequent response is: "I'm too old to start now," as though passion and *joie de vivre* have an expiration date. I always reply, "Too old to get lost in a world of delight? Too old for something that lights you up? Too old to have fun?"

Whether you're 25 or 85, what would it take to put away the concept of progress toward a lofty goal and, instead, focus on enjoyable hours doing what you love? What's the worst that could happen? You'll wake up looking forward to your day and have it end even better than you thought? What's the downside to that? Maybe, just maybe, putting in your 10,000 hours doing something you love is enough. Progress can happen later, in its own time.

After living in the art world most of her life, Carmen Herrera sold her first work of art at 89. At 101, she had a solo show at the Whitney Art Museum in New York City, and at 104 she had her first public art exhibit. If Carmen had used the *Too Old* reason when she was 40 or 50 or even 80, she would have shut the door on herself, never knowing that others would open the door wide for her one day. In the meantime, she had years of satisfaction doing what she loves.

Today, more than any time in history, people can follow their passions and get paid for it. Gamers earn five figures per month because others enjoy watching them play. Makeup-obsessed teenagers earn big paychecks demonstrating and reviewing products.

People with the gift of gab light up the world from their own back yards. Helen Wyatt is a great-grandmother from Georgia who loves making outdoor crafts like cement bird baths and mosaic table tops. She has a beautiful Southern accent and a sweet personality. When her grandson first urged her to start a YouTube channel, she said, "Who would want to watch me puttering around with my silly projects?" but she tried it.

Now she has more than 120,000 subscribers. Comments pour in from house-bound subscribers who tell Helen she brightens their day with her long monologues about rain clouds and coffee. Those subscribers send her stacks and stacks of cards, little handmade gifts and letters filled with love and good wishes. They add joy to Helen's life in return. In her videos, Helen often says she feels like she's won the lottery—doing what she loves and making friends with thousands of people.

So, what is that thing for you?

Find it, and follow it. Once you do, you'll feel like you've won the lottery, too.

www.LanaMcAra.com

A speaker who teaches and a teacher who inspires, Lana McAra has been on hundreds of stages around the world. A radio and TV show host, she has shared the stage with media personalities such as Loral Langemeier, Janet Attwood and Fabienne Fredrickson. Her work has been quoted by Carol Roth and Dell.

Lana is an award-winning, best-selling author and ghostwriter of more than 30 titles with a million books sold (writing under the name Rosey Dow). She won the national Christy Award for her fiction in 2001, and one of her ghostwritten books received review acclaim in Publishers Weekly. She is a writing teacher and provides private coaching for budding novelists.

Lana also has a personal development practice, helping clients dissolve painful childhood memories, anxiety, and limiting beliefs. She is a graduate of the San Diego Hypnosis Institute, Hypnosis for Health, and Transform Destiny. She lives near the Delaware beaches within driving distance of Washington D.C., Baltimore and Philadelphia. Visit her web site at www.LanaMcAra.com

Leadership is About Connecting

When Was the Last Time You Connected with Yourself?

By Lisa Wilson

I used to believe that as long as one part of my life was working, I could handle anything life threw at me. If work was stressful but my personal life was going well, I could manage. Or if life was stressful but work was manageable, I could handle it. It's when the two parts were difficult at the same time, then I couldn't handle anything. Business, Life and the Universe are very entwined. When all three are working together life feels easy, when they are not, things seem to fall apart.

Staying in line with the belief that work and personal were two separate entities. I went into every job I held believing that I would NOT make friends, because I was in Human Resources. It took a special person to be my friend because they couldn't ask any questions. I had a lot of information that I couldn't share. I did everything I could to keep business and personal life separate.

On top of that I showed up in business and personal life in very different ways. In business I was controlled, organized, and while I still brought in laughter and fun, the wilder part of myself was hidden. In my personal life I was doing things like bungee jumping, travelling for 6 weeks on my own, mountain biking, snowboarding, scuba diving, anything to get the adrenaline rush.

I could not have been more wrong in this belief. You are you, no matter where you are. While you don't have to share everything that is going on in your home life at work, I assure you people know when there is something happening. This lesson was brought to me on several occasions.

Once I worked with a Union Steward, while we didn't agree on everything business-wise, we got along very well. She walked into my office one day and said "Did you let that guy back in your life?" I responded "Yes", wondering how she even knew, I had not discussed it with her. The next thing out of her mouth was "Get him out, he is ruining you!" And she left. I couldn't ask more questions; she was done talking. I still have no idea what she saw, I didn't know that I was behaving any differently. I had been talking to an ex-boyfriend again. It wasn't a healthy relationship and somehow she saw it.

It became very clear when I started my business full-time that being two different people, one at work and one at home wasn't going to work either. To run a business, you need that wild side. The one that is willing to take risks. At the same time, you need that organized and controlled side. I had to be all of it at once. Actually, I GOT to be all of it at once. It was a relief.

Initially, I struggled in my business because I wanted to be both a life and corporate coach. All the marketing experts told me I had to pick one and I couldn't because they are so closely related. Separating your personal life and your leadership role is almost impossible. You might be able to avoid talking to people about your marriage problems, but that doesn't mean you are separating the two. How you show up in your leadership role is always affected by what's happening elsewhere in your life. Even if you think it's not. You can see from the story above, I was not doing a good job at hiding what was happening in my personal life. I had learned this lesson before starting my business, and it was going to be hard to unlearn in just for the sake of marketing.

I worked with someone once, who signed on for business coaching, but we mostly talked about giving her permission to go home early. She ran the business with her husband. She felt pressure to stay at work for long hours but she also took care of the bulk of the work at home. It took a long time just to decide that leaving at 4:00 p.m. was not only allowed but it didn't matter whether her husband understood or not. For her, personal and business had a very strong and obvious connection.

How I came to a mix between the marketing experts and what I wanted for my business, was I focused on leaders. I didn't need to tell people in my marketing that we were going to talk about their personal lives too, they just came to me and we ended up there anyway. Recently I had one person apologize for talking about her personal life. I reminded her it helped me to know what was happening elsewhere in her life to better understand her.

Six months into starting my business I had a surgery that left me tired for years. I had to make a lot of changes. Initially, I fought it. I tried to remain the person I thought I was before. I would continue to push my body and it would continue to fail me. It took me almost five years to accept where I was and that I needed to listen to my body and let it rest. While I'd been preaching self-care I didn't really understand it myself.

I think the words "self-care" have lost all meaning. I think that we believe self-care is bubble baths, massages and pedicures, or a good night out with friends. While it is all these things, it is so much more. Self-care involves listening to your emotions and intuition. Knowing what you need in any given moment. Paying attention to your personal energy and what exactly is causing your stress. When you know this, you know whether a bubble bath is what you need or whether you need to pay the bills. Sometimes you need the bubble bath but you won't relax unless you pay the bills first. So, you need both, you just have to pick the order.

Prior to starting the business, during a particularly difficult time in my life, I was offered a job at a company I'd previously worked at. It was in a different city, a different group, but the same company. I knew I didn't like working there, but I convinced myself that since this was a managerial role I would have the ability to make some changes. I was very, very wrong. This was the first time in my life that my primary focus for taking the job was money and not the job itself. I was in a tough spot financially at the time and I convinced myself the salary at this company would compensate for the fact that my values did not match theirs.

While in the interview they complimented me on the ideas that I was bringing to the table, once I arrived, they had no interest in my ideas. They said things like "Assimilate Lisa". I had been honest about who I was, I wasn't a person who assimilates. I was a person who was always looking to make things better. While they had presented themselves in the interview as a company that wanted to hire people with ideas, they were not.

I am a very strong-willed individual. I did not change who I was, but three years of constantly hearing you are wrong and being repeatedly put into situations where there was no way to succeed, took its toll. My health was not good. I had tons of tests and procedures to figure out these symptoms and eventually my Doctor told me to take a vacation or he would put me off on stress leave.

You know it's bad when the Union Steward you refuse to speak to, because he bully's management, tells people "She's too good to be here". I stopped speaking to this man after several incidents where his behaviour was unacceptable and I was told I could NOT manage him.

I was blessed with a layoff from this job, I knew the next step was going into business for myself. Yep, that's the one where the surgery left me exhausted six months in.

Both of these experiences for me follow a time I did not listen to my own intuition. With the job, my first instinct was NOT to work there, but I let myself be talked into it because of a large salary. In the first month something happened that told me to "run" but I was in the middle of selling my house and buying a new one, so I pushed on. I let my fear of being without money rule my decision and ignored my intuition.

The surgery was worse. I had a full-on panic attack and everything inside my body tensed up and I heard my own voice in my head say "Don't have this surgery". What I didn't mention earlier is that the surgery was a mistake. The best explanation we have is that it was a typo. I had a part of my body removed because of a typo! As well as, my inability to listen to my intuition.

Once I committed to both mistakes, I just kept trying to make it something it was not. The job I tried to make it better by starting my coaching business and working out all the time. After the surgery I tried the same plan. This time, run the business, volunteer at three organizations and keep trying to work out even though it exhausts me every time.

Obviously, it didn't work. What I needed to do was take a review of my life and accept things for what they were. Had I accepted that I was never going to be able to make changes at the company, I would have just moved on sooner. After the surgery, if I'd just accepted where my energy was and given myself the grace to rest, I would have heard my instincts telling me what I needed to do to feel better. The universe was speaking to me. I just needed to listen.

I can't say it's all bad though. Every experience has its positives and negatives. I made some great friends at that job. Even those I don't keep in touch with come over and hug me when I see them in the community. I was laid off in a restructuring and over 20 people showed up for a dinner that was planned for me, against the advice of my boss who told them to stay away. Obviously, I was still doing something right.

The illness has taught me that it's OK to slow down and the importance of setting up your life to be one that you love. It taught me to look at my life and what's important and then plan accordingly. I stepped away from all the volunteer roles, except one.

Through both experiences, while my behaviour changed, my values did not. While I was being pressured to do things in a way that didn't meet my values, I never did. Even when my boss directed me to talk to the Union Steward who had been a bully, I flat out refused. If he couldn't be disciplined for his behaviour I didn't have to put myself in harm's way.

I also learned that your ability to give yourself grace, increases your ability to give others grace. The only way I see to do this is through self-care. Paying attention to your energy levels and allowing yourself what you need. When I started taking better care of myself, I was a much nicer, more patient person.

I left most of my volunteer roles because what I really wanted was a successful business and happy family life. The volunteer roles were not taking me to either of those places, they were taking time, space, and energy in my day. One in particular was difficult to leave, because I had promised one more year. It took everything in me to put myself over the organization.

To be a strong leader you need to lead yourself first. To create a solid foundation ask yourself these questions:

- What gives and takes your energy?
- Where are you headed (Vision, Mission)?
- What are your values?
- What are you giving your time to?
- What is your intuition tell you?

When you get straight on the above, you need to act towards it. If you know your Vision but are giving your time to everything else then it's time to make a change.

When you are clear on the answers, you will become more consistent in how you behave. That makes it so much easier for people on your team to follow your lead. Giving yourself grace, makes it easier to give the same grace to your teams. You will attract people who want the same things you do, and those who don't will find a place they fit better.

I did not go through any of this alone and you don't have to either. Please reach out if you have any questions or just want to talk. Let me help you unlock your full leadership potential. Find me on my website and book a free call at www.lmwconsultation.ca

www.lmwconsultation.ca

Lisa Wilson is a Leadership Vision Coach and Human Resources Cultural Consultant. Her passion is teaching small and medium business leaders to effectively lead their teams by creating exceptional workplace cultures. Witnessing the impact of both poor and great leadership she now devotes herself to coaching leaders so their teams can experience the excellence they deserve.

Lisa believes that leadership is not only about the people around you. It's about leading yourself in a way that allows you to show up for your team as the best version of yourself.

Her signature program "Leading With Ease", an 8 week online program that provides a mix of both teaching and coaching, provides a foundation for leaders. Once the foundation is solid, decisions become easier. Allowing space for the leader to look at the big picture and creating an environment where the team feels valued. The course runs three times per year.

Lisa holds a Bachelor of Business Administration, is a Certified Human Resources Leader, a Certified DiSC and True Colors Facilitator, and holds a certificate in Advanced Dispute Resolution. Most recently she finished all the requirements to be a Distinguished Toastmaster.

She also holds the titles Step-Mom to two teens and Mom to her fur baby (dog) Sandy.

With 20 years of experience and training, she is set up to fast track you to become the leader you want to be. Lisa knows that great leaders can take their teams to amazing heights and she invites you to find out how.

Living Out the Universal Synchronicity of Creating Your Legacy in Life and Business

By Lori A. McNeil

No matter where we are currently in our life or in our businesses, we impact and influence others...and we do it daily, whether we realize it or not. Living out a legacy is much deeper than most people realize. The imprint you give to this world causes an enormous ripple effect across multiple generations. Right now, today, this instant, the world is waiting for you to show up — your significant other, the kids, your parents, your business partners, and your clients – they are all waiting with anticipation for you to show up in the manner that you were created for. Our world is interconnected. We are not meant to live in isolation, but to live in community, where each of us brings our piece to the puzzle.

How we show up in our world creates a flow which stretches beyond what we can perceive sometimes. Especially after we are gone more than our memory will live on. Life, however, doesn't desire us to be gone from this world before it reveals our legacy. In many cases, people are not living out their full potential and are not being remembered for the things that are most important OR are not being remembered as was intended. Legacy is bLU TALKS

so much more than your bank account, your possessions, or family. It is greater than a name on a building, white letters on a street sign, or giving to a charity for a worthy cause, albeit great elements to support.

Origins of Legacy

Do you know where your legacy originates from? Most people associate legacy with how one is remembered once they have passed away. One day, we will pass on... it's one thing that we all have in common. Knowing this, we have an amazing opportunity to point our life in a way that builds legacy while we are still very alive. Ask yourself how you want to be remembered in life, today! The benefit of creating legacy is that we have complete control over how we show up. If we do not like how we are showing up or how people perceive us, we have an opportunity to change that perception! Legacy is about building those key areas of life daily that you want to not just be remembered for, but to be *known* for.

The most remarkable thing happens when we realize that we are the ones responsible for our legacy... we tend to take strategic actions to build it. Awareness is one of the greatest gifts that we can receive and/or give ourselves. Awareness is that piece of life that presents us with the ability to see beyond who and what we are. Those passions and visions that we have inside of us intertwined with the capacity to see beyond ourselves and our current circumstances, bring us to an accountability to take certain actions that inspire us to hit the next level which is living beyond ourselves, thus developing legacy. We see this in many ways. One of the most common is through media, whether social or more mainstream channels. The once heralded phrase "15 minutes of fame" may be true inside of today's TikTok™ or SnapChat™ spaces, however finding yourself in the mainstream allows for a wider audience to know you, thus expanding your exposure and intensifying your impact. So, how is creating a legacy accomplished? In the next section, I will break down eight steps to creating a legacy that will not only outlive you but can be implemented in a quick, effective manner that is designed to help you begin (or level up) your legacy today.

148

Creation of Legacy

The below eight step checklist for creating your legacy, whether personal, family, business, or any combination of the three is vital since *the world wants to hear your story and know who you are.* Each of us deliver value into our worlds. Ask yourself, what are my values? How am I building my legacy? As you read through this checklist, take a walk down the path of self-discovery and determine which ones of these you are living in now and which one of these need to be reviewed, renewed, or rejuvenated:

1. **Launch Your Vision:** What are you most passionate about that makes you want to get up and do every morning? Is it something that is bigger than you can accomplish on your own? Passion is the impetus for vision. Vision is the desire that uncovers motivation. Motivation leads to making it personal. When you make your vision personal, the desire and dedication it takes to make it come to fruition will drive you towards action.

2. **Leave Your Mark:** Try this. Write a letter to your future self. Make it a good one too. Provide as much detail in it that you can that will describe who you will be and what you will be doing. Then read the letter out loud to yourself in one year. If you have hit your 'goal' from that letter, then great! If you didn't, then take the time to write another letter and aspire to those goals. Many people that have gone through this step in my programs stop after a year, especially if they are not hitting all their goals. The key here is to not make it personal or irrational. If you don't hit a goal, this is the time to use your awareness for just that... awareness.

3. **Level Up Your Resources:** Where do you need to grow at? Who do you need in your corner? These are some extremely important questions. Taking your spirit, your mind, or your body to a whole new level requires resources. Some of those resources may be other people, some may be other ideals, some may come through reading, and still others may come through meditating. Now is a

great time to look at your "Ideal 5." The Ideal 5 are quite simply five lists of people who are your ideal clients, advocates, influencers, investors, and important people (family and friends) who can/are willing to help you level up.

4. **Live In Your Value:** What qualifies you to live out your vision? What work have you done to prove to yourself that your values align with your vision. This is one of the most important pieces. The closer we align our values to whatever we are doing, especially our vision, the more we will walk in our integrity. This translates to a more authentic life which in turn help drive our legacy.

5. **Leverage Your Toolbox:** What makes you unique? How do your skills and knowledge afford you opportunities? Each of us are unique. We are individually created for a purpose, and I believe our job is to discover that purpose and lead that life. Partnerships are two people with two separate visions who get the awesome opportunity to create a third purpose, one that is shared... whether that partnership be a marriage or in business, it doesn't take away from the point that each of us have the ability to develop and live out a legacy. When we realize what we have and who we are, we are now positioned to be afforded opportunities. Each opportunity is a moment designed to allow us to leverage what we are good at, what we are known for, or what knowledge we can impart that creates pockets of legacy.

6. **Look Past Your Future:** Your legacy, *your true legacy will outlive you.* This one can be hard for us at times. When we think about legacy, we often think about it being something that occurs after we die. The point here is to look past when we die, and maybe even into two generations past you...your great-great grandchildren. Imagine if you found a journal from a great-great grandparent who spoke highly of their one day great-great grandchildren. How heartwarming that would probably be. This is the moment where I want you to think in the terms of after you pass. What

is it that you want to be remembered for? If you were to meet an unexpected death, is the current path you're on one that would be worthy of legacy?

7. **Locate Your Integrity:** Ask the challenging questions that create growth and alignment in all areas of your life. Integrity, like being a truth teller can take years to build and the mere mention that you may not be what you say you are that can completely destroy you. Integrity is how you live out your character. The closer you can become to being a real, authentic person, the quicker you will locate what you are living for. This integrity is what builds your reputation. Those who aspire to lead a life of integrity will also find themselves in the middle of the public eye. Why is this? Deep down inside each of us have a desire to see, be, and be known as someone with superior character. There is no better place to demonstrate that than inside the public arena. When out integrity and character are aligned well together, everyone around you will see it and feel it.

8. **Lead Your Life On Purpose:** Your results are a direct response to actions you take. Remember becoming aware. Awareness breeds accountability which in turn creates action. The more action we take, the more opportunities we have so be accountable to those actions, and the more aware we become as to what we are doing and who we are doing it with. True leaders will lead from a place of purpose not power. Anyone can develop power, but it takes a special person to develop purpose. It wouldn't hurt to take a moment right here inside this book, on the margin, or even on a scrap piece of paper to write down three ways you can lead with your life on purpose. You have created awareness. Now that they are written down, you can be accountable to do them, and in-turn make action a continual thing.

Where Should We Go From Here?

Take time to reflect upon the checklist and ask yourself, "how many of the eight steps am I currently engaged in?" A better question may be, "which step of the eight needs the most attention?" The steps build on each other and yet they are independently whole on their own. Each of us sit in different places on this journey and where you are is perfectly aligned for you. Perfect in that whether you are at checkpoint one or checkpoint eight, there is something to be learned, perhaps something to revisit, or maybe it is something you need to do. The best thing to do is to...

Start today. Show up today.

Remember, *tomorrow, your legacy becomes what you did today.* Every day we don't step into our purpose becomes another day that we may have to undo what we have done. That 1000-mile journey that starts on step number one needs to know you are serious. How are you resonating with this chapter? Did any step cause you to pause and evaluate your current actions? What are your ***three action steps*** you are taking to live your life on purpose? What awareness have you come into? And about that letter... are you ready to write it?

 www.lorimcneil.com

International Educator, Speaker, and Business Coach, Lori focuses on the missing foundational tools needed for long-term success. Experienced in public and private sectors, Lori helps new businesses grow, and established companies re-strategize. She has successfully grown grassroots programs from zero to millions which lead to National recognition and a United States flag flown over the White House in honor of her success. Lori is also a Curriculum Designer, a retired Business Professor, and has helped grow countless organizations organically (including her own International company that includes Legacy Leaders Unlimited, Media Secrets, and Driven Mastery — all brands that assist Entrepreneurs to build a true, long - lasting purpose). Lori has been featured on ABC, NBC, CBS, FOX, & 500 various media outlets per year. She has authored several Best -Selling books; including co-authoring an International Best-Selling book with Kevin Harrington, the original Shark of the hit TV show, Shark Tank and Pioneer of "As seen on TV." Lori works with organizations globally to support literacy, cancer research, young entrepreneurship, and military support programs. More information can be found on her global efforts at www. lorimcneil.com. She was an invited guest at the National Celebration of Reading in Washington D.C where she helped raise over Three (3) Million Dollars for Literacy and was recently awarded the Lifetime Presidential Service Award for her long-term success in working with communities Nationally. Most recently, Lori was selected as one of the official featured speakers for the Think & Grow Rich World Tour and was honored with the prestigious Outstanding Business Coach Professional Award. In 2020 was named Most Inspiration Woman in Entrepreneurial Coaching & Media Relations.

SIMPLE!

By Maggie Slider

Do you have a blueprint for your life? You know, all the hopes, dreams, and aspirations that you have thought about since you were a kid. The story of how you believe your life should be!

Which areas of your life do you really feel good about?
Is life not turning out the way you hoped?
Are you looking for happiness outside of yourself?
Are you blaming others for your situation?

Do you know that life happens 'for' us and not to us? If it doesn't match your blueprint, it leads to unhappiness and makes you feel you have no control. You are basically out of alignment with your inner self. This can lead to depression, feelings of being worthless, guilt, loss, and blame. Are you spending the majority of your life worrying and stressing about minor things? This causes a dis-ease in your body, which eventually turns to disease. So, we end up getting more of what we are vibrationally asking for.

The only way it gets better is when YOU get better. It doesn't change by chance, it's all about choice. When you realize that you do not need approval, acceptance or to apologize for being you, amazing shifts take place. The only thing you can control is how you respond to whatever comes your way. It's all about letting go of the need to control.

As a Law of Attraction Practitioner, I am aware that everything is energy, energy that vibrates. In humans it vibrates from within and through our thoughts. Think about this...everything was a thought before it was a thing. Our thoughts lead to our perspective, which leads to our behaviour. It vibrates out to the Universe and basically gives us what we ask for. For instance, if you focus only on what you don't want, you will attract exactly that, more of what you don't want.

I am amazed by The Law of Attraction but I am also amazed by the human psyche, the more I learn the more amazed I am. I am not a clinical therapist, or psychologist. However; I am a trauma survivor, I have survived and risen above many of life's traumatic experiences. I am not a so-called expert, but I am an expert based on my own challenges and experiences. It is due to these experiences and my stories that I am able to inspire and guide others to choose better and want different for their own lives. You see I totally believe that life is SIMPLE, not easy but SIMPLE...I will explain this in a bit.

Allow me to give you a little background...

I believe we are souls with a mind in a physical body having a human experience. Our souls have already agreed to everything that is going to happen 'for' us on our life journey. Our souls and the Universe are a step ahead of us, and will give us what we need when we need it, not what we want when we want it.

I believe as babies we are born not actually knowing much, (although there are debates) other than how to breathe, their parent's voices, and their natural instincts for hunger, pain, and discomfort. We learn from watching and mirroring others and from how we are treated by others. Usually, our parents are our role models. We do what we see them do, not what they tell us to do. How many of you have ever thought of your parents as hypocrites for telling you one thing and they do the other?

We are born with neuropathways in our brains, which kick in the minute we are born if not before. What was a dark, safe, muffled-sounding place, is now a place where light hurts the eyes, the air makes the bare skin feel cold, and the sounds hurt the ears. The cut from the umbilical cord causes a new pain - hunger. Diapers placed on our bottoms cause discomfort. We now start to learn about people and the world. The hunger pain, tummy aches, or soiled diapers causes us to learn how to cry. If someone attends to us, feeds and comforts us almost right away, we are learning, love, trust, attachment, and that the world is a good place. Your neuropathways are already learning that crying will get you comfort.

When you learn to cry because of discomfort and no one comes to comfort you. You are learning to distrust, fear, a sense of unworthiness and detachment. You are learning that the world isn't a great place and that you are unlovable and unworthy.

Up until about age 7/8, everything is real to us as children. We are only aware of what is, until the subconscious is formed. Once this is formed, we begin to see and experience life differently. Our reality is formed, and perspective created. We begin to form our thoughts, our beliefs and limiting beliefs, our reactions, our judgement, fears etc. which all lead to our perspective and again leads to our behaviour.

These patterns and beliefs are formed from three common denominators...

1. Our parents and caregivers...teachers, coaches, aunts, uncles, even older siblings

2. Repetition...we have so much of it in our young lives, repeated schedules, school, discipline, punishment, the stories we are told over and over, the way we were spoken to, our hobbies and interests, and so much more.

3. Trauma...every single one of us has experienced trauma of some kind. None of us are exempt, it is just that we deal with it differently. It's really based on our perspective, strength, resilience, coping skills, and our support systems. Trauma can be first-hand something which happens to you, something happening to someone else, or hearing stories from someone else. It can be what we see on television or what we hear on the news. These can all lead to trauma, which as a child is often stored deep and they try to forget about it.

I call these common denominators because none of us are exempt from them. We were all raised by someone, all had years of repetition and all have experienced trauma. These three common denominators set our default reactions or responses which we continue into adulthood. They are creating who we feel we 'should' be not who we are 'born' to be. Not who are souls are here to be.

Many of us will feel a quiet sense of unfulfillment, like something is always missing. Most of us fall into the people-pleasing category, where we are afraid to say no to others because we fear they won't like us or maybe will even call us a bitch. We feel that gravitational pull by society to live our lives by societal norms, even if that feels off. If not, people may judge us, and be disappointed in us. We give our own power away by allowing others opinions of us to be more important than our opinion of ourselves. We are more worried about hurting others feelings than we are about breaking promises and disappointing ourselves so we lack in setting personal boundaries. We compare ourselves and feel we are in competition against others who always appear to be 'better than us.' We even at times, end up self-loathing and totally disconnected because we have no idea of WHO we actually are. We feel that no matter what we do we will just never be good enough. It's a vicious cycle.

What's my point to all of this?
Glad you asked.

Remember this...you always have a choice. You can choose to take the chance to make changes in your life. You can start taking responsibility and stop blaming others. YOU get to choose what kind of life **you** want to live.

Remember the blueprint, is your life what you want it to be?

If it isn't, think about your mindset and making changes. You can either have a positive mindset and an attitude of gratitude. You speak kindly and lovingly to yourself, you nurture and love yoursel,f and know your worth. You figure out your passion and your purpose for being here. Or...you have a negative mindset, you do not trust, you that feel you have no self-worth or that you even really matter. Sometimes we can have fabulous parents and a great childhood, but experience trauma at the hands of someone else and this can affect us for life. Depending on those three common denominators we will usually form our own mindset. But no matter what, it's your responsibility to take responsibility for your life.

Even if you had bad parenting, or faced trauma, you can still have a positive mindset. You get to choose.

The positive will be filled with joy, gratitude, self-love, self-esteem, worthiness, happiness, great opportunities, and way more.

The opposite, a negative mindset, will have feelings of being unworthy and unloved, never good enough, too fat, too thin, not smart enough, anxiety... all of this negative thinking leads to more of the same.

It's a known fact that what we focus on expands, where our focus goes our energy flows.

Are you aware of how often we talk to ourselves in our heads? How often we tell ourselves that we will never measure up. Never be liked enough, never be good enough. This is total bullshit! Change this speech! Start telling yourself the exact opposite. Remember the repetition I spoke of. Repeat positive affirmations and mantras, speak to yourself with love and kindness, turn that frown upside down!!!

Your past isn't holding you back, your present self is.

Brene Brown a well-known author, speaks about courage and vulnerability. I see vulnerability as a strength as she does. Many feel it is a weakness, because it is about intimacy...in-to-me-see! This is a really scary concept for many. You may feel people will see that you failed at something, that maybe you had a time when you were challenged with depression. Maybe you become paralyzed by anxiety and fear. You don't want anyone to know that. Bull! None of us are exempt from anything. It's all about perspective and what our individual realities are.

Denzel Washington in a University Grad speech said this: "Your ego wants everything to be perfect but your soul knows everything is perfect just as it is." Don't fight that, allow yourself to be content in the knowing that all is as it should be, right at that moment.

We only get one shot at this thing called life. Our days are numbered. No one knows when they will take their last breath. Some of us will go early, some much later, but we will all pass. Your soul knows its journey, your higher self has everything within that it needs to be, do, know, and have the life it is here to live. Focus on what you want your life to be like, know why you want it, and how you want to feel. Let go of always focusing on what you don't want. Instead of always saying 'what if" focus on all the things that could go right. It's your life, your timeline, your journey. It isn't for others to understand or even for you to try to explain to others. Just live it your way.

Life is SIMPLE ...this is all you need

Strength...you are stronger than you could ever imagine and this will build resilience!

Intention...live life with intention, live in the moment not for five years down the road!

Mindset...and mindfulness are everything, choose happiness, be grateful, don't ever give up!

Purpose...you are here for a purpose and that is to find your passion that drives you to serve others!

Love...is our natural born state, all others are learned. Do everything from a place of love!

Evolve...strive to be the best you possible, never stop learning, growing, and thriving, otherwise you are merely surviving.

https://www.facebook.com/maggiemcslider

Maggie Slider is an intuitive Life Coach, focusing on Self Love and acceptance, she is A certified Law Of Attraction Practitioner, Published Author, Workshop Facilitator, Real Estate Investor, Former Special Constable and Personal Trainer.

Maggie studied Social Service work at Seneca where she graduated with Honors. She has worked in group homes, schools, a nursing home, and the justice system. Her youngest client being 6 months and the oldest 99 years.

Her passion is people. Her purpose is helping others and giving back., which brings her to present career.

Using her experience and Intuition she guides people to uncover and release fears and limiting beliefs, to replace fear with courage, to find their authentic selves, get clear on what they want rather than what they don't want. Believing that we all have abilities and potential Maggie encourages her clients to use that potential to create a life they love through Hope ,Courage and Strength.

Staying fit, eating healthy, playing the djembe drum, getting out in nature and traveling are some of Maggies interests

The Emotional Entrepreneur

By Miranda Horvath

Let me ask you a question. When you think of the phrase "getting emotional", what is the first thing that comes to mind? Do you think of someone crying, or overreacting? Do you think of someone becoming hysterical or unreasonable? Think of yourself when you start to get emotional. What is the first feeling that rises up inside you? Is your instinct to feel embarrassed, or to hide your emotions? Do you think of this term as a positive or negative term?

Many people say there is no room for emotions in business and I want to prove otherwise. I want to talk today about my reasons why emotionality can be a powerful tool to create a thriving business. I want to talk about the benefit of being an emotional entrepreneur.

Accepting your emotions helps to utilize them for vulnerability and connection with yourself and your clients. Feeling deep emotion allows you to then learn emotional temperament which allows you to make space for others in a calm and positive way.

Let's change what "getting emotional" means to us from something negative to something positive.

My name is Miranda. I'm a registered massage therapist for the last five years and online holistic business consultant based in Edmonton for holistic entrepreneurs for just over one year now. I came from very humble beginnings, raised by a single mother on Vancouver Island, Dad was not in the picture, and I was on my own by the time I was 17. I entered into the workforce very young. I had average grades. I went to a modest high school, and an equally modest college for massage therapy several years after moving to Edmonton when I was 20. I paid for my first crappy car, it was a Pontiac Sunfire, and for many crappy cars after, and for my own college education. I have no business background, I used to be severely tech-challenged and there is no special reason that I would earn the success I have today.

Yet, here I stand before you; a successful entrepreneur, running two successful companies. My massage therapy business that is always booked weeks in advance, and the most previously tech-challenged woman ever, creating and running a constantly growing online holistic coaching business from scratch. I've now hired employees, I've been able to even support my friend's businesses by offering them freelance work that supports my client's needs, and I've crushed every financial goal I've set out for myself. My success has allowed me to travel and live a lifestyle I previously could only dream of, and I honestly still can't believe I've come this far. It has not come, however, without some challenges, of which include accepting my sensitivity and my emotionality as an asset, not a hindrance.

Like anything in life, you can choose to run your life, or let your life run you. You can choose for your emotions to run you, or you can choose to utilize your emotions as a catalyst to achieve any goal you set out. There are a couple ways that you can harness your emotionality to cultivate and grow what matters to you.

Think of a particularly difficult period in your life. Maybe you're going through it right now. What were the emotions you felt at that time? How did you get through it? How did you cope, and eventually heal? Use the obstacles that caused you to feel that intense emotion; that gave you the ability to navigate through and overcome, that created an emotional healing experience that you can forever pull upon as a way to relate to, and connect deeply with your clients. The power of harnessing a difficult situation and turning it into something good, teaches you then how to level yourself to navigate through difficult emotional situations in your business which can be the catalyst to allow your business to launch off of.

I'll be honest, and I bet some of you can relate, I have a complicated relationship with a member of my immediate family. It's been like that for as long as I can remember. Whatever that was caused by in the past is not relevant here unless we're having some wine, but what I find fascinating now, is that the lifelong practice of forgiveness, of understanding, of leveling my emotions to try to understand her, to attempt to deeply accept another's flaws has become an infinitely powerful tool in handling the needs of my clients and their emotions to this day.

I remember this when a client may want to engage reactively in their own way, and I could never have learned to temper my emotions without having felt deep emotion in the first place.

I'd like to give an example of when I first understood the power of connecting to others through our emotions, and when I realized that I wanted to be a holistic coach; addressing not just the business, but the person as a whole with the business and how this is a catalyst to connecting deeper with my clients now.

I worked with a very successful and blunt male business coach in the past. He made it clear when we began coaching that he does not wish to engage in the emotional aspect of coaching, only to teach you the technical steps of the business which was fine with me at the time. I understood this when going into his program.

However, as time passed and the business growth challenges became increasingly difficult, I was definitely feeling emotional during the breakthroughs. So, despite the upfront clarity in his teaching style, I still reached out a couple times to express the pain I was feeling during these stages, but I never received a reply if it was to express an emotion or struggle I was feeling.

I realized after this experience, even though I learned a ton, that I want to be a coach you can express your emotions to. I want to celebrate that emotional part because it means a breakthrough is coming. Then we can share in that breakthrough together and the bond grows deeper. If we choose to separate that emotional transformation from our business, we are losing out on one of those very reasons that we are human. Emotions connect us. Our transformation and our breakthroughs are what makes up our business, it's where ideas and value for the client materializes.

Being emotional and successful in business crushes stereotypes that there is no room for emotion, particularly emotional women, in business. Knowing that I am breaking the mold, that I am crushing it in my business in part by showing my emotions and showing my true self to the world, makes me feel brave, and confident. In an awesome twist, my vulnerability makes me feel more confident than ever. Thank you Brene Brown, raise your hand if you know who Brene Brown is. I step into my light, I know who I am, and I bare it all.

I'd like to give another couple examples of two incidents, one in my massage business, and one from my consulting business, to show how my ability to make space for a client's reaction with compassion helped me to mitigate a potentially negative fallout and instead create a good client experience.

When working in my previous clinic, a previous clinic I worked at used to require credit cards on the account before making an appointment. My front staff girl was speaking to a client over the phone and she was becoming irate because she did not want her credit card on file. She was threatening to cancel her appointment when the receptionist phoned to get her credit card.

The front desk girl comes up to me and says she wants to cancel her appointment. So, I offer to take the phone, and ask the client why she does not want her credit card on file. She says it's because she's had her credit card information stolen before. So, in understanding this, we came up with a compromise of her adding her credit card after her initial appointment with me. I established trust with the client and came up with a compromise that we were both happy with instead of getting irate back to the client, or panicking, or simply canceling her appointment.

Here is another recent example. A little while back, I had a potential client that I was going to work with once. We did a free consultation, and some time later she decided to move and start her own practice on her own, which is great.

Some time after this, my business was expanding into working with the inter-personal relationships and client retention for teams, so multiple practitioner group sessions. I reached out to her old clinic, and long story short, there was an unfortunate assumption that I revealed private details of our consultation to her previous boss which I absolutely did not.

This was a situation where I steadied myself. I could have been emotional in the typical negative way that people think of when they think of "getting emotional", angrily replying to say you assumed the worst of me and personally attacked my integrity. Instead, I used my emotional personality for compassion in this situation. I thanked her for reaching out to me, clarified the intention of my communication with her previous clinic and assured her that I never spoke of the details of our call. I never even mentioned that she and I had had a consultation.

This was such a rewarding experience, because I would have been way more reactive and upset to have my character questioned in the past. But this time, I clarified, took a breath, and let go. In turn, the misunderstanding was simply cleared up and it ended up being a positive interaction for both of us.

Understanding and accepting the emotions rather than controlling them, forcing or hiding them allows you to utilize them to level yourself out and steady your emotions and the emotions of others around you. It creates a positive ripple effect, like dropping a stone into still waters.

So don't curse your emotionality or think that it doesn't belong. Celebrate it! It's the reason you are as strong as you are. Without our emotional intelligence being challenged, we would have no emotional maturity and we would all still be savage kids! We would have no way to grow and in turn handle other's emotions with considerable skill and care if we don't practice owning our emotions, and accepting them. Without having emotional obstacles, we cannot practice emotional temperament. Without the ability to practice tempering our emotions, we have no ability to feel the confidence that we get from overcoming our hardships that allow us to apply that skill to our relationships, our businesses, or anything that matters to us.

Your emotions are your connection to others, your personality, it's YOU! Without your emotions, there is no you. Without you, you don't have a business. So own your emotions and use them for good. Use your emotionality to create deeper connections, and to learn when to utilize the past emotions you've experienced to deepen your understanding of yourself, what you're capable of, and your client's emotions, so that you can be there for them when it matters most. Being emotional means that you care. We are all emotional beings. People buy emotionally and justify it logically. Nobody is immune to being swayed by emotion, so understand and accept them as being part of you. It's a blessing to be an emotional entrepreneur in business. Thank you.

 www.massagebymirconsulting.com

✉ massagebymir@gmail.com

Miranda Horvath is a lifetime entrepreneur; from her first entrepreneur venture as a mobile piano teacher, teaching children at age 17, to running a thriving massage practice and online holistic consultant business today, she is passionate about inspiring you to skyrocket your practice by reaching your untapped potential just as she has.

She created MassageByMir Consulting to draw back the curtain and reveal how you can create a thriving practice as the holistic entrepreneur you know you can be.

She found a calling to close the gap for practitioners who are amazingly talented but lack essential business skills to thrive. She specifically serves holistic practitioners like you, who know they are meant for greatness!

Her message to you is don't listen to anyone that tells you that holistic therapy is just a side job. You can have a purposeful and lucrative career helping others; you can have it all!

She is consistently booked between 4-8 weeks in advance in her practice and frequently booked out in her consulting business as well; she would love to get to know you better and work wonders with you.

To see if you're a good fit for the MassageByMir 8 Week Intensive, head to her sales page and feel free to check out testimonials from other happy clients, book your free consultation and submit your application at www.massagebymirconsulting.com.

Questions? Email her at massagebymir@gmail.com and she will be excited to hear from you!

Thanks For Showing Up

By Nancy Agnes / Bromley

"Thanks for showing up", he shouted at me from across the bank. What an odd thing to say. Caught off guard, I simply called, "Thanks, you too!". I was puzzled for a while and then on the long walk down, I reflected on all the times I was called to show up.

This particular moment felt pivotal in how I came to view much of my life's journey so far. I was out on a small solo hike up to a little waterfall. The hike itself was more of a walk, with wide paths and big trees up a steady incline. The top of the hike featured a brook more than a river with a pretty little waterfall. It was a beautiful serene space but nothing overly spectacular. Just peaceful, natural and accessible. I planted myself down on a little log over the water and took in my surroundings. I was noticing the sounds of the water and how the light played on it. The life buzzing around me and the breeze rustling the leaves. I was vaguely aware of the people present as well. A family, a photographer, a couple, and a few others came and went. There was one fellow, stepping on the rocks near the falls. I only took any notice of him because he looked like he might be indigenous. My relaxed, wandering mind pondered which indigenous groups initially populated that area. I was familiar with the groups around my home but not there. That was about as much thought as I gave him. At some point he was there, and at some point, he was gone. Then I heard someone shout "Hey!" in my direction.

I looked up and he was standing across the back and yelled out. "Thanks for showing up." Then he left. I never saw him again and have no idea who he was, but he had a profound message for me. You see, while I was walking up that path, I was talking to my guides, and I was asking, "What's next?". I guess, a deeper showing up was next. It was acknowledging the power of showing up in all the ways that I showed up in throughout my life. On the walk back down the hill I began thanking myself for all the times I showed up. I could write a few books about different aspects of my life where I was called to show up. I am limited for word count so I'll just highlight a few to make the point.

When I was seven, all I wanted to be was a dancer. I was fascinated by dancing and danced every day in my living room. I was enrolled in ballet, as dance options were a little limited back then. I had my first exam, and strangely enough, I remember it clearly. I was nervous in my white, testing dress tutu, and my ribboned ballet slippers. I had practiced, but I had something stacked against me. Back in the late 70's there was only one type of body allowed to be a dancer and I was not it. I was told I had great rhythm but I was not made to be a dancer and I should take piano lessons. My mom pulled me out of dance and I was not allowed to take dance lessons again. I thought she agreed with them. It was not until adulthood that I found out that she was angry, didn't want me hurt, and tried to protect me by pulling me out of dance. However, I didn't stop dancing. I still danced daily in my living room. I watch every dance show I could find. At some point in my 20's I showed up. I saw an ad for belly dancing lessons. I thought, "You can have a belly and be a belly dancer", so I signed up. I was so insecure I would put myself just behind a very beautiful classmate and pretend that her body was mine. I didn't dance in the first recital, as I was ashamed of my body, but I was good at it. I kept at it. I showed up. Even though I was too insecure to get up on stage that first class, I later went on to dance professionally and create and manage a very successful performance troupe, called Vibe Tribe Gypsy Circus. It took almost 20 years but I eventually showed up.

Throughout my life, I showed up when my marriage was horrible and lonely and I had the strength to leave. I showed up when my son came out as trans. I showed up when my daughter got pregnant at 18, giving me a beautiful granddaughter. I showed up at work, as a teacher and administrator; being innovative, leading, and challenging myself, even though I never really enjoyed it. I showed up in many little ways too. Celebrating natural beauty around me, enjoying friends, grateful for family. Continually showing up and finding moments of gratitude daily.

However, after that message on my hike I have decided recently to truly show up to my gifts. The abilities I have chronically downplayed because I didn't understand them.

There are many things that happen that we can't explain and brush off as nothing, as coincidence, a dream, made up fantasy. But part of showing up is acknowledging those things, living in them, celebrating them and then taking responsibility for them.

I have always been sensitive, overly aware of the energy around me. I didn't really understand it, so I didn't give it much consideration even when it stared me in the face.

My first acknowledged experience with channeling came in university. I was taking a course I was not at all interested in. Our final project was a big one and I was partnered with a very ambitious young lady who took course work very seriously. I had good intentions, but her keenness and my procrastination were not a good combination. Presentation day could have been a disaster if I hadn't shown up last minute.

It was a lecture style room and the professor sat front and center. Her dark rimmed glasses halfway down her nose, giving her a permanently condescending look as she cocked an eyebrow to examine you from above them. She was intimidating and on the presentation day she pulled out every ounce of the scolding librarian she carried.

As each group went up, she ripped them to shreds with her matter-of-fact inquiries that she knew they could not answer. Watching them sweat and stammer, and knowing that they were infinitely more prepared than I was made me swallow hard as we stood for our turn.

The guilt of how I was about to let down my partner, who put in countless hours doing work, was weighing heavily. It was her work alone we were floating on and I knew it. At that moment I felt an intense and profound gratitude for her. Time stopped while my heart was overcome with the desire to do something to show her how much I appreciated it. Then my gut-wrenching guilt began to subside and something in my head or heart, I'm not really sure which, told me it was going to be ok. I exhaled slowly and I listened to her present the information 'we' had gathered.

Everything seemed to move in slow motion, and it is difficult describe what happened next. I listened without hearing but felt like my heart and my mind were opening up. I was suddenly listening to everything. It was like in that instant I could intimately feel everyone in the room. It was beyond that. For that moment I had the complete understanding of the connection that exists between everyone and everything. As if everything was underwater, a part of my brain was still registering the words and the reality of the event. It all came into focus as the bullet of a question was fired at us. I felt my partner's energy change to panic, and all of a sudden time reinstated. I was strangely calm and I just knew. I said, "I can answer this if you like." She looked at me with a mixture of fear and disbelief.

I turned and looked at the prof and began to answer. I have absolutely no idea what I said or how I knew any of it but I orated and watched the prof stop, and push her glasses up and smile. She sat back, crossed her legs and nodded as I went on. When I was finished, she clapped, and said, "Excellent work ladies!" We sat down. I exhaled.

My partner looked at me dumbfounded. "How in the hell did you do that?"

"I have no idea." I replied.

I showed up then, profoundly, but dropped it for many years. I didn't even talk about it because it felt like fiction and I was afraid of judgement.

Since then, I have had many experiences, unexplainable like that, almost magic. I have now accepted them, but it wasn't until I was shouted out to, about "showing up" that I have stopped hiding, stopped telling only parts of the story.

Probably the most unique story that I have, is how I actually received my gift of soul telepathy.

I was working with my mentor, to help understand my sensitivities when I had a "dream" one night. I say dream in quotations because I am not certain it was exactly a dream.

I dreamed I was at a resort in Mexico, and there were people everywhere and we were having a good time. That part of the dream was disjointed and more like my usual dreams where things make sense or don't, randomly. At some point in the dream, I decided that I needed to be somewhere else. That is the only way that I can describe it. I became aware that I needed to be somewhere else. In the dream I told my friend I was going to go back to the room and began to walk there. There was a path leading to the hotel room but there was another path that went off from that one to a destination I couldn't really see or determine.

As I began to walk, the quality of the dreamscape began to change. The sounds turned from partying happy people, to a muffled silence. The air changed. I didn't remember being aware of the air in the previous part, but this air was comfortably cool, still and heavy, like a fog but completely clear. The landscape seemed endless on the periphery of my vision but I knew it would disappear into a sort of nothing if I looked. I didn't want to look, my eyes were fixed on a being up ahead of me on the path. He was beautiful. I knew on some level that he was a male but perfectly androgenous. I can't even begin to put into words how beautiful this being was. It was like looking at the most spectacular sunset or having your breath taken away while walking in an old growth forest. It was a visceral sense of awe and wonder as I gazed on this being and continued to walk toward him. He was patiently smiling at me, waiting for me to approach.

He was beyond beautiful. He had long straight blond hair tied back from his forehead, but loose down his back. His eyes were so warm, loving, endless and abnormally large. They were the richest blue; deep and immeasurable, like the facets of a sapphire, a cloudless sky, and the ocean all rolled into one. I was lost in them as I approached.

He reached out his hands to me and I held them. Instant warmth and peace flooded through me. Although I don't actually remember him speaking, I remember hearing his words. He welcomed me. He said that I was doing good work. He said that *his people (started with a P)* wanted to give me a gift to help me with my work. I didn't question any of that at the time, I just gratefully and humbly received.

At that moment he embraced me and put his head to the right side of mine. In that moment, I had complete understanding of everything. I understood love, life, God, the interconnectedness of everything. The understanding flooded through my whole existence. Then he released me saying that I couldn't keep that because it was too much for my human form. It was given to me to remind myself and anyone that I worked with that we all have access to that knowledge deep inside of us, accessible when we need it. I was still full of bliss from that gift but felt a slight loss as I felt that knowledge leaving me. The he said that his people, had a gift that I could keep and my job was to use it to help people evolve on a soul level. He said they were giving me the gift of telepathy. I thanked him/them and he released my hands and I went back to my dream.

The part of that story that I almost never tell, because I am afraid of judgement, is that when I told my mentor about it, she asked me if the name of the people was the "Pleiadeans". I had never heard of them before, but that was the name he said. Then she showed me an artist's rendition of a Pleiadean and although it couldn't come close to the beauty of the being I encountered, it was an artist's best shot. If you are not sure what the

Pleiadean's are, I encourage you to look them up. I did and was fascinated, honoured and, I'll be honest, a little afraid.

However, after that experience, I am able to channel what people's own souls are trying to tell them in order to move forward, to evolve. I call it soul telepathy or intuitive counselling.

I am so grateful for the gift I received, but I am even more grateful to the man who called out, "thanks for showing up" across the bank. I have fully begun to show up now, not just to the plain sight life experiences but also to those I can't explain. I encourage all of you my dear readers, to also show up. What is your soul path guiding you to do and share? No matter how ordinary or esoteric. What gifts have you been afraid or reluctant to own? We all have a path and a purpose, you only need to show up.

 www.nancyinspired.com

Nancy Agnes' purpose is to inspire and empower others to reach their highest potential and soul evolution. Whether in the realm of education, leadership and consulting or intuitive counseling, writing and public speaking, she touches the hearts of her audiences and ignites them to follow their own inner wisdom to become the best version of themselves and in turn inspire those around them. You can find out more at www.nancyinspired.com

Step Into a Larger Dimension of Yourself

By Nancy Showalter

"I'm a Star. And so are You—shining your Light in this magnificent Universe."

Do you instinctively know that there is more to life than what you have been taught? And you are not afraid to explore beyond conventional belief systems?

We are living in unprecedented times. And the Universe just keeps transcending itself, shaking us, and pushing us to move to higher levels of consciousness.

And it's time.

It is time to step into a larger dimension of yourself and bring forth that part of you that was made in the image and likeness of the Divine—that part that is uniquely you. The part of you that has a specific purpose that only *you* can fulfil and is powerful beyond measure.

In this world, we all have our traumas and challenges. Whether they be great or small, emotional, psychological, or physical, they are ours to overcome.

You may have parts of you that are fearful, hurt, angry, even devastated. But there is a part of you that is *not*.

And it is *this* part of you that can heal the painful and unresolved issues you deal with. It is your Source of life, intelligence, and abundance. It is your protection, guidance, and inspiration for navigating life in this dimension. But only if you are aware of it and tap into its limitless power.

From a spiritual perspective, there is only one Source, one creative energy and we all come from that one Source. Even science agrees with this, although many do not see it.

Looking at science, it tells us that everything is a manifestation of energy. And energy is subject to the law of conservation of energy, which means that it can neither be created nor destroyed. It can only be transformed.

From a scientific perspective, energy is the common denominator of all things in our physical universe. According to its vibration and frequency, various manifestations are produced. And the Big Bang theory suggests that at some moment all matter in the universe was contained in a single point.

Our spiritual traditions refer to this source of life as God, as Light. The concept that there is but one God—one Light, one Source—from which all things were created parallels the scientific concept of all things being a manifestation of energy and at one time being contained in a single point.

So really, where is the disconnect? There really isn't one.

Each time the universal Father-Mother God speaks the Word, the One is individualized. (In the beginning was the Word and the Word was with God and the Word was God. John 1:1).

And that Word is "I AM." A unique manifestation, or Presence, comes into being and that "I AM Presence" is you and me. It is the Source individualized as each one of us.

This is who you are. You are a luminous being of great light, an energy field of unlimited potential that has its origin in God/Source. Your soul has descended into the realms of time and space to experience this physical world while your Higher Self, the I AM Presence remains in spirit.

Think about it. If you really believe that there is one Source from which all things come, and you are made in that image and likeness, then reason tells us that you too are a manifestation of this pure, light energy.

You have been endowed with free will and given dominion over the earth to choose what kind of world you will create for yourself, and we together, will create as a whole. That means you are a co-creator in this dimension. You come with a purpose that you are compelled to fulfill.

You may be familiar with the story in the Old Testament when Moses was on the mount and God appeared to him in a burning bush. Moses asked God, "Whom shall I say sent me?" And God answered to tell the people that "I AM that I AM" hath sent you. And He further said that this is His name forever more. (Exodus 3:14-15)

This is a great key for us.

When you speak the words "I AM," you are literally calling for your Divine Presence within you to create whatever condition you speak following those words. Your words are commands to your super-conscious Divine Self and to your subconscious to create the conditions that you speak.

Descartes said, "I think, therefore I AM" but when we understand our divine origin and identity, it is better said, "I AM, therefore I think." "I AM" signifies being and self-awareness. No other species on our planet can speak these words or make choices to change beyond their natures. But we can.

You are not a victim of circumstances. You are a co-creator with Source/God/All that Is/The One/I AM—whatever you choose to call it. If you speak negatively about yourself or any aspect of your life, you are creating those conditions by investing your energy and attention in that which you do not want. Your speech is a powerful creative force in your life every day.

There have been many experiments and demonstrations of the power of sound and how it impacts the physical world, including probably the greatest experiment that we read about in the Bible when God said, "Let there be light! And there was light." And the Bible is not the only place we find this action recorded.

In the ancient Hindu Vedas we read, "In the beginning was Brahman with whom was the Word, and the Word is Brahman." And Hindu, Buddhist, Christian, Jewish, and Sufi mystics all believe that it is this Word that creates, pervades, and sustains everything that exists. And this is one of the ways we create in this world—either constructively or destructively.

There have also been contemporary experiments that have brought forth some amazing revelations about sound and its effect on matter. One example is the late Dr. Masaru Emoto's experiments with water that he conducted in the 1990's that are well documented.

Dr. Emoto performed a series of experiments observing the physical effect of words, prayers, music, and the environment on the crystalline structure of water. He had photographers take pictures of the water after it was exposed to these various conditions and then frozen, which formed crystalline structures producing remarkable results.

Prior to the experiment, the water did not really have any particular structure—just sort of random shape and form. But after being exposed to various words, both positive and negative, the water took a definite form. In the case of positive words or in the case of prayer, beautiful forms resulted. When negative words or phrases were used, the water took on ugly formations that were not geometrically balanced.

So how do you access this power—this kingdom of God that is within you?

It is through the doorway of your heart. This is where the spark of life that is the Power, Wisdom, and Love of your I AM Presence is anchored within you.

When you focus on your heart and cultivate your awareness of that particular vibration or "space," you enter into the eternal Now. You transcend your experience of time and space in this dimension and the magic of the Divine happens.

It is here that you can experience the mind and heart of God—the magnificence of your true Self. It's transforming and healing. And truly, it is communion with your Higher Self where you can receive the answers to your questions before they are even asked.

Much scientific research on the heart in recent years has established its intelligence and recognizes it as a source of intuition and perception. And there are many techniques, both ancient and modern, to help you access your heart intelligence and your I AM Presence.

Heart meditation is the quickest way to connect to the Divine within. There are many forms of meditation and all have their benefits. In fact, experiments have proven that meditating has definite physical and psychological benefits. Reducing stress, controlling anxiety, greater emotional health, and lengthening attention span are just a few.

The single greatest benefit of heart meditation, in addition to all of the documented benefits of meditating, is its ability to directly connect you with the Divine, the I AM.

"I AM" in and of itself is a statement of "Being." It is the center core of who you are. It is not doing, it is not becoming. It IS. And in that Presence, you have all that you need. "Neither shall they say, Lo here! or, lo there! for, behold, the kingdom of God is within you." (Luke 17:21)

If you already practice meditation, entering your heart space may be familiar. In addition to deep breaths to relax your physical body, you may find it helpful to visualize a drop of water falling from your head to your heart. As it falls, feel your awareness falling with it, letting go of all thoughts and tensions.

Imagine this drop gently hitting a still pool of water in your heart. See and feel the ripples of peace flowing out and let yourself be in that space. Or you may simply imagine a bright sun superimposed over your heart in the center of your chest. The idea is to place your attention on your heart and enter into the energy of that space.

In addition to "being" in this sacred space and letting all tensions, worry or concern drop away from you, it is also the time that you can pose a question or present a problem and ask for guidance.

You may receive answers as thought impressions or as words in the form of a thought. Others may receive it as an inner knowing, a picture, or with a distinct feeling through your intuition. And sometimes the answer may not come at that exact moment but revealed in another way.

Keep in mind that while meditation assists in the process and may give you a deeper experience, it is by no means required. You can enter the peace of your heart space and receive divine guidance at any moment and in any place. It is a matter of moving your awareness into that sacred space, which only requires the choice to make a shift in consciousness.

The more you practice, the easier it becomes until you are more in your heart than not and you maintain constant communion with the Divine. Once you have a little experience, you will find it quite easy to enter your heart space at will. Or you may never leave it.

The beauty and benefit of stepping into this larger dimension of yourself is that you can transform and heal yourself by talking to the vulnerable part of yourself from this higher perspective. It's almost like speaking to a child from the mature adult perspective. But in reality, you are speaking to your soul from the perspective of your Divine Self.

And you do this by literally speaking to yourself, either out loud or silently. Say your name and reassure this "child," this vulnerable part of yourself that you love him/her and that you have his/her back. Figuratively embrace this one and love, love, love. Just as you would with a child that is afraid or has been hurt, reassuring that one that you, the "adult," will handle whatever the situation is.

There may be times when you need to listen to your soul who may have felt that you have let him/her down and cannot trust you to protect it or even care. By listening, you will learn about yourself and what feelings or experiences you may have suppressed that need to be dealt with.

There may also be times when you discipline the soul. When this part of yourself wants to throw a fit or scream hateful things, you can step in and say, "No, we aren't going there. I'm handling this." Then you respond from the balanced perspective of your Higher Self.

Another way to heal painful memories, fears or phobias is with the violet flame. This is a spiritual frequency of energy that transmutes, or frees, energy locked into imperfect patterns. Visualizing spiritual violet fire surrounding your physical form and using mantras is the most effective. Here is a simple mantra:

I AM the Violet Flame, Victorious and Free,
One with God I AM, for all Eternity.

https://www.nancyshowalter.com/

 https://www.spiritualityforpoliticallyincorrect.com/

Nancy is the author of It's OK to be Rich: The Entrepreneur's Guide to Increased Wealth and Personal Mastery, endorsed by T. Harv Eker. She is the host of "Spirituality for the Politically Incorrect" podcast.

For over 30 years Nancy has mentored and coached individuals and groups, including conducting seminars, conferences and leadership training in the United States, Canada, Latin America, and Europe. She hosted a 26-day video tele-summit with 26 experts in personal development and was co-host of the worldwide "Prophets for the New Age Radio Show."

Nancy currently speaks, conducts seminars, and does client coaching and mentoring. She brings creativity and a unique integrated perspective to her audiences and clients who find her coaching and presentations to be both practical and personally transforming.

She has a Bachelor of Arts degree from Western Illinois University in Liberal Arts with a concentration in Peace and Conflict Resolution, including traveling in the Middle East to Egypt, Israel, Gaza, and the Golan Heights, meeting and discoursing with Israelis and Palestinians on their perspectives and hopes and dreams for a peaceful future.

She is also author of two mini-books, Quantum Living: Keys for Transformational Change and Ascent Back to God: Wisdom Teachings for the Journey.

Lessons from My Father

By Sangeeta Bhatnagar

It was the evening of May 2nd, 2019. I was with a group of my industry peers as we were winding down from our Awards Gala. The usual chit-chat was going on, we were cleaning up, folding banners, picking up tabletops, extra name badges, etc. Chatting with some of my peers, my sister received a text. It was around 10:15 p.m., she turned to me and said, "We have to go, Dad is being admitted to the hospital". I sunk physically into a chair. My heart sunk into the pit of my stomach.

From that point on, I have minimal recollection. I know some good friends loaded our car and gave us good wishes.

When we reached the emergency room, we saw my dear father in a separate room with my brother. He looked fine – just a bit swollen. As my sister and I entered his room, he gave us a huge smile. We caressed his head as we always did, and he gave us his million dollar smile!

Long story short, my Dad stayed in for more testing. He looked great, lots of laughter, and his trademark joke telling. The night of May 3rd, he had a rough night and then finally went to sleep as my brothers nurtured him. The next day, the nurses tried to wake him up for the morning rounds and he was unresponsive. My sister called me early in the morning as she was already at the hospital. She was calm but emotional. I rushed back to the hospital, not thinking. I felt like I was looking at things happening to someone else.

The Dr. came and said, "I have good news and bad news. Good news – your Dad is not in pain, bad news – his body is filling up with CO_2".

It was as if we were watching a movie. Calmly my sister and I said, "We do not want him to suffer or be in any pain as we love him more than anything else."

Just like that, in under 48 hours, my dear Dad, my advisor and mentor, my "Captain Obvious" was gone! It is as if with a snap of a finger, this amazing man left this plane and went onto another.

On day one of his passing, May 4th, I was very cognitive, calm, cool, collected, and logical with no hysteria. The next day, I woke up and felt a pain, an emptiness and wondering if I had a bad dream.

Like most people who lose someone, we went through the motions. My natural temperament is to be upbeat, positive, and not to show anyone my vulnerabilities. I tried that for some time and then hit the wall by August of 2019. Everything caught up to me. The months of not sleeping, emotional eating, and constant anxiousness with butterflies in my stomach hit me like a brick. I had no desire to do anything which is horrible when you are self-employed. I felt frozen, numb, and not sure how to do anything to move forward. I stopped taking or making calls, and hid behind emails where I could fake happiness and enthusiasm. I could hide and pretend that everything was fine. I could avoid meltdowns that were happening anytime I spoke with my caring friends and even clients. Instead I cried, rather sobbed, for hours on end, day after day staring out my living room window.

I could see myself starting to spiral downward in every area of my life. How could my father's daughter let this happen? He did not work so hard his entire life for me to throw everything away. I was blessed to have some great friends and one in particular said "feel what you feel". That resonated with me and I thought, I would definitely acknowledge what I felt and then at the same time take small steps to move forward.

I never knew what constant anxiety looked or felt like – now I knew. I did not have faith or desire to do anything even though I knew my Dad would always want me to move forward.

The Universe has a way of taking care of us. My faith in God has always guided me through life. While planning a conference, one of our keynote speakers served as a guide. He said, *"You are so close with your father, once you tap into his energy, you will see exponential growth"*. *"Your Dad will still guide and help you."* I share this lesson in the hopes that it can help others who are grieving, feeling lost, and not knowing how to move forward.

I never knew what despair was until August of 2019 (four months after losing my Dad). I sat staring out my living room window wondering "how do I pick myself up?" I have to work as I knew my Dad would want me to be strong. I had to acknowledge that I was having some mental health issues, which I had never voiced before. My greatest lesson is "feel what you feel" and then do what YOU need to do to move forward. It took a few months of me sharing with some trusted friends, sharing my emotions and vulnerabilities, and then trusting in the universe and in the strength that my Dad gave me that I would come through.

From nowhere, I received a call from someone to help with a difficult Talent Search. It was a random call from someone I knew from years back. This served as a nice distraction and started me to get back in the groove. I knew without a doubt that my Dad sent this opportunity my way to help me. I am glad that I was aware enough to recognize the energy and blessings around me.

As I reflect on where I am today, I am so grateful of the lessons my dear father taught me. Sharing this journey is a small way to celebrate my Dad's honourable, well-lived life.

Although my father was not a businessman himself, he taught the timeless success principles to us. His lessons have helped me so much in my life and business ventures. I am sure each of you have lessons you remember from your parents/ grandparents/ elders in your life. Here are a few lessons that my father taught my siblings and me. I recognize how blessed I am to have received these lessons.

Here are a few lessons from my father:

1.   **"A man (person) cannot be weak".** My Dad always said that there will be tough times in life, challenges to overcome, but you cannot crumble and be weak. Have faith in yourself, work hard, work smart, be kind and always be grateful and you will be strong."

2.   **"You've got to do, what you've got to do."** He said this when we would complain over how much schoolwork we had or how challenging our jobs were. *"Whatever the task assigned for school, work, home, volunteering, do it and do it well!"* He always said that no matter what the job is, **do what you need to do.**

3.   **What you give with your right hand, even your left hand should not know.** This lesson has shaped my life in a major way. I am sure many people have been taught this lesson to serve and give so humbly that your own ego should not think about it. There is no need to broadcast what you do or give personally.

4.   **Serve those people that will never be able to help you back — be selfless.** I see many people will support a charity if their boss or an executive is collecting but what about just giving to a homeless shelter or any place where the recipient has no idea who you are. When we give from our heart, we end up being the biggest recipient of good.

5.   **He believed, no matter what the ailment — physical or mental — take a nap!** Things are always clearer after a nap!

6.   **Live below your means.** *Only buy what you need, and not everything you want!* Be responsible with your money and do not finance anything other than your house.

7. **Live with honour, protect your name.** My Dad always said, *"your actions will either build your name or destroy it. Live a life of character, do what is right when no one else is looking!"*

8. **Be the biggest giver and do not think about taking!** We were encouraged to knock on doors and be the biggest collectors of funds for our local walkathons or selling chocolates and other items so that we could be the biggest givers. He told me as a child, that he did not come to Canada to take anything but rather to add value to the community. My Dad loved Canada and said we should look for every opportunity to give back!

9. **If you are going to do something, do it well or do not do it at all.** Do not do anything half-hearted! My Dad always said, *"do not have the mentality of it's good enough"*

10. **Be kind to everyone. Serve anyone who comes to your house with respect and full hospitality.** I remember every guest, tradesperson, and repairmen who came to our house were treated with respect and offered a drink and something to eat. Regardless of their "status" in society, each person was treated as if they were the most important person ever!

11. **Study, study, study!** *"No one will ever be able to take your education away from you!"*

12. **Do not use words like *"I'm tired, I can't or it's too hard."*** He would remind us of how hard it was when he came to Canada with nothing more than $25 and a dream. He told us to never shy away from effort and hard work. We were taught to have the best work ethic but even more importantly, have a great attitude.

Defining success is difficult as everyone measures it differently. The perception of success varies, it may be the big job titles and lots of money, to others it is simply serving others in your most authentic manner. My Dad came to Canada with very little money in his pocket and was eventually able to educate four kids fully through university and college without ever asking us to give anything back in return.

My Dad showed me what success was when I saw him overcome a major financial adversity. After years of saving, proper investing, never spending on himself as he only spent on his kids, he went into a bad business deal by trusting an old "friend". In doing so, my hard-working humble father lost $250,000 and we almost lost our house. I saw my Dad lose all that money, lose his job, all the while he had three kids in university. Did he crumble? No. He said, *"this is why you live simply and think of your blessings"*. This was a firsthand view of **Resilience 101!**

My Dad had years of legal expenses and added stress, but he kept a positive outlook and knew he had to do something. After losing his job as a supervisor in a pulp and paper mill in Trenton, Ontario, he immediately thought he could start selling bulk confectionary items to the smaller stores. He drove from store to store, all day long in the heat, in a non-air-conditioned car, waiting to get sales orders from grocery store purchasers less than half his age.

After trying this business for a while and being such a strong believer in education, at age 75 my Dad decided to take the Canadian Securities course so that he could sell RESP's. He studied so hard and passed in the 80th percentile! He did this successfully until age 80 when our family convinced him to stop and to enjoy his retirement.

I live with complete faith in a greater energy, faith in God and faith in all elements of the Universe. It is only with faith that I was able to overcome some of life's challenges. I believe it is faith in something more than yourself that helps drive you to *make this world a better place than how you found it.*

We all have the power to influence others to do more, serve more, give more, and be more.

I am proud that I was able to write this chapter without having a complete meltdown, although I had a couple of mini episodes. I feel I can pass on the lessons I was blessed to receive. I hope this chapter can show the strength of my Dad coming through. I was taught to always be grateful for what I had in life, for the opportunities, and all the blessings around me.

To anyone who has had a struggle with losing someone and not knowing how to move forward, please know that the memory, teachings, and spirit of our close ones can always be with us.

I dedicate this in memory of my life mentor, success advisor, true "influencer", friend and my "Captain Obvious", Dad – VP Bhatnagar.

Below is a photo of my **"Captain Obvious"** Dad who told us to make sure that while taking this shot, we do not miss capturing Peyto Lake in the picture!

 https://www.sbglobal.ca/

Sangeeta Bhatnagar is Founder of the boutique Human Capital firm SB Global, which focuses on talent acquisition and training (live and virtually) for top-tiered Contact Center & Customer Experience professionals. With an emphasis on Human Behaviour, Sangeeta helps companies to attract, retain and develop top talent using behaviour models, strategies, and Emotional Intelligence principles. Sangeeta is a frequent contributor to industry publications, conferences and webinars focused on creating memorable human experiences. Sangeeta was selected as one of ICMI's "Top 50 Customer Service Thought Leaders on Twitter." She also co-authored the Amazon #1 best-selling anthology, "Called to Action," and she is Chair of the Greater Toronto Area Contact Centre Association.

The Inside Job

A Revolution of Love, Light and Personal Power

By Sarah Grace Knutson

In the year 2000, I was 20. Life was a little crazy. I'm sure my childhood and formative years looked normal enough on the outside (even with the rebellion and black eyeliner). I have good parents who did their best, but it wasn't without big challenges. By the time I was 20 I had been violated enough times to count on two hands, and things had fallen apart more times than I cared to think about.

Despite my quick mind, I dropped out of high-school, made risky choices, hung out with risky people, and then said, "see - that's what it's always like!" when someone betrayed or pulled one over on me. When I was accepted to college simply by challenging the entrance exams, I really tried to make something good happen, but the patterns of self-sabotage, substance abuse, apathy and anxiety took over regularly enough that I was not thriving on my noble path.

I say "noble path" because my chosen mission was to get a degree in psychology, followed by a post-graduate diploma in art therapy. I planned to work with troubled kids who couldn't express their feelings because it didn't feel safe to be themselves. I was going to save the kids that nobody else could make a difference for. One night, while standing outside of the bar I worked at, I told my plan to a good friend. He smiled lovingly and said, "That, Sarah, is very noble." I felt myself glow - his words were the recognition I craved. Sarah the noble.

I had a plan for those hypothetical kids somewhere in my future; the only problem was I didn't have a plan for me.

I remember drawing a picture in my sketchbook one late night in my downtown bachelor apartment. It was a boldly coloured charcoal drawing, titled "victim of circumstance". It was like Lady Justice with her blindfold and scales, but the scales were tipped way off kilter and there were little demons all around her, representing "circumstance." They haunted her. I felt proud of my profound and insightful statement about "how the world works".

I told my dad about my drawing on the phone—we've always had good chats. I was frustrated when he said, "be careful what you're putting out there." I felt invalidated. I wanted people to understand how much circumstance had played into my hardships. I wanted to prove that it was never my fault when things fell apart—there was always someone or something I could point at as the "reason" for it.

I can see now how totally immersed I was in being the victim, and how enraged I was about it. I can also see how upside down that all is. I was raised on the law of attraction, but I still didn't grasp how my beliefs about my circumstances were creating more of the same, or that I ALONE had the power to get myself out of the spin cycle. There would be no saviour, save myself. I could and would only start digging myself out of a messed up outer world by changing my inner world first.

Fast forward 20 years. It is the year 2020. Life is a little crazy.

The world is locked down in a global pandemic; people are viciously polarized over who is wearing a mask or not. Countries are burning, hatred and oppression appear to be tearing apart the fabric of the world's societies, intense accusations are being made about scams, mass manipulation, mind control, nefarious intentions...and the second it all started, I bolted upright with a deep inner knowing that every second of my life (and all the ones previous) had prepared me for this moment. I was witnessing the catalyst for the world to wake up—en masse—all of humanity—and that I had a role to play. I was ready to step in. Nothing has ever been clearer to me.

It's been eight years since what I would call the start of my "awakening journey." In that time, I have completely transformed in mind and soul. I found the courage to look into the darkness of my previously troubled mind. I learned to shine the light in there and lovingly change the things that were messy and not working for me. I boldly walked away from everything that was ever abusive or toxic in my life, and re-created myself in a way that feels good, and true, and right. I have since become a women's empowerment coach with a specialty in transforming and healing from limiting belief systems and toxic life patterns.

What does this have to do with the year 2020 and all the chaos that's been happening out there? Well, let me tell you a story.

In my meditations, I found myself communicating with an ancient goddess who told me I was going to write a book about personal empowerment. "The New Power" she called it. When I asked her what that meant she just said, "You'll see when it's time." When I felt frustrated that she wasn't satisfying my curiosity fast enough, she just typed "Love, Love, Love, Love, Love...it can only come from pure unconditional love."

I considered that perhaps my sanity had broken. It hadn't.

I also found myself processing a ton of rage—most of it was from a time I was burned at the stake, and all the other lifetimes I'd been persecuted just for showing up in full divine feminine power—so there was also terror. I realized my mind wasn't the only place with dark, scary corners. Some were carried in my soul too. I undertook the process of healing these insane emotions. I'm beyond grateful that I was already a seasoned pro at clearing traumas and brutal mental patterns from this lifetime. It meant I had the strength and willingness to do it with even deeper ones from before. I would be lying if I said I didn't need support. I got help. Always get help!

I started sitting down at my computer regularly, getting grounded, aligned and connected, and just letting words flow out my fingertips to see what came out of me. Much of it was poetry.

One morning after meditating, I opened to my creative source, and a pretty little poem poured out of my fingertips.

It's not about who has the money
It's not about who thinks they're right
It's not about who said something
That made you want to fight
There's only one thing that you need
to do to find your might
Look within and find your power
Look within and shine your light

I did not check the news that day before posting my poem publicly on social media. Turns out it was offensive given the world climate. It wasn't offensive to everyone—many of my friends who identify as light-workers, energy healers and mindset coaches celebrated and "liked" my poem, so I got lots of fresh dopamine hits and good leverage on the Facebook algorithms.

Then came the one comment that ripped my pretty little poem in half. I didn't see it coming.

To be honest, I only check the news about once a week. I choose not to give energy to things that drag me down, for my own wellbeing and for my family's wellbeing. While doing my best to stay informed and educated, I limit exposure and stay off mainstream media completely because I do believe they are manipulating and pushing narratives that don't help us.

I wasn't writing a poem about a specific world challenge. I was speaking of personal empowerment, which is the very thing I believe will shift the global population out of the challenges that are being faced.

On that day, however, the world stage was playing out a game of oppression. My post was interpreted by one friend as if I think "ignoring all the problems and just connecting with spirit will make all the problems go away". They said my perspective was dangerous; that I was going to lead people further into oppression by spreading this kind of message.

"Oops." I thought, "They misunderstood me." I got busy clarifying myself. I wasn't implying that people shouldn't look at injustices. I meant that when we are connected with our innate power and clear the thought distortions that have kept the narratives of victim and oppressor going for so long, we won't need to change the systems because the people inside the systems won't perpetuate their victim or oppressor roles anymore—they will have risen above these mindsets. Simple explanation right?

Wrong.

I was told I was victim blaming.

I was told personal inner work and self-empowerment are all fine and well but they do nothing to help humanity. This friend said that focusing on ourselves is selfish, disregarding our duality and responsibility as part of a collective.

Of course, they said, it would be lovely if everyone on the planet did their inner work but it's not going to happen so revolutions are necessary because no radical change has ever happened peacefully.

In my privileged position; white, Canadian, not currently struggling, food on my table, no guns in my house, not afraid of cops, able to relax at night and meditate in the morning, my friend thought I couldn't see the hardships that plague so many; the ones who were right in the thick of it in that very moment!

At first I felt personally attacked, and I struggled for a moment with needing to defend my position. Then, I chose to breathe, go for a walk and nourish my body. I decided I had nothing to prove and I let it go, but I still had something to say, so it became the topic for this chapter.

You see, compassion runs in my blood and in my tears. I see the struggles of humanity and I resonate deeply. I have lived through a grueling journey, hauling myself out of torturous relationships riddled with every form of abuse, including the insidious psychological abuse of a manipulative narcissist who exploited my willingness to devalue myself.

While I was in this place, convinced that I was valueless, I could not make my life work and I was vulnerable to anyone who knew how to control people, but I made a conscious choice to break the chain; inside and out.

Today, after eight years of personal development, healing old patterns and toxic belief systems, I have learned to listen to my soul when I need answers. Once I did that, I found the source of my power and my life changed before my eyes. However, that doesn't mean I can no longer see the struggles that others are immersed in. I have extraordinary capacities for both compassion and clear vision.

But compassion doesn't mean I have to enter into the struggle with you to help you get out of it. That's codependence. Compassion doesn't mean I have to act from a place of rage—in my work I help people to rise out of the rage and transform it before taking action. Compassion doesn't mean rushing in to be a saviour, it means holding space for the person who is struggling to rise into their inner power.

So from this place I declare that personal inner work and self-empowerment through expanding consciousness is the best thing that each of us can do to catalyze great shifts for the global population.

Einstein said, "We cannot solve our problems with the same thinking that created them"

I do not say "ignore the problems," I say "rise up out of the mindset that created them," but I also see what is challenging people so much in accomplishing that.

One challenge we are facing is that the whole human collective (oppressors and victims alike) is dealing with generational trauma from thousands of years of oppression. This means that people in general are still programmed with the same kind of thinking that created the issues we are seeing, even if they can't see it in themselves.

Generational trauma means that belief systems and situational reactions are passed along in our DNA, or by social conditioning based on ideologies presented by the family in the first seven years of life.

In other words, hundreds of years ago, groups of people dealt with psychological abuse from manipulative aggressors who convinced them they were valueless. Today, the descendants of those people (on both sides) have inherited many of the core beliefs their grandparents had, but they probably don't even realize it because it all happened when they were teeny little kiddos, or even through their DNA. These core beliefs could look like "My people are looked down upon" or "I'll never be able to succeed" or "The world is just like this."

The beautiful thing is that we can change our situational reactions, our deepest belief systems, and our thought patterns to allow us to rise out of the generational patterns that have been keeping us stuck. And when we change our belief systems, we actually change the fabric of our realities.

The fields of epigenetics, neuroplasticity, subconscious reprogramming, learning theory, heart coherence and quantum reality would fill a gigantic library. You can google any of them and find masses of profound work from scientific and psychological pioneers as well as self-help and spiritual masters. (Bruce Lipton, Ali Jawaid, Michael Skinner, Johannes Bohacek, Suze Casey, Joe Dispenza, Gregg Braden, Deepak Chopra)

All of it is all relevant to the work of rising out of generational trauma, which IS the work we all have before us, and it is the work I am devoted to doing for as long as it takes. You don't need to know the science to do the work—it's a basic process that anyone can accomplish. Several ingeniously simple yet profound systems have been created. I know one of them inside and out, and there are millions of helpers, lightworkers, coaches, therapists and other people devoted to this same work in their own unique ways.

The point I so badly wanted to make in the comment thread that I abandoned so that I could write a chapter instead—is that I am ALL FOR tearing down broken systems and holding oppressors accountable for their atrocities—but tearing down external systems when the individuals involved in them are still programmed with old thinking...well, it's not going to work!

Do conventional activism and revolution work? Maybe for a little while, but they don't necessarily get to the center of the issue, which is the socio-spiritual wellness of the people who are playing out the patterns (which is all of us). I believe the collective heals on an individual basis first, and trying to change things on the outside without each one also shifting things on the inside won't *really* get the job done. History would repeat itself yet again, so instead, I propose tearing down the system from the inside.

It has to be an inside job; a revolution of love, light, and personal power.

Without blaming anyone, I am saying that each individual holds accountability for the way that they are contributing to their own set of circumstances. And yes—they deserve support—but maybe meaningful help will be different than what they're used to.

So, 7.8 billion people changing their inner worlds—seems like a lot, hey? Except that it is 7.8 billion walking, talking, breathing transmitters and receivers of energy. When I raise my energy through healing and consciousness, it DOES have an effect on all the rest. A group of people in a room create an energy field that is transmitting information constantly. If one member of the group consciously shifts their heart-coherence, the nature of the whole energy field shifts and the emotional experience of the other group members changes. This also happens (in a not-so-great way) in a riot or flash-mob. When we use this consciously for good, we can have great impact on the world around us just by controlling our own energy and vibration.

When we are caught up in survival mode ourselves, we're not actually wired to be of much use, and important decisions made when we're in sympathetic nervous system overload don't typically turn out well.

When I really look within, beyond the wounds and shadows of my inner child, beyond the egoic games that we have been programmed to play, I find the source of my love, my light, my true power and innate worthiness. When I live every possible moment from this place, and I build into myself the tools to remain calm and neutral, observing, and thoughtfully responding to the outer world rather than getting shaken up and blindsided by it, THEN I am in a position to take aligned action that can be truly meaningful.

When I am standing so solidly in who I am that not a soul on earth could pull the rug out from under me, then I am in an empowered position to make changes in the world—and when all the humans realize that their power comes from within, that no one can give it to them and no one can take it away, when all the humans know their innate value and purpose— then the systems of oppression and victimhood fall away on their own.

We all have the same potential for personal power, and it is the generational traumas, old belief systems and broken thought constructs that are stopping people from knowing the power of love so deeply that they simply walk out of the drama.

I believe revolution CAN be peaceful and just because we have never seen it before doesn't mean it isn't possible. I believe we CAN take down the toxic, patriarchal constructs of control from the inside, with LOVE.

I believe humanity already IS doing its work collectively and what we are seeing now is the flushing out of everything that was hiding in the dark.

Things are not getting worse, they were already worse, they are coming to light and this is the first step of healing on a global scale.

I believe that the more individuals simply walk away from the constructs of control (in an empowered way, not a reactive one), that the systems will deconstruct on their own.

I believe it is already happening, but things might look crazier before we start seeing that they are getting better.

An awakening human goes through a dark night when the awakening process begins. I believe what we are seeing in the world is billions of dark nights of the soul at once. I also believe that it will pass.

I will continue to declare that the best thing any one human can do for the collective is their own personal work first, and then ripple it out to 20 people, who will ripple it out to 20 more. The result is more exponential growth than any virus, and more energetic catalysis than any flash mob.

When the water rises in the harbour, all ships rise. I'm using my light to bring in the tide.

/…

🌐 **Complimentary discovery call**
www.soul-birth.com

🌐 **The Soulfully Empowered Mother Course**
www.soul-birth.com/goddess

✉ sarahgracewellness@gmail.com

⬛ sarahgracesoulbirth

⬛ sarahgracesoulbirth

✈ soulfullyempoweredwoman

🎵 @sarahgracesoulbirth

Sarah Grace Knutson is a Best-Selling Author, Founder of 'SOUL-Birth Personal Empowerment Coaching for The Soulful Woman' and Licensed Belief Re-Patterning® Practitioner. She is the creator of the 'SOUL-Birth Signature System' of transformation, and 'The Soulfully Empowered Mother" online course.

Sarah specializes in guiding Soulful Women, especially mothers, to rediscover their unique identity, liberating them from unhealthy beliefs and societal programs, helping them reconnect with their authentic truths so they may create meaningful lives of empowered confidence, joy, passion and purpose.

Her work combines elements of energy-work, guided meditation, direct intuitive coaching, Belief Re-Patterning® and simple yet profound personal practices. Her Soul-Birth Signature System focuses directly on alignment with your soul, clearing the mind and nervous system of traumatic memories and old patterns, building confidence through personal empowerment, divine self love and drawing out the valuable pieces of you that make you YOU.

By encouraging and assisting women to embrace their light and ripple it out into the world, she is contributing to an empowered future for all people, our children, and our world. While our stories are unique, the challenges we face are universal and the hunger to rise up is present in all of us.

Sarah Lives in Edmonton, Alberta, Canada with her loving partner and two sweet children, enjoying music, laughter, and walks in the woods.

The Journey to Self-Love May Be Challenging But the Destination is Worth the Adventure

By Sarah Willoughby

2020 is a year that will be etched in people's hearts and minds for generations to come. The year that the whole world stopped. The year that physical contact was forbidden, and hugging people outside of the household became a thing of the past. How I miss those hugs!

I'm currently in an extended lockdown in Melbourne, Australia, the longest one in the world. As I sit here wondering how we came to be awarded this badge of honour and where it all went wrong, many people are struggling. If you are doing it tough right now, know you are not alone. In my experience, wisdom and better times often follow great adversity.

Reflecting on what has helped me navigate through 2020, I conclude 2009 was a pivotal year for me. The year I strapped myself into an incredible rollercoaster ride where I learnt the harshest lessons life has ever afforded me. My memories of 2009 continue to be instrumental in maintaining not just my sanity in 2020, but also hope. Hope for the future and faith that all will be well, no matter what happens. I wish this for you too.

2009 was the year it became crystal clear that life is incredibly fragile. It's not a dress rehearsal. I'd been guilty of acting as if I were immortal, procrastinating and avoiding difficult decisions. Despite the discomfort of being stuck, this familiar feeling was easier to deal with than leaping into the unknown. Does this resonate with you? Frozen in fear, I inadvertently compromised my happiness because I subconsciously didn't believe I was deserving of the joy, connection, and fresh start that I so desperately craved. Then I had the biggest wake-up call imaginable and my life changed forever. For this I am grateful.

In 2009 I had ventured over to Norway from the UK with my husband, three-year-old son, and mother-in-law for some In Vitro Fertilisation (IVF) treatment; a routine procedure. We had planned to enjoy a relaxing holiday afterwards to take our minds off the torturous two-week wait and anticipation about whether I could be pregnant. But an ultrasound revealed that my ovaries had overreacted to the drugs, dangerously swelling with fluid to several times their normal size. After the egg collection, I took a rapid turn for the worse. The IVF cycle was cancelled, and my embryos were frozen; I was shattered.

Ovarian hyperstimulation syndrome (OHSS) ravaged me. Lying in intensive care, unable to breathe, nauseous and with pain coursing through my body with such intensity I felt I may explode. Morphine brought me no relief. Vulnerable and scared, the constant beeping of machines filled my ears as I drifted in and out of an eerie fog. Days later I had fluid on my lungs, an enlarged heart and my organs began to struggle and slowly shut down. With the doctors unable to stop the deterioration, they could only treat the symptoms and make me as comfortable as possible while we waited for the condition to reverse itself. The rest was up to a power much greater than me.

The day of our planned return flight to the UK arrived. Still too sick to be discharged from hospital, saying goodbye to my son, Isaac, was my lowest moment. As I lay in my hospital bed blinking away the tears that began to fill my eyes, I wondered whether I would ever see him again. The pain in my expanded body which had rapidly filled up like a balloon with 20kg of leaky fluid prevented me from hugging Isaac. My heart began to pound with despair.

Overwhelming thoughts bombarded my mind.

Will I be able to hold Isaac in my arms again and breathe in the fragrance of his newly washed hair? How I love that smell.

What happens if I'm not strong enough to survive this?

Will I see Isaac learn to ride a bike or attend his first day at school?

I hope Isaac doesn't understand what is happening.

My stream of consciousness was abruptly broken by Isaac's whisper.

"When will I see you again Mummy?"

"I don't know darling," I replied.

Isaac looked up at me with sadness in his beautiful deep brown eyes.

"I love you Mummy; I'll miss you."

"I love you too Isaac," I smiled, stroking his soft, gentle face.

Isaac slowly turned away; it was time for him to go to the airport with his Grandma. Watching him walk out of the large, wooden hospital doors holding his small, well-loved jangly rabbit in his hand, I had never felt so devastated.

As Isaac disappeared out of sight, I broke down and began questioning my decision to go through IVF. I had not made this choice lightly. Our three years of infertility had already been filled with physical trauma, miscarriage, and emotional pain. With such disturbed hormone levels and an erratic cycle, IVF had been our best chance of having another baby, a sibling for our son. But now guilt and shame for putting my body through an elective procedure, despite the low risk, bubbled within me. *What have I done?*

My recovery became a mindset battle, and one I was determined to win. Because if I wanted to raise my son, I needed to get through this. My meditation and mindfulness practices were my saviour. Without them, I wouldn't have survived those difficult weeks in the hospital and months of healing. The excruciating ascites drainages, chest x-rays and heart scan would have physically defeated me, and mentally I would have been crushed by the fear of what lay ahead.

I learnt the hard way, gasping for air, that our breath is our life force. When we're stressed or pressured, we often forget to breathe correctly. Meditation can help us focus on our breath and wellbeing.

The promise of better physical health, more restful sleep, reduced stress, anxiety and blood pressure, relief from anger, depression or distress are reasons people are drawn to meditation. Meditation also attracts those searching for a more meaningful spiritual connection or to improve their intuition and decision making. A regular meditation practise facilitates mental, emotional, and spiritual growth, as well as changing and restoring the brain. No longer stuck with what we're born with, we can proactively improve our experiences. I encourage you to try the guided meditations that are available on my website. Breathe into your heart and see which ones you are drawn to.

Facing my mortality in 2009 was the most humbling experience. For the first time, I comprehended how little we can control. Instead, we must choose how we respond to circumstances that come our way. When visiting hours were over, being alone with my thoughts, unable to move, and staring for hours at the same white walls, pushed me to my limits. But it also created an opportunity to re-evaluate my life and tap into gratitude. In my darkest moments, I promised myself that if I recovered, I would pursue my desire to live in Australia and strive to be my best version. After 30 years, I finally understood that the connection between our mind, body, and spirit is pivotal for our happiness. My infertility was a journey to self-love, the most significant gift of all.

Gratitude is in alignment with the highest vibration; love. Have you noticed that when you are thankful, you can feel your heart open? Being open-hearted attracts more love and abundance into our lives, even during turbulent times. Abundance such as more connected relationships, improved wellbeing, increased joy, and material wealth.

Practising gratitude means we are practising love; we all need more of this. Delve into gratitude by writing down three things every morning or evening that you appreciate in a notebook. Do this for 21 days to feel the subtle shifts that gratitude brings. When you acknowledge the small things such as a warm shower, a conversation with a friend, or the sound of birds singing, you will naturally attract more experiences to be grateful for.

Engaging the whole family in the practice of gratitude is easy. Every person writes down or draws what they're thankful for on pieces of paper and pops them in a jar. During family dinner on Sunday evening, all the week's blessings can be read out loud. Children love this activity and it enables everyone to start the next week with an open heart and positive mindset.

I believe it was my open heart and mind that encouraged the ovarian hyperstimulation syndrome to eventually reverse itself and for my body to start to heal. My kidneys kicked into action, fluid was released from my body and the pain caused by the excessive weight gain was relieved. When we were finally reunited, Isaac's love nursed me back to wellness.

Later in the year, a return trip to Norway for a frozen embryo transfer resulted in a pregnancy with twins. I was ecstatic but miscarried them both. Despite my grief, my inner-knowing that things would improve was stronger. My second chance at life was not wasted. In November 2009, I emigrated to Australia with my son and husband and surrendered to all that was meant to be. I could do no more. The next month I fell pregnant naturally, against all the odds, and welcomed my now ten-year-old daughter into the world, a child I thought I may never have. I left the corporate world, set up my own business and four years later cradled another daughter in my arms, she is now six.

Whatever you are currently dealing with, know that this too shall pass. Everything is temporary, just like your emotions. I hope my story will inspire you to keep going because the world needs you. The world needs your unique talents, perspectives, and compassion. The world needs you to heal your past hurts and walk along your path to self-love. To forgive yourself and others. One thing I know for sure is that we are better united. Each of us may only be a tiny drop in the ocean, but when we connect, we make up the entire sea. Together we are a powerful wave of hope and potential.

Know that the answer to every problem lies inside you. How amazing is that? Quietening your mind enables you to hear the messages. Whether you weed the garden, go for a run, sit in silence or dance in your living room, it doesn't matter. What matters is that you connect to yourself so that your loving inner voice can rise to support you out of your current struggles.

Being in nature slows your breathing down, makes you feel calmer and lessens your repetitive thoughts. Your brain is given a well-deserved rest.

Try grounding to reconnect to the earth. As you draw energy into your body, you will re-energise and feel your energy shift. The simplest way to access this natural energy is to walk barefoot on the surface of the earth, lie on the ground to increase the skin-to-earth contact, or immerse yourself in water. Being in water relieves stress and releases your stuck emotions. When you are grounded, you move out of your mind and into your body. This is where you need to be to make your best decisions and positive change.

2009 and 2020 taught me about self-love and acceptance; I am indebted. Your challenges provide valuable insight into where you need to focus. They can also help you step out of fear to move forward. This journey may not be easy, but the destination is always worth the tumultuous expedition. Because what lies on the other side is strength, wisdom and an ability to connect so profoundly with yourself that you no longer doubt your intuition or heart; your master thinker. When you're brave enough to tune into the signs you receive and then respond, life will unfold in miraculous ways. And never forget that your time here is short, so grab life with both hands and make every moment count!

sarah@sarahwilloughby.com.au

www.sarahwilloughby.com.au

www.facebook.com/SarahWilloughbyAustralia

www.linkedin.com/in/sarah-willoughby-2019

www.instagram.com/sarahwilloughbyaustralia

www.youtube.com/channel/UCj7B9AAPLyGDci2Y6tvoMVw

In April 2009, Sarah Willoughby lay in intensive care following a disastrous In Vitro Fertilization (IVF) cycle. Sarah promised the universe that if she were blessed with a second chance, she would face her fears to make positive changes in her life and the world.

Sarah emigrated to Australia with her family in November 2009, leaving behind her ten-year corporate human resources career, degree, and professional qualifications. Listening to her intuition to re-train and set up her own business, Sarah began empowering people to heal, love themselves, be peaceful and transform their lives.

As a Personal Growth Coach, Speaker, Author, Spiritual Mentor, Reiki Practitioner, Intuitive Energy Healer, and Infertility Coach, Sarah has always been intrigued by what connects us and why we are here. Her inspiring articles on life and spirituality have been read by thousands of people all over the world. Sarah's book on self-love through secondary infertility is motivated by a desire to provide hope to anyone navigating this difficult path and help break the silence surrounding infertility.

Sarah loves spending time in nature, sitting by the fire in winter reading a book and having fun with her three beautiful children, who are her greatest teachers.

How Permanent Stress Changed My Life?

By Stephanie Schaffner

A few years ago, I worked as a controller for a university in Germany based near Frankfurt. I lived with my husband and our two kids together and we had a very unhealthy relationship. From day to day, I felt more sick and my stomach felt like a stone.

I had to raise two school kids and run through a very hectic job. My husband was not much support back then.

Every kind of food I ate seemed to want to leave my body right away. In the end I weighed just 83,7757 lb which corresponds to 38 kg. I was hospitalized and had to remove large parts of the intestine in an emergency operation.

The diagnosis was Crohn's disease. Crohn's disease is still uncurable.

As I spend a long time laying in this intensive care unit, I questioned myself: should this be everything? Should I live a life without love and stay in this unhealthy relationship?

Does life have to be like this? Do I have to live a life that my husband wanted me to live?

I didn't want to show my kids a false picture of human relationships.

I wanted to show them that with kindness and understanding for other humans everything is possible.

After months of convalescence, I decided to leave my husband and live with my kids as a single mum.

I questioned myself more than one time: will I be able to raise my two kids in a positive way and what will it cost me? Would it cost my inner peace? No it wouldn´t.

I would loose my inner peace by staying where I was.

I changed my job and went back to the software industry where I worked a few years prior. I worked as a sales manager and was responsible for new business and the expansion of sales.

It did not become less stressful. So I had to raise the kids, lead my houshold and work in a responsible position.

To work in sales means that you have to travel a lot. From customers to conferences, to the next workshop. I changed to another company, hoping to travel less.

But I was wrong.

As the head of new business, I was responsible for the development of the sales department and additional operational sales activities.

I woke up one morning in a hotel room and had no idea which city I was in that day.

I called my mother to ask what conference I was at. She told me that I was in Düsseldorf.

By the way, I didn´t drink alcohol or anything like that.

This was the day I decided my life had to change.

Looking back, many things have been reactions of my body to stress.

Yes, Crohn's disease is an autoimmune disease, but the severe course of the disease flare-up was intensified by the constant external and internal stress.

Permanent stress damages the body and organs. In the event that the adrenal gland continuously releases cortisol, inflammation develops in the body.

It took me several years to get where I am now. I worked with NLP coaches to change my way of thinking.

I had to work on my inner drivers and learn to not be so much of a perfectionist. Perfectionism is a thing that increases stress.

I learned a lot about visulization and how to reach the goals you set yourself.

As I watched the movie "The Secret" everything started to change and turned my world upside down. I was invited to the Digital Enterprise Show in Madrid.

In Madrid I met Catherine B. Roy for the first time. I had no idea that to meet Catherine would change my entire life.

I didn't know Catherine B. Roy in advanced. We had a great time at this day in Madrid.

After my return from the Digital Enterprise Show I bought her book "Live From Your Heart and Mind".

We stayed in contact and I made a decision that changed everything.

I took the risk to start my education as a Certified Trainer for stress management and a coach for burnout prevention.

I had the vision to help people to manage their long-term stress in a healthy way and to transform it into high performance.

Without the contact with all the positive people arround me I wouldn´t have the strength to walk my way.

In my point of view you receive what you give. Being supportive and kind is the way I always choose. And so everything falls in place.

Catherine B Roy became my Business Strategy Coach and played a big role in my founding process.

After completing my education sucessfully, I founded my own company "Die Stress Managerin" in the year 2019.

Meanwhile I'm writing these words we are in a Covid19 crisis. The restaurants and bars are closed, the stores were closed for a while and we had to stay at home with our loved ones.

Football games and concerts were not allowed and our kids aren't allowed to sing in school.

Even visiting older people in the hospital and in nursing homes was forbidden.

These times are very stressful and many people suffer under the changed situation and the lockdown situation around the world.

To keep in balance in times of more working from home, it is really important to keep a structured day, even with kids in home schooling.

What keeps us in balance?

A really important thing is how we look at things.

Are we able to see the positivity even in a negative situation? Or are we lost in negativity?

We can train our inner attitude and see the positivity even in hard times.

Often, we cannot change the life events or change very little the circumstances that we encounter. But we can always change our inner attitude towards it. We alone have the opportunity to change the way we look into the future.

If you want to change your thinking create an **action plan** and think about **exactly** how you want to be in the future.

How should you think, act and feel? How should you react in the future?

Write it down.

Divide your big goal into many small goals. And do not be afraid, you can do it!

Be proud of every little step that you take.

Reward yourself for every small step forward and be proud of how far you have come.

Knowing that you want to act differently in the future is the first step.

Setbacks are part of any development and should be seen as progress.

Life is not easy for any of us. But you can make your life easier with the way you think. You cannot avert fate but you can adapt your style to respond.

The key in every situation is a positive mindset.

In times of struggle and overwhelming self-care and the right strategies have a really huge positive impact.

You can train and implement strategies and self-care into your daily routine.

Block your routine into your calendar as you do it with your business events and meetings. Your private appointments are just as important as your business appointments.

Give yourself the permission to rest, if needed. Be aware of the signs your body shows you. Even little signs like back pain and a headache are important and should not be underestimated.

Take yourself into nature and go for a walk. To see the green outside helps you to rest your eyes. A walk through nature is like a little meditation and helps you to breathe right, like the walk meditation from Thich Nhat Hanh you are able to be more focused afterwards.

You need to breathe right to reduce your cortisol instantly.

Try the breath exercise for three minutes:
Left nasal ventilation
It is easy to do, quickly calms the breathing rate and thus calms the autonomic nervous system.

By taking in air through the left nostril, the energy is directed to our "moon side" (left half of the body), which is responsible for relaxation, regeneration, and letting go. In addition, the li. Stimulated frontal lobe, which among other things is responsible for controlling "positive states of mind". This means that this activation makes it easier to get into a positive mood.

- breathe in deeply through the left nostril, slowly counting to four (four seconds)
- hold your breath for a moment (pause)
- if you like, visualize the area behind the left front side, which is now stimulated

This breathing exercise directs the energy to the left side of the body, calms the vegetative nervous system through breathing, activates the parasympathetic nervous system, and relaxes and calms. In addition, the activation of the left frontal lobe in the brain stimulates the experience of a positive mood.

And one thing changed a lot for me. I just want to give you one of the important messages, that can really change your way of thinking.

A few years ago I had the opinion that I have to solve every challenge or problem by myself.

Every deadline that had to be kept, I felt responsible for it.

My inner driver was perfectionism.

I want to tell you today one important sentence that you can tell yourself every day.

Asking for help isn't weakness! Asking for help is strength.

You don't have to save the world by yourself.

This message is one of the most powerful messages I've ever heard and it can change your way of thinking.

And sometimes it doesn't have to be 100 percent perfect. 80 percent in times of a high stress is enough. Give yourself the permission to not be perfect.

You see knowing the right strategies can change a lot for your stress levels and your whole wellbeing.

If you ever had the feeling in your life that you are not in the right place at the right time, take the risk and change it. You have the opportunity to win. If you aren´t happy with your current job — take the opportunity of the Covid19 crisis and start that side hustle you ever dreamed of.

If you're trapped in an unhealthy relationship, take the risk and break up. Give yourself the permission to find your personal luck.

If you ever dreamed of another job or founding your own restaurant—do it!

We all have just one life—and it can be over faster than you can imagine.

Yes, sometimes it is scary and sometimes it takes a lot but you have nothing to lose.

Your mental health is the most important thing. It is the basic for your physical health.

Without health success means nothing.

After every negative event in my life, I managed to get up and grow in the situation.

And that's what makes resilience.
Resilient people are solution-oriented, goal-oriented, network-oriented, optimistic, accept responsibility and leave the victim role.

And always believe in the power of yourself.

Love Stephanie

http://www.diestressmanagerin.com/

Stephanie Schaffner worked for many years in business for international companies such as Lufthansa. In the past few years she worked as a Sales Manager & Head of New Business in internationally operating software companies before becoming a certified trainer for stress management and a coach for burnout prevention.

Stephanie is focused to work onsite with the client and their team to manage stress in a healthy way and to transform negative stress into positive stress to reach high performance.

Stephanie is official Contributing Author for Thrive Global by Arianna Huffington and as a international guest expert in various podcast broadcasts and live shows.

She was nominated in the Health category of the Digital Female Leader Awards.

Stephanie is an international keynote speaker on the Digital Enterprise Show in Madrid and Thinkers 360 has chosen her among the top 150 female thought leaders in B2B to follow in 2021.

The Masks We Wear

By Sue DeCaro

August 2020

It was the summer of July 2020. The heat was almost unbearable outside in the low country of Hilton Head Island, South Carolina. As I sauntered through Wholefoods on my weekly grocery haul, I suddenly felt hyper aware of all of the masks around me. Everywhere I turned, there they were: masks. My thoughts and awareness stopped me in my tracks and truly made me think about the significance of these coverings made of fibers and fabric, fitting over the nose and mouth. Don't get me wrong, I am pro-mask! I am all for the safety and protection of others and myself in regards to the public health crisis due to the COVID-19 pandemic, but I couldn't help but see this as a metaphor. I was stopped in my tracks in the middle of the produce section, trying to decide between peaches or nectarines, having a greater, more significant epiphany. We are all masked. In this moment of awe looking around at people with half of their faces covered, I realized that many of us wear masks all the time—a different type of mask, an invisible one.

There is a different kind of pandemic that we have been facing every day. It's called disingenuity and lack of authenticity. In this case, these are the masks that we hide behind not to protect us from a virus or illness, but to protect us from allowing the world to see us for who we truly are. They are masks that we have developed over time, intentionally detaching us from our true selves, yet protecting us from shame, fear, and judgment that caused us to develop the mask in the first place. This façade becomes a way of life, until we encounter a reason to dismantle it. Our greatest fears are often about allowing our true selves to be seen by those around us. Thus, this metaphorical mask becomes an object of protection from external fear and judgement.

In order to take a deeper look into the metaphorical mask, we must first have a clear understanding of how the mask actually works. Sometime during our life, usually early on in our childhood, we begin to learn the art of creating a protective exterior. The protective exterior shields our true self from the world while simultaneously detaching us from who we really are. This mask, also known as our idealized self, is developed from fear.

As children, we unconsciously establish an idealized self to avoid experiencing shame or pain we may encounter from our families for our beliefs, thoughts, actions, and reactions. Once we feel protected (read: less shame and pain), we begin to see our masks' significance. When we have that aha-moment that putting on a mask works for us to keep negative, uncomfortable, and detrimental feelings away from our own hearts, we lose a little piece of ourselves. This begins at a very young age and then, unless addressed, continues through adulthood.

Many of our parents, including mine, carried expectations of how we should behave as children. When we don't meet their expectations, their reactions can create feelings of shame and guilt. For example, in my personal childhood experience, I can remember feeling a great deal of shame when my behavior was greeted with spankings, timeouts facing bare white walls, and being left at home as punishment when all others went out. When punishments are repeated over and over, many of us learn to avoid them by suppressing parts of ourselves that may "get in trouble" or evoke these kinds of punishments as a response. Therefore, while it is an unconscious process that we are conditioned to continue, wearing a mask saves us from shame. This has long-lasting implications that extend into adulthood.

I grew up in a family with high standards. It was in my nature to rebel or challenge the system. I was not obedient. I can remember one particular instance that ultimately led me to shield a piece of who I am from my entire family for a significant amount of time. On one spring day in my hometown of Pennington, NJ, my three siblings and I were lined up in our Sunday best as a photographer was trying to take our picture. I remember all of my siblings teasing me incessantly, and suddenly, I burst into tears. Then, they laughed and teased me even more. After that very painful incident that the entire family still recalls, I learned to conceal all of my emotions caused by teasing. I never let them see me sweat, no matter how much they were taunting me or how it affected me internally. This mask is often described as having a hard exterior, while hiding the soft sensitive interior. Each one of our masks has a different feel, look, texture, and color; they are developed and expressed in different ways.

This concept of presenting a hard exterior is not new. As a society, we condition young men to wear this mask at all times, or else they shall be perceived weak. We tell them to 'suck it up,' when they express their internal emotions externally. However, we rarely tell young girls to 'suck it up' when they cry. This innate response that society has towards boys and young men has significant and detrimental effects on the emotion-processing abilities of adult men.

We are born into this world both naked and exposed as our true selves. This unsullied authenticity is quickly demolished, as our familial, societal, and cultural norms set up an entire script that we learn to conform to. These scripts chip away at our true selves. Perhaps you admire a style of dress and immediately are met with disapproval from family when you express it. Most of us conform to the expectation by wearing what was approved of and discarding both the item and sense of self and individuality that accompanied it. These types of judgments are carried with us throughout life. While some are heavier burdens than others, they all ultimately create a façade that we find useful, allowing us to fit in, receive acceptance, and eliminate shame. As we move through life, we create and manifest our identities. Our masks become second nature; they become a part of our identity.

We wear and adopt a mask to fit in, feel like a part of a family, community, organization or group. It becomes the focus of our behavior. We learn the rules governing the places we step into and begin to conform to these often-unsaid rules or expectations, thus perpetuating the false sense of self.

The mask becomes a system of beliefs that we hold to replace or neglect our true beliefs and feelings. Letting go of our mask, breaking the exterior, peeling away the pieces, is where truth and authenticity exist. When we are not connected to our authentic or true selves, we are living a life of ingenuity. We slowly fade away from our authentic self and become this masked, conformed, and idealized version of ourselves. Therefore, we are living in falsehood.

When you live with a mask on, no one knows the real you, including you. Not only does this hold us back from a true, rich, and authentic life, it creates a deeper disconnect from who we truly are. When our real and ideal selves are fragmented and lacking congruence, we are in a constant state of unease, teetering between these seemingly conflicting selves.

For many, the mask or false self is focused on pleasing others. This holds us back from experiencing the unadulterated world around us. It restrains us from experiencing the self-awareness, self-confidence and compassion that becomes unavailable when the mask is on. Having embarked on the journey of discovering my true self, I can tell you that the freedom it offers is extraordinary. Once we are aware of the façade we embody and dismantle it, a process that can take years, we experience life as it was meant to be lived— authentic, real, and uniquely ours.

During these unprecedented times of COVID-19, the opportunity of reverting to our most modest and undecorated self has been provided. For those of us who have transitioned to working from home or are no longer working, these past few months have allowed us to just be as we are, without makeup, fancy suits, or elaborate adornment. This alone has offered me personal freedom to breathe, allowing a small piece of my mask to be released.

However, it isn't always a walk in the park. Freedom from the masks we wear allows us to experience a dichotomy: one where we are able to be our true selves and at the same time, experience judgment and rejection. Part of living our truth comes with feedback and judgment. As we move toward freedom and shed our external protective shell, we need to learn how to adapt to and tune out the noise of the outside world, the family, the community, and friends. The expectations and pressures of others become unimportant and less powerful. The truth that lies within us is what we allow to shine outward. The world's judgments begin to fall on deaf ears. But with or without a mask, we are all *imperfectly perfect*.

Just like social media, we have been conditioned to show our best selves, our highlight reels. In reality, when we show our true selves, we honor the vulnerable individual that we arrived as when we entered this world. When we live with expectations that are set by us, rather than the rest of the world, we honor our authentic selves.

I stopped trying to please those around me, be who I was told to be, and suppress pieces of me to feel worthy years ago. It has been an extremely transformational and intentional experience. The truth is, there is pain with or without a mask. It is valuable to release the noise from the outside world, and deal with pain as it comes rather than constantly being in defense of it. When you shed your mask, you live a life that fulfills you, the most important character in your plot. Commit to living life as you, for you. Releasing the mask; drop the protective exterior; find your most authentic identity. You are worthy of living a life untethered by society's unwritten rules, pressures, and expectations.

Let's Get in Touch!

 https://www.suedecaro.com/

sue@suedecaro.com

Worldwide Coach & Educator

Sue is a heart-centered coach, educator, motivational speaker, and writer, working with individuals, corporations and families around the globe to navigate life's daily challenges.

While integrating education, consciousness, and coaching, Sue helps individuals to feel empowered, grow and thrive. Her passion is to help people deeply connect to themselves, to their children, and of course, to the world around them, creating a brighter future.

Sue also serves as a member of the Wellness Council for the Unionville-Chadds Ford School District, focused on researching and identifying best practices related to improving student health. She served as a Guest Parent Specialist/Coach for Mindvalley University Training and an esteemed member on the 24 hour virtual help desk support team for Mindvalley.com month-long summer event in Pula, Croatia, 2019.

Sue has had writings featured in various online publications and magazines. She has presented at events featuring Dr. Shefali Tsabary, Neale Donald Walsch, Marianne Williamson, Anita Moorjani, and John O'Sullivan. Sue has been an invited guest on radio shows and podcasts and has also appeared on Television, on The Dr. Nandi Show as well as a number of appearances on FOX 29, Good Day Philadelphia.

My Empowerment Story

BY SUSANA SALGADO

From Riches to Richer

The Princess
The spoiled girl in the community
There I was driving a white Escalade
Fancy dark black designer sunglasses and diamonds dressed me ...
Days spent shopping, spoiling myself and my daughters and
always my loved ones as I've always been a giver...that was me...
But was that me??
The giver yes
But everything else no...

What no one knew was that I was paying a price for all the material I had.

All those fancy things were covering my pain and also holding me back on
my purpose and what my soul craved most

FREEDOM!

How did a free-spirited girl get there?

Feeling trapped, unfulfilled and in pain.

I met the father of my daughters at 14 years young, yes, I was just a baby...

The first years were fun adventurous and sweet as we both were just two kids experiencing love for the first time.

As we got older, growing more and more into ourselves and me into a young woman

Wanting to express myself even more...

See I was always wild and unique in my ways always doing things different as a child and the older I grew, the more I needed to express my wild unique nature.

Never wanting to follow society or what everyone else was doing.

Always creating my own world!!

Here I was a girl wanting to live in a house of colored rainbow walls which I did!

Dressing in all the colours of the rainbow, I loved to dress up and express my creativity freedom and sensuality through my clothing, style and way of being!

All these things made me happy, colour, creativity, freedom and expressing my divine feminine essence.

He loved it all at first, as he was the opposite.

But then the insecurities and control began as he did not enjoy the attention I received and it really didn't go well with the more conservative man he had grown into.

That's when the once sweet love story changed and I began the fight of my freedom and expression that lasted 15 years...

We got pregnant and I had our first daughter when I was 20, he was 24.

Both being hard workers we bought our first home by the time I got pregnant with my second daughter, I was 25.

He started to work out of town, as he wanted to provide for us completely and wanted me to be a stay-at-home mom.

His success grew and we bought a bigger home, had our third daughter, and we began our travels, living a very comfortable life...

It all seemed like the perfect successful life to the outside world,

But no one knew all the fighting and toxicity that actually happened when no one was watching...

Through it all I would keep myself busy being the best mother I could be, volunteering at my girls school, being a dance mom, driving my girls to all their classes, cheering them on at every class and recital, and organizing the best birthday parties and play dates for them.

I created so much magic for them, it made me happy seeing my kids smile and also to make up for all they had to witness with me and their father and of course I kept smiling to the world.

What did I do for myself?

I would shop.

It became an addiction as it was a way to feed my hurting soul that was yearning for more...

Through all my trauma in my marriage and also personal challenges I was overcoming, I developed major anxiety.

I was not well at all, I was 29 years young, anxious and not happy, suffering actually as my soul couldn't take anymore fighting and suppression.

I sought help and began my healing journey, went to my first Reiki Session!!

That was the day my life changed and where my life's purpose was shown to me...

I began healing my soul through continuous reiki, yoga, meditation and diving into every self-help and spiritual book I could find!

While I was healing, I was empowering myself without even knowing it!!!

I loved these practices so much as they allowed me to feel so good, I knew I wanted to share them with the world and help people with what was healing me!

I went on to get certified in both reiki and yoga!

Became a Reiki Master & Yoga/Meditation Instructor!

I knew this was my calling and my soul's purpose!

At 32 years young, another episode/fight happened and once again he was apologizing...

He drove me to a big peach coloured house that I always wanted, closer to the lake, in the lake community that we lived in. It had the big for sale sign right on its perfect landscape, that was filled with roses and every flower of my dreams!

He parked in front of the house, expressed how sorry he was once again and how he wanted to buy this house for our family.

A bigger fancier house...

Looking right into his eyes I said

No.

It's over...

Those words changed my life!!

Other times the trips and the gifts were accepted.

When he was sorry...

This time I chose my soul's freedom that was the best gift I could ever receive from anyone and it came from myself!!

Don't get me wrong, the house was so beautiful with the most amazing garden, but it was time to grow the garden of my soul, and allow it to flourish through my temple, my real home!! My most important home! Me, all of Me, needed to BLOSSOM!

It was time to fully FLOURISH and untether MY WINGS!!

The separation and divorce journey began...

I moved out of our home and bought a smaller home and began the journey of solely taking care of myself and my girls for the first time in my life!

I only accepted two years of alimony, as I just did not want to fight and really, I just did not care about money anymore...

I shocked so many with my decision as they believed I left so much...little did they know of all I was going to gain...

Was I afraid of this new life?
YES!!

Was I excited for this new life??
FUCK YES!!!

As soon as I moved into my new home, I began my healing business.

Lotus Love was born!

No business coaching or training on how to run a business, I just went for it with my certifications in hand and a heart full of LOVE to help people!!

Business was slow like any other starting business but I was happy as I was living my PURPOSE! I was also falling in LOVE for the first time in my adult life!!

I met a man that loved and supported all that I was, while encouraging and allowing me to be free and feel FREE!!

(That's another chapter, stay tuned)

As the two years of alimony ended, the financial stress began as child support and my small growing business was not enough to support my bills.

I knew I had to put more work and energy into my business, which I did, I gained more clients but still not enough to sustain from, so I had to get a full-time job while still running and growing my business.

I was not going to give up on my calling and purpose!

I went back to a publishing company I worked at in my early twenties

There I was, back in an office staring out of the window for eight hours, feeling like a fish in a bowl wanting to break free!

I felt so trapped stressed and exhausted.

I did that for a year and a half!

I continued working MY day job, teaching a couple yoga classes at different studios, growing my business, plus mom duties, I was exhausted...

One day I was told by my Spirit Guides "TRUST"

Leave your day job and focus all your attention on your "SOUL BUSINESS" On "YOUR SOUL'S PURPOSE"

I listened and did it!

I left my day job and gave all my energy to Lotus Love!!!

Again, was I afraid??
YES!!

Was I trusting?
YES!!

I jumped!!

I started promoting my business but not just my business, this time myself.

Sharing my story.

Sharing my challenges.

What helped me.

What began to happen next, I did not expect.

What once was only a healing practice, began to transform into empowering woman!!

Through my stories, more and more woman came to me for guidance, empowerment, and healing as they saw themselves in me!

They felt my heart and soul in every session!

As I gave it my all to each one, I recognized myself in every hurting woman...

All I wanted was to see them rise like I did...

And I did, every woman that came to see me began to rise!!

I began Moon & Goddess circles to heal and empower woman. I created my Energy Activations to empower and guide woman through their transformation!

I held my first Nude Goddess Awakening Retreat in 2019.

Did I think I was a little crazy?

Doing this?!
YES!!

Did part of me fear the judgement?
YES!!

Did part of me believe it wouldn't be a success?
YES!!

But I did it!!

And yes it was a success, and yes I did get judged by some, but did I care?
Fuck No!!

I was doing me, following my purpose, and that's all that mattered!

I just hosted my second annual Nude Goddess Retreat this summer!!

Total success once again!

At the moment, I am planning my first Winter Wonderland Nude Goddess Awakening Retreat and of course, next summer's event is already in the works!!

As I write this chapter

I will admit I was nervous to begin writing my empowerment story and to share more of myself to the world!!

But again, I let go of my fears and I am doing it!!

All my challenges, all I overcame was immensely hard, but it made me into the woman I am today, the woman I was always meant to be!

Inspired.
Flourished.
Untethered.
And Free!!
All I ever desired!

I share my story to empower and inspire you to let go of your fears, insecurities and to allow yourself to live your best life!!

The life you are worthy and deserving of!!

The life of your Goddess Dreams!

You too, are a Lotus.

FLOURISH and RISE GODDESS.

I dedicate this chapter to my three beautiful daughters. You three are my biggest inspirations, all that I do is for you to be inspired to grow into healthy conscious powerful women.

Mom Loves you!

Through the cosmos and back a zillion times!

Angelina Navas - Salgado
Elizabeth Navas
Persius Navas

Also a huge thanks to my supportive and loving family I love you!

 www.lotuslovelightworker.com

Susana Salgado founder of Lotus Love. She is a Spiritual teacher & Empowerment Coach

Susana began her healing journey 11 years ago when she was in search of healing and truly discovering herself and her soul's purpose.

She discovered holistic healing through Reiki, Yoga & Meditation it completely changed her life. She then went on to get certified in Reiki, Yoga, Meditation, Crystal Therapy, Soul Coaching & other holistic practices. She performs a range of healings and practices, presently her most active practices are the Yoni & Goddess activations. Her activations unleash the Goddess in every woman that comes to see her!

Each Goddess feels absolutely beautiful, sensual, empowered and yes, orgasmic!

Her Yoni Activation has helped many women dealing with sexual suppression

Low sexual drive

Orgasmic issues

Fertility issues

Menstrual and menopause issues

Sexual traumas (this life and past) which are usually the cause of everything listed.

Women have experienced amazing sexual healing through this activation that she created herself, being an energy healer and meditation instructor. She says it works with the energy she puts in through her guides, angels, her divine, and the universe of course, as well as her meditative powerful words which have a lot to do with every success story through this magical activation!

Women have become orgasmic, so empowered, and shine in such incredible divine feminine Light after her sessions!

Her mission is to bring healing awakening empowerment to as many women as she can. She believes with every woman she can guide through healing will heal generations before her and after her, allowing our planet to heal and flourish. Women are a huge part in the healing of our planet, which is also a mission of hers, as she is a huge animal and environmental activist.

Her loving nature and powerful practice attracts many souls to her. Having people drive hours to come to her classes/healings and some even have flown to see her!

Her joy is seeing woman flourish and rise into their most Radiant Goddess light!

Growing her Goddess Tribe!

That is her gift each time and why she continues to do what she does.

Testing the Universe's Patience, and Finding I am Loved Always

BY TAMMY YOUNKER

Warning: This chapter contains stories of self-sabotage, trembling fear, then faith and miracles. And if I didn't learn the lessons the first time, I repeated this pattern over...and over.

So let's go!

In all my years it has become exquisitely clear that there is so much more than this life as Tammy Younker: farmer's daughter, lover of the ocean, energy worker, mother, wife, and friend.

I have come to know myself as an energetic being filled with love, care and compassion; in truth I am, an essence that is larger than my physical being. As I believe it is for you. Yet, as you may attest to, it's never always simple. It is through light language and energy work that I have come to truly understand all that I am. I am humbled and blessed with the power and wisdom that comes through me for myself, Mother Earth, and for my clients. I allow sound energy to transform and transmute stuck, dark, and clouded energy from negative beliefs, worries, stresses, and anxiety. If it had not been for the love of the Divine, some synchronicities and me saying YES in pivotal moments in my life, I would not be where I am today. I know in the depths of my soul that I am guided daily - whether I listen or not. I am so grateful for the many miracles in my life!

237

This 'Stuff' Really Works!!

In 2007, I took a cruise out of San Diego, California for seven days with the teachers of *The Secret* for a total of $132US! I put the laws of manifestation and attraction, and my sanity to the test. I was doubtful, nothing in my life made sense, timing was completely off to even think about travelling from Prince Edward Island, Canada to California! A coast-to-coast trip! For li'l ol' me?! I was just about to open my coaching business, as I hadn't had one client yet, but from somewhere deep in me, I did not care. I believed I would be on that ship.

In this blind faith, I danced, I sang, I envisioned, and I made clear intentions...and most of all, I religiously gave thanks for this dream to come true every day until it did...on day 30. A $5500 coast-to-coast round trip turned into $132, with an email, a call from a friend, the stroke of a family member's pen, a gift of flight points, and a whole load of commitment to this dream. On this trip I made friends for life, great business contacts, and learned even more on the journey to and from San Diego than expected. From that moment on, I knew I could conspire to dream and manifest anything when I worked together with the Universe.

Short-Lived

Then I came home and shortly thereafter fell off the "I can do anything!" wagon. My energy and enthusiasm dropped, as doubt crept in. All the negative self-talk hung out: "This feeling can't last. You can't do that again! Who are you to have whatever you want?"

I did the long and arduous negative self-talk dance for some time afterwards. Life was good, but I lost the feeling of that confidence I felt before and on that trip. I used my energy techniques to manage and release what I was able and ready to at the time, but it wasn't until I was bold again that I could see another large example of how much I was loved and guided.

Road Trip!

Throughout most of 2011 I had a difficult battle with C. Difficile, a bacterial gut infection, which was a beautiful example of how I was not taking care of myself. I was spreading myself thin by running too hard with university, volunteering, and working. It was then that I said yes to a dear friend who needed help to move to Ottawa, Ontario. I was feeling much better at the end of August, so we loaded my SUV with most of her worldly possessions and off we went. I had never done anything like this before or experienced driving in rush hour traffic in Montreal! Heck no...barely a highway trip to Moncton NB from PEI! She was the perfect co-pilot and we had a beautiful experience together. Little did I know that before the year was out, I too would move to Ottawa and then meet my future husband in his living room in less than 24 hours of moving to the city!

The Sign

One of the biggest reasons this all came to be, was as Shelley and I sat in a restaurant together that late day in August, I asked for a sign. It had to be specific and incredibly clear. I had toyed with this tool over the years but would doubt the signs, make up stories of why the contrary was true and lead myself down a long and arduous path of my ego's doing. Certainly not the easy path the Universe was trying to show me. I was consistently my own worst enemy.

I was overcome with the sense that I could really see myself living here. Ottawa is beautiful with all the parks, trees, canals, rivers, and hills. It felt safe and comforting. My friend, being the open person she is, says "Ok, what would that look like?" We chatted over supper and it felt more like a doable adventure for me.

My sign came to me in the form of a lovely young college student who was our server. We chatted trying to get to know her—as all East Coasters do—and I had a 'movie moment.' I receded into my mind away from the conversation and said to myself "OK Tammy, if this Ottawa thing is right for you then you ask this girl what she is studying and if it is the same as what you are, then it is confirmed. You move to Ottawa."

So, tuning back in to the conversation, I looked up at her and asked "What are you studying?" Her reply, "psychology." I'm sure she wondered what just happened because I burst into tears. I was majoring in psychology and religious studies at UPEI, and that was a close enough sign for me.

Now, 100% convinced and now crying out of shock, gratefulness that God still cared enough to give me a sign, and out of fear of "Oh s**t! Now what?" Which quickly turned into "Ok, when do I move? Go home and come right back? Go home and finish another semester, then come up in January?" (I had gotten a scholarship for the fall so it seemed tempting to do another few courses.)

A Course Correction

I had to go back to PEI to plan my move to Ottawa. Back in PEI, all made perfectly clear that I had **not** made the correct decision of the return to classes for another semester. Within a week, I was sick again and in more pain than I had been in the spring, and now battling a viral gut infection! I was forced to drop all my courses, return the scholarship, and work on getting well. This time I took the hint. I wasn't meant to stay in PEI any longer.

By the time I was recovered and was ready to leave, it was December 29th, 2011. Yet the Universe was still not done with me and challenged me on this solo road trip. My car broke down less than 30 minutes into New Brunswick and then I hit a blinding snowstorm. I distinctly recall stomping around my car with great determination and declaring to the sky and my car: "I will leave you here and rent a van. I don't care! I'm MOVING TO OTTAWA!!" I was pushed hard—my boundaries and my level of commitment were challenged. I was stressed to the max! On day two of the drive—after gliding into a car shop at the 11th hour, that just happened to have the exact part I needed for my car left in stock and getting a good sleep in a hotel while the snow howled—I had a perfectly working car and was rewarded with the most spectacular sunrise over the hills in Quebec. I felt I had passed the test this time and was gifted with nature's beauty.

I did arrive safely on the 30th to a warm hug from my friend, a soft place to land and spent some time to really collect myself. This was a bold move for me and my body was trying to catch up with my soul's confidence. I literally vibrated with a whirlwind of emotions.

Bride Home Delivery

To take the edge off we went to a New Year's Eve party the next night. Little did I know what the Universe had in store for me. I was delivered right to my current house! To my future husband, father of our son, and partner. We laugh to this day about how it all came together. I know it was another way of being blessed, and being gifted another confirmation that this move was perfectly in alignment. I was exactly where I needed to be.

A Whole New World

Since the move, life has opened up to me. I am more alert to the ways the Universe speaks and guides me. I am no longer the same person I was in 2011 and am grateful for the constant guidance. Again, sometimes I don't listen, but I am guided nonetheless. Wide-eyed to the synchronicities, life lessons, energy courses, and beautiful souls, all of which have been placed along my path and lighting the way to bring clarity and confidence to my purpose.

It hasn't been easy and I have veered off course many times, but what has been consistent is the way the Universe provides course corrections. When you are standing in the realization of one it is so joyful! You realize that you are loved enough to be guided back to where you need to be. You are forgiven for not listening and loved unconditionally. What a confidence boost! You know that you can do what your ego mind wants to do and ignore your intuitive knowing, your guidance, and that you can be realigned again!

A Declaration

I choose to be a team member of energy workers needed to be part of the healing solution. I am, if only a tiny part, here to assist myself and others to be more loving, compassionate, and whole. I encourage you to be the same. I know that the Universe has sent many messengers in all shapes and forms, to this earth to guide us along the way. We are all evolving and we can't help but feel it. In these current times of 2020, we are bombarded with the shifting tides of energy. It is the rise in our voices. It is the rise in our action. It is the removal of our complacency, and the removal of fear. It is the boldness in our words, and it is the boldness in our feet. WE are here to be the change we wish to see in the world. Humanity needs you. Yes, even you!

At the beginning of the pandemic, I chose to protect my mind like a precious jewel. I watched very carefully what I fed her; what she heard, what she watched, and what she interacted with. Energy can be very powerful and overwhelming in a negative way if we continue on autopilot. You are being asked to be aware of and no longer be on autopilot.

Ask Yourself...

What feeds your soul? What nourishes your mind? What FEELS to be the next action step for you? Can you discern the difference between what is in your best interest and what is programming or expectations from media, family, and society? What is really best for you? What tools and resources do you have or use that keeps you clear and grounded so that you can feel this tone the earth is nourishing you with? She wants to love you and she wants you to love her back. When we heal Mother Earth, we heal ourselves. When we heal ourselves, we heal Mother Earth. Compassion then flourishes. Love is what you feel. What you vibrate and what you radiate out into your home, your neighbourhood, city, and country, thus manifesting the energy and change we intend to see in the world.

When love is your guiding force you are a being of power—true power—a strength unlike the world has felt on en masse in a very, very long time.

We are being asked to be love, to reach down in and embrace that inner you and hug her/him/them. To cradle the hurt you inside and to sing to them. To be love. For true clarity, certainty and confidence are tied together only with a rope of love.

A note about Light Language

If you haven't heard of light language, I encourage you to try a session. At first your brain will try and make it familiar, make sense of it, and decipher it. The key to remember with any light language healing session is that it speaks to your soul and not your mind. Light language is channeled messages for you to aid in your healing and evolution energetically. A light language soul is calmer, compassionate, and conscious, with some wonderful side effects. Boundaries are set with compassion. A voice rises out of you that is a tone stronger than you had before. It rings clear. Actions are thoughtful and with greater purpose. Your purpose is clear, if only the next step. I want you to rise up, whole and loving, out of any stress you have. I believe you can be the change we intend to see in the world right now. The Universe has always been there, ready to show you how.

Peace and Much Love,

Tammy.

 www.inspiredspiritwithin.com
tammy@buildingalegace.com

Tammy Younker - is an author, teacher, coach and Light Language Healer. She is trained in Reiki , EFT (tapping,) Ho'oponopono, and Integrated Energy Therapy but her main focus is in Divine Light Language transmissions and Crystalline Heart Energy Therapies. She is a strong believer that everything is energy—a thought, a word, a song, a movement, an intention, a shout, and an embrace. Choosing her energy carefully she teaches others to rediscover their inner inspired spirit. This inspired spirit within is your soul's song, your life purpose, your voice. Let us all use it wisely.

Tammy was born and raised in picturesque Prince Edward Island, and now resides in Ottawa, Canada with her husband and son.

Visit www.inspiredspiritwithin.com or email tammy@buildingalegace.com for a personal virtual energy session.

8 Simple Steps to Make Your Visual Story Irresistible

By Tetiana Voronina

You probably already have a great story that you want to tell the world. Maybe you've already written a cool speech that will help you get your message across to your audience? Practice facial expressions and gestures?

If not, then it's time to start.

If yes, then I invite you to comprehend the following information.

The human brain perceives information from the world with the help of the senses: sight, hearing, smell, touch, and taste. The world's most successful companies and products integrate touch, taste, smell, sight, and sound with amazing results, turning human senses into essential allies in building communication, delivering information to the audience, and convincing it.

(Source: Martin Lindstrom, Brand Sense: Sensory Secrets Behind the Stuff We Buy).

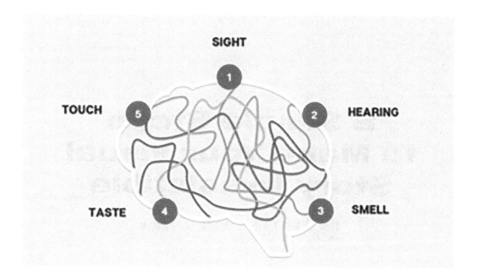

Thinking of our story as a product, we will understand that we can engage almost all human senses—the smell of coffee, delicious treats during coffee breaks, comfortable chairs, an inspirational story told by a confident speaker's voice, and visuals reinforcing and supporting speaker's message.

Involving some of them (smell, touch, and taste) is an area of responsibility of the organizers. Still, the two remaining channels of information exchange—vision and hearing—are the space of the speaker's opportunities.

We will focus on the vision.

People are incredible at remembering pictures.

Tell people your story, and three days later, they'll remember 10% of it.

Add a picture and they'll remember 65%.

(Source: Dr. John Medina, Brain Rules)

Memorable is just one metric that cool visuals can improve—important, but not the one and only.

Another dramatically important metric is attention span.

We live in a world of high speeds and technologies, where the audience's attention is simultaneously trying to grab social networks, podcasts, YouTube channels, and many other sources of interesting information that can be found...in a pocket/purse. More precisely, on the phone, located in a pocket/purse.

This makes the presenter's position extremely vulnerable, leaving him only seven seconds to grab the audience's attention entirely or lose it forever.

Only seven seconds...think about it.

In theory, a speaker with great actors' skills can cause the desired emotions, convince, and captivate the audience with his story, without using additional visual effects, but believe me, as a person whose journey into design and marketing began with scenography. In practice, impressive scenery helps even cool actors and show business stars to strengthen performance effect.

Thus, I would recommend applying practical experience, and handle such a powerful marketing tool as presentation design, which will help the speaker:

1. Grab attention

2. Convey the speaker's message to the audience

3. Make complex processes, data, and abstract ideas easy to understand.

4. Evoke appropriate emotions

5. Create prerequisites for the speaker's ideas to be remembered and excited by the audience in three days, three months, and even three years after the presentation.

Are all presentations evenly helpful?

No. Moreover, poor presentation design can make the action boring and lead to loss of audience attention.

But knowing and following these simple rules will help you avoid making dramatic mistakes and make the visuals a powerful supporter and loyal ally for the speaker.

8 simple steps to make your visual story irresistible.

1. **Audience is hero**

   You probably would like to tell how good your idea or your new product is going to be in the performance. However, people sitting in chairs, most of all, are interested in themselves. The ideas of your speeches are interesting to them only if they resonate with their interests and answer their questions like "How can this help me? How will it improve my life, my incomes, and career prospects?".

   Considering your presentation's ideas and suggestions as useless, the audience will easily forget about them five minutes after the end of the conference, which will be held behind the surfing of the internet using a smartphone.

   On the contrary, having found something that coincides with its interests in your presentation, the audience can become your mouthpiece and "lawyer".

   Conclusion? Do not spare the time and effort to study the audience you plan to tell a story about your product or idea. Moreover, visualize and imagine the person you are creating the presentation for during each slide's creation.

   In this case, success will certainly be on your side!

2. Three second rule

If we think about which type of media is closest to a presentation slide, we will find the answer to be (billboard)—the same set of distractions and, as a result, limited attention span.

So, working on the presentation design for a speech, we must always remember that we only have three seconds in stock, during which the audience must be clear about the idea that this slide is trying to convey to them. Otherwise, the audience's attention will turn to something else.

Understanding this fact leads us to a new rule.

3. One slide - one idea

Hierarchy is one of the main keys to a harmonious presentation. Therefore, the question of analyzing and structuring information almost becomes the most important task in the process of creating a presentation. Many next steps, for example, the choice of fonts, colors, will be based on how well you have worked with the information you would like to convey to your audience's mind and heart.

I think during the process of writing the story, you determined the Key Idea, the one for the spread of which you initiated the whole action. You have probably decided on ideas-arguments that support and prove the importance of your Key Idea and motivate the audience to experience certain emotions and make the journey you need from point A to point B, where the person becomes your adherent and advocate.

If not, then it's time to do it—each of our slides should contain a visualization of only one idea, made in such a way that its meaning is clear to the audience in three seconds.

So, it's time to move on and advance to visualization planning.

4. Visualization planning

In this step, we need to write out each idea on a separate slide.

The number of slides in a presentation directly depends on how dynamic your presentation promises to be, but it is 1-2 slides per minute on the average. So, at this point, you can decide on the number of slides in your presentation and, accordingly, the ideas that are worth visualizing and creating a separate slide layout. Be ruthless, choose only those ideas that can make a lasting impression on your audience, supporting your Key Idea, and cut out any unnecessary things.

Now we can go through the idea slides (remember: one slide - one idea) and ask one important question:

Will the information on this slide represent a process, data, or abstract concepts?

The answer to this question will allow you to easily decide what type of visualization this information needs: infographic, diagram, photo/illustration.

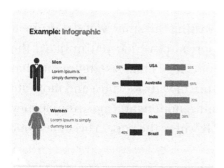 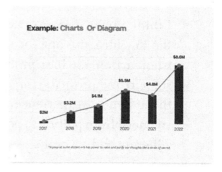

Now, knowing the exact number of slides and the type of information planned to be placed on each of them, we can start creating the layout design.

5. **Consistency - the path to harmony**

Several uncomplicated fragments can create a sense of consistency in presentation design

- Typeface

- Colors

- Illustrations / photos

- The arrangement of individual elements

All these components are part of the consistency. Failure to adhere to gives the impression that all elements are "playing in a different league".

Therefore, choosing color palettes and fonts, keep in mind that the colors should contrast well, and the fonts should be readable even from the back rows, and appeal to the audience.

6. **Simplicity and adherence to the visual hierarchy rules**

I won't get tired of repeating and recommend constantly keeping the thought in mind while creating slide layouts - you only have 3-5 seconds for the audience to understand your slide's main message. Otherwise, you will lose their attention.

So, simplicity is the only sure way to create an irresistible presentation.

In this case, the visual hierarchy becomes that critical tool, knowing several principles that will allow you to establish the visual flow and lead the audience's journey around a slide, where it can easily differentiate the main from the secondary.

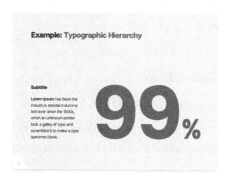

Size and Scale - use them to highlight important elements.

Color and Contrast - use color and contrast to emphasize what's important on each slide.

Typographic Hierarchy - distinguish the main from the secondary with different font sizes and typefaces.

Alignment - Organize and structure your design with alignment. This makes a layout look clean and polished.

White Space - large spaces between layout elements help guide the audience through the page and prioritize the focus area.

7. **Metaphors**

Leave on the slides as few words as possible. Replace the rest with visuals.

This does not mean putting a lot of pictures on one slide. This means conveying the slide's key message in one visual solution: infographics, diagram, map, large number, photograph, illustration.

By choosing a photograph as a metaphor for your slides' key messages, define emotions when planning how you want your audience to feel at these points of your speech.

8. **Dynamic and interactivity**

The animation is another glorious way to capture and repeatedly return the audience's attention to the spectacular visuals that accompany the speaker's speech, greatly increasing the chances that the audience will remember the presentation ideas.

As we said at the very beginning of our chapter, every person in the audience has in their pocket a device that can completely distract his attention from the speaker's presentation. Let's make it our ally by posting on the closing or Q&A slide links to interesting additional materials and our contacts in the form of a QR code.

Voila—a person who is keen on the presentation ideas will be able, not only to ask additional questions, but immediately receive links to any additional materials on their phone.

We established long-term contact with the audience and increase the listener's likelihood of becoming a supporter and advocate of our ideas!

• • •

To conclude this chapter, I would like to say that presentation design and data visualization are interesting topics worthy of an entire book and more. Therefore, I did not set myself the task of describing all the subtleties in one chapter, the understanding of which takes years of study and experience. On the contrary, I tried to create a practical tool describing the essential steps that my dear readers can take to dramatically improve their presentations and take their design to the next level.

Use the "8 simple steps" as a guide when creating a presentation and as a checklist for making sure of its quality, and I am sure—the level of your presentations will delight you right here and now.

I will be happy to be a positive part of my readers success stories!

Hello!
I am Tetiana,
Founder of Voronina & Partners
Marketing Solutions

Being a student, I started working as a Personal Assistant, and then as a Junior Graphic Designer with one of the best Moscow Set Designers, and this was a life-changing experience.

Within ten years, I worked in every capacity: Designer, Creative Director, Account Manager, New Business Development, Marketing Consultant, and Founder in 2005. The agencies served clients such as; Lukoil, RosAviaConsortium, Nestle, Knauf, Sally Hansen, etc.

After fifteen years of amazing work, I parted ways with Moscow to establish a marketing and design consultancy company that works exclusively with an English-speaking audience.

So Voronina & Partners Marketing Solutions was born, and it specializes in presentation design, marketing planning, strategies, and execution.

Over the 5 years of its life, Voronina & Partners Marketing Solutions has successfully collaborated with Christie's, Microsoft, public speakers and many large (mainly American) businesses and small startups from various industries.

Singing My Way Home

How I healed my relationship with my body with song and sacred sound

By Tiffany Sparrow

Most of the music I write and sing today is about finding courage, solace and even peace through the dark, difficult times in life. This music is inspired by my own journey.

There was a time in my life when I deeply hated my body and myself and was in complete rejection of being here. I first developed anorexia at age 11 and struggled with multiple eating disorders over several decades. I spent years of my life so uncomfortable with myself, my body, my voice, and my place here in the world...

This is the story of my journey through to the other side of body loathing, into full body love and self-acceptance through music sound, mindful embodiment practice, and devotion.

Out of Sync

I can't pinpoint one particular thing that triggered my decision to stop eating. The culture shock of leaving my first childhood home in Peace River - a place where I was free to be creative and playful – moving to a new town where I felt I didn't fit in and was confronted with pressures I didn't understand was probably a big part of it. Being uprooted like this was a very literal external representation of my internal discomfort of not feeling at home inside myself. Combined with my over-achieving, perfectionistic tendencies, this scenario created the perfect storm.

I started to feel less and less comfortable in my own skin in grade 6 – like my bones and muscles didn't fit, or like I had a layer of film on the inside of my body that kept me from settling. Through the summer before grade 7, I tried to get rid of this feeling and made a conscious choice to eat less and less. Though I knew about anorexia, at that time I believed I was in control of this decision and could stop or start at will.

It all went off the rails quickly and the fall of my 12th year is a blur in my memory. I dropped 25% of my body mass in a matter of only a few months until one evening my father sat me down to tell me I was being checked into an Edmonton hospital. I remember feeling shocked, not believing this was necessary, and vehemently resisted the decision. Looking back at the few photos we have of the time, I didn't realize how dire the situation was; I was definitely more emaciated than I felt or thought I looked.

Disharmony

Eating disorders were and continue to be mysterious and difficult to treat. At that time, there wasn't an eating disorder unit in Edmonton so I was placed in a children's general psych unit. Although something needed to be done, I can't say that hospitalization was the best idea as I didn't receive the kind of support I needed to heal. My doctors didn't trust me, often looking for symptoms that weren't always there (like when they thought my hair was falling out when it was just pinned a different way). These professionals didn't seem to understand the nature of what I was facing - most people couldn't understand why I just wouldn't eat. I was prescribed an anti-depressant but even then, I knew medication wouldn't offer me a long-term solution. Other than two nurses who calmly listened to me and taught me the value of saying NO to assert my boundaries, the treatment strategies I was offered didn't present any real long-term solutions. I felt really alone and remember thinking I would have to figure it out on my own.

After two months on the unit, I was discharged, having gained back about half the weight I had lost.[1] Over the next few years, anorexia morphed into a form of bulimia. I would go for months with "normal" eating and then relapse into restricting or throwing up after meals. During this time I saw a handful of different counsellors, though none really resonated.

My first big turning point came when I realized that talk therapy wouldn't help me fully heal - I could talk circles around my problems and counsellors. I now know that talk therapy couldn't address the somatic, felt-sense symptoms nor the spiritual components of my eating disorder. Also, it couldn't help me fully accept that being thinner in my body and getting rid of heaviness from food wasn't going to get me what I actually wanted – deep inner peace and a long-term solution to my inner feelings of discomfort and hatred.

Finding My Voice

Through junior high and high school, I got into music, playing oboe in the school band, taking piano lessons, performing in musical theatre productions, and taking voice lessons. Gradually, singing became my main musical focus. Something instinctual pushed me to learn to express myself through my voice, to overcome its breaks and shakes and quirks, feeling this would be helpful to me. Looking back, this draw to voice work is interesting to me, given my body challenges. A vocalist's, body is their instrument and learning to navigate and use it for performance also means learning to connect with it. For me, it has also meant that the familiar judgements for my body manifested similarly towards my voice.

---

[1]   I've since learned that gaining back all the weight lost before hospital discharge has a much longer term recovery projection.

A few years later I was accepted to the University of Alberta as a music major, which was both exciting and terrifying since my childhood love for performing had been replaced by intense stage fright and anxiety. I experienced a culture of competition and judgement, an emphasis on ideal sound and a "one shot to nail it" mentality, all of which felt super terrifying and threatening to me. In this high-pressure performance environment, my perfectionism and bulimia again reared its head.

Near the end of my first year, my mom heard about a profession called music therapy and helped me set up a phone conversation with a local Edmonton music therapist. Based on her recommendations and my gut feeling, I decided to move to Ontario to do the training. In music therapy school, music is seen as a point of connection to others and used to support others in their overall wellbeing, a concept I found very liberating. I was also taught to work improvisationally, to experiment, to be creative, and make "mistakes" rather than trying to replicate a gold standard performance. Focusing more on the healing qualities of the music and others' needs really helped me move through some of my anxieties with musical expression.

Embodied Sound and Soul Connection

As long as I can remember I have believed in spirituality. The religion I was raised with as a child set the stage for my exploration of alternative healing and new age theories around the relationship between spirituality and embodiment.

I first discovered yoga in my mid-teens in a women's health book and experimented with postures on my own, finding some relief in the breathing and moving. While in university, I started attending weekly yoga classes offered through the school. Though part of the initial appeal of yoga was the physical exertion, the spiritual foundation really distinguished it from other forms of exercise for me. I eventually went on to become a yoga teacher and initiated a daily physical and mantra-based practice. Through yoga I began to forge a relationship with my physical and my nonphysical layers.

In my 3rd year of university, I developed a mysterious throat pain that affected my breathing and my ability to sing. Specialists couldn't find anything physically or structurally wrong and this added fuel to my curiosity and desire to find alternative solutions to physical conditions. I came across a book about the chakras and their symbology, and started following its recommendations for using breath, affirmation, and repetitive movements. I also started semi-regular sessions with a reiki master to help with the spiritual-emotional links to my physical symptoms. I have since trained in energy healing methods including reiki, pranic healing, oneness blessings and Ignite Your Spirit healing. Energy blessings can be given through the voice as well as hands – or so I've been told.

Spiritual practices, though very helpful, can be very tricky and deceptive. I've learned that its not what you do but how. With spirituality, it can look like you're doing "good" when you're just repeating patterns with different actions. For me, even years after the initial onset of anorexia, I still disliked my body and was afraid of fully being myself. While I was definitely looking for solutions, it was easy to hide behind spiritual bi-pass, rationalizations and dishonesty with myself.

Devotional Song, Devotion to Self

I discovered important pieces for my transformation in my midtwenties: devotional chanting, song writing, and sound meditation. I first encountered kirtan, call-response chanting, while staying at an Ashram near Nelson, BC. During kirtan, I could feel something happening that I couldn't exactly put into words. I felt both deeply inside myself and expansive at the same time. When I later took a trip to India to complete another yoga training, my teacher, Yogrishi Vishvketu, advised me to keep teaching posture yoga but also strongly suggested for me to focus on chanting and to make that my main practice. I hadn't been waiting for permission per se but his comments were like a door opening in my heart. While still India, I bought a knock-off guitar and began writing original songs and kirtan chants which I began offering publicly.

The next four years became what I lovingly call my "gypsy phase." I lived out of my backpack, travelling through India, Canada, Australia, USA, Peru, and Bali, co-facilitating yoga teacher trainings, learning about healing practices and performing music. I actively shook up my life like a snow-globe to let the pieces resettle in different orientation. I recorded two mantra kirtan albums during this time and trained in more sound healing. Writing original songs at this time also became a way to be more bare with others, to share my experiences and thoughts more openly. I started documenting my reflections and healing experiences in song, with themes about pain points and struggle, offering poetic perspectives. Through song-writing, I connect to a more personal truth that can have resonance when shared. Song writing and mantra chanting have grown to be two important points of connection: One to the deeply personal and the other to the universal. Both are valid and both are needed.

The Rhythms of Home

Near the end of 2011, I knew I still had work to do and that it was time to leave Bali and return to my roots and to the solid flat earth of the Alberta prairies. Even after all I'd been through, bouts with body hatred and restricting food would still flare up from time to time, with the old sensations of discomfort in my skin. Though travelling for four years had created a lot of freedom in my life, I knew I was still avoiding and managing rather than integrating residual parts of my pain. I needed to let the pieces of my snow-globed life land and to let myself sink in and feel. To make a strong statement to myself that I would no longer stand for destructive patterns, I enrolled in an eating disorders day program. Though I quickly found the program was not for me with its familiar medication and talk-based therapy, most important was this self-declaration, this deliberate act of will. This was a major turning point for me, one I was ready to make, thanks to all the work and healing I had been doing. I drew a strong boundary, committing firmly and lovingly to stop running. Though I knew unwinding patterns would bring discomfort, I also knew deeply that I was trading a lifetime of managing and avoiding for truer, more sustainable freedom.

What followed was a tumultuous, and at times quite painful, few years for me. I was regularly sitting in the discomfort in myself without the escape of running away, or physically purging anything out. Some days my insides honestly felt like they were on fire. Thank goodness for my daily sound-mantra practice as my beacon as well as monthly kirtan session. I almost always felt relief when I could put what I was experiencing into sound. Also important to note that I didn't forge ahead alone. I committed to working regularly with a healer/therapist who combined sound with shamanic journey work.

Bit by bit, the pain and discomfort dissolved, integrated, transformed. And, one day a few years later, I was able to look at my naked body in the mirror with real love and appreciation. I was able to enjoy the feeling of eating, of being nourished and socializing around food. I was able to feel valuable and proud of myself and my music.

And now, the fact that I'm no longer weighed down by the chains of body hatred feels like a miracle at times, albeit one that came with a lot of perseverance. Though I still have moments of discomfort – which I now call humanness - I have so much comfort and love for myself , my shape and feel so at home in my skin. I'm very grateful.

And I'm here to share my story so that anyone who reads it and resonates with any of it – the body loathing, food tension, physical discomfort, pain, shame etc - can know that there IS a way through. There is a way home.

 www.sparrowharmonix.com

With sun-kissed tones and soulful lyrics, Tiffany Sparrow offers music not only for its entertainment value, but as a way to connect and heal. As a singer-songwriter, certified music therapist, sound healer, yogi and body image coach, she's passionate about accessing sound as a powerful tool for physical and mental health in both difficult and joyful times.

Tiffany has performed around the world and many of her global experiences continue to influence her music today. Based in Edmonton since 2012, she's been an active member of the Western Canadian music scene, performing original songs and carefully curated covers, and offering group chanting and soundbath meditations. The music she writes is a testament to the healing journey. You can hear her recordings online including two world-music mantra albums and two new albums of original songs.

Tiffany is devoted to providing music for wellness is because she experienced its impact herself when she faced multiple eating disorders. Sacred sound reached into places that talk therapy and medication couldn't and Tiffany is now committed to helping others find similar deep acceptance and liberation. She's founded the Hangups to Harmony initiative, a shamanic sound coaching program to help others dismantle body hatred and baggage and find true radiance, confidence and whole self-love. Music, intention and grace have tremendous power to remind us of who we are.

The Secret to Creating Connection: Choosing to be a Guide

By Valerie Canino

I am the mom of two amazing teens, Joshua who is 16 and Rachael now 19. I never went through the "terrible teens" like a lot of my friends. My kids and I have a really close relationship. Every day, I am so in awe of the human beings they are now and continue to grow into. My relationship with Joshua and Rachael has taught me so much about unconditional love, which I am extraordinarily grateful for. Over the years, lots of family and friends have made comments to me like, "your kids are so great and you are all so close. What's your secret?" After being asked enough times, I started to reflect on how that happened. Some people might say, "wow, you really lucked out," but looking back "luck" had nothing to do with it. While I saw many people around me struggling to connect or maintain a connection with their kids as they entered their teen years, I didn't have that experience. In fact, I found so much peace in my relationship with my children, even when my outside world, that I had no control over, seemed chaotic at times. I can honestly say, the most valuable wisdom in my life has come from my journey of being a mom. One that I was not so sure of at first. I truly receive back as much as I give and every day brings a new awareness to my life. My children have been my greatest teachers.

Here in this chapter, I want to share how I grew this connection over the years and continue to nurture these two most important relationships in my life. I hope this small snapshot of my journey inspires and helps someone else.

Before I became a mom, I worked as a lawyer in a small firm that focused on upholding individuals' civil rights. My job became my life and at times I was working over 80 hours a week. While I was good at my job, I just felt that there was just no way that I could balance work and have a family. So, I left and took a contract position at a local community college as an Assistant Professor teaching law in the criminal justice program. Soon after, I became pregnant with my first child, Rachael.

When I was eight months pregnant, I had a profound spiritual experience that changed my life. I remember every specific detail like it happened yesterday. That night, I got into bed around 10:00 pm. I positioned myself around my body pillow, which made it easier for me to get comfortable and fall asleep. I laid my head down on the pillow, pulled the covers over my shoulders and settled into bed. As I started to fall peacefully asleep, I gently rubbed my tummy, telling my little girl how much I loved her. The next thing I sensed was someone calling my name softly over and over again, then a gentle tugging on my arm. Unknown to me, this was my husband trying to wake me up from what he later described as a deep trance like state. As I started to slowly open my eyes, I saw a beautiful woman's face. She had dark brown hair, her skin was like porcelain and there was a blue veil around her head. I immediately recognized this beautiful soul as the Virgin Mary. Then, I felt my body flooded with a deep sense of peace. There was no sense of struggle, pain or loss, only pure divine love. It felt like I was wrapped in a warm soft blanket, cared for, nurtured, all my needs were met, and there was no wanting for anything. I had never experienced anything like that in my life. As I started to come back to the awareness of being in my bedroom, I could feel the tears streaming down my face. I looked around and realized I was not laying down. I was instead kneeling upright, and my hands were clasped together in a prayer position. I heard my husband's voice ask me if

I was okay. I couldn't answer. I just sat there frozen, sobbing uncontrollably trying to understand what had just happened. I wanted to go back and feel everything I did in that moment but I knew I couldn't. There was a deep sense of joy that I wanted to experience again and again. I looked over at the clock and it was 3:00 am. My husband told me to lay back down and go to sleep. But I didn't know how I could. Mother Mary had just bestowed a message and blessing to me about my little girl that was about to be born. Although my mind did not hear the words, I knew my soul did. I felt a newfound confidence in myself that I did not have before about becoming a mother. It was like already knowing how to ride a bike when you have never even gotten on one or when you are up for a promotion and you feel like you already have the job. In that moment, I knew that I had all the wisdom inside myself that I needed to be a mother to Rachael, so she would thrive in a world that was so uncertain. I really needed that assurance.

Before I got married, there was a point in my life that I didn't really know if I wanted to have kids. Not because I didn't love children but because I was unsure about the type of parent I would be. These thoughts came from my own story of growing up. I really struggled emotionally, especially when I hit my teen years. In my house, it was my dad's way or the highway. Respect was big but I never felt that respect was mutual.

Many times, I felt like I was in the fight of my life to be heard, loved, and understood. The messages I received were that my own opinions, thoughts, and desires did not matter. This was so difficult for me because deep down I would have such a knowing about something but I was told I was stupid, wrong, or just not worth being listened to. But that knowing was important, which I learned later was my intuition guiding me. So instead of listening to my intuition, I let my dad's opinions, beliefs, and judgements guide my life and I was absolutely miserable. What I eventually realized was that like the many generations before him, he had parented like a boss. This is what he knew, experienced, and understood. I love my dad and understanding the "why" of how he parented has helped set me free to appreciate the many other lessons that he had to share with me, like the meaning of loyalty, perseverance, and courage.

Even though I had come to appreciate the good in our relationship, I still knew I didn't want to be a boss to my children. I wanted to be a different type of parent, but I just didn't know what that would look like. A few weeks after Rachael was born, I got my answer. I was sitting in my glider, gently rubbing her back while she was swaddled in a blanket. Rocking her, I felt a strong sense of knowing that she picked me to be her mom. I realized that Rachael was born to experience her own journey here on earth and her journey was not about what I wanted for her, who I wanted her to be or what I believed she should do. My role as her parent was to honor, respect, embrace, and support that journey. Then I asked myself the question, "how do I do that?" The voice inside me said, "you are here to guide...she leads, you guide. You know what she needs, remember to listen to what your heart tells you." I immediately recognized that voice. My intuition was speaking to me again, that same intuition that I had lost long ago as a teen.

All of a sudden, I felt so grateful for what my dad showed me. I was the one in my family line that was supposed to break the pattern for the future generations of parenting from the old school paradigm that hurt us all, including him.

So, when I wake up every day I make the conscious choice to parent like a guide. Parenting like a guide begins with connecting to the vibration of love in your heart and then using your intuition to make decisions, take actions, find resources, support, connect, nurture, and communicate with your child. This is my secret formula.

While love in God's world needs no definition, love here on earth does and continues to be a practice for all of us. Actor Will Smith uploaded a great six minute YouTube video that embodies the practice of love that I want to share a part of the narrative here. He illustrates this by talking about the relationship a gardener has to a flower.

> The gardener wants the flower to be what the flower is designed to be.... [Love is wanting] the flower to bloom, to blossom and become what it wants to be...not demanding it become what you need it to be for your ego. Anything other than all of your gifts, wide open-giving, and nourishing this flower into their greatness is not love.

...[L]ove really demands an in-depth understanding of their hopes and their dreams, fears, needs and [struggles]. Giving and sharing our gifts for the purpose of nurturing them, empowering and helping them to create their greatest joy... [this is love].[2]

The "anything other than" that Will Smith refers to is the stuff that gets in the way of "connection." This "stuff" is the limitations, negative emotions, stories, pain, judgements, fears, expectations, blame, control, programming, and beliefs that we get from the external world. Often without realizing, we let this stuff parent our kids instead of our gifts even when that is not truly who we are. None of us were born into the world with this "stuff" and we are not here on earth to let it parent our kids or run our life. No matter how we were raised, what we experienced, or who is in our life telling us what to do, we get to choose in each moment whether we connect to the stuff or love.

What I have learned is that the greatest gift about choosing love is that our intuition has permission to come in and flow. Intuition is where our greatest wisdom lies, not only to parent our children but also to help us create the life and vision we dream for ourselves.

Intuition is an extremely powerful life tool. It is our highest source of inner knowing. Intuition gives us a path to a goal, helps us solve problems, find inspiration, leads us to take the right action, find our passion, embrace the good, and so much more.

Sometimes intuition can be an immediate knowing, like you just know what to do, say, or take action on.

Sometimes intuition is a random thought popping into your head, telling you what to do, say or take action on.

Sometimes intuition is a sensing in your body, leading you to what to do, say, or take action on. Like a gut feeling.

All of us have this inner knowing, we just have to recognize it, trust it and listen. This is where our greatest happiness lies not only for us but for our children too.

---

[2]   https://www.youtube.com/watch?v=9tVkWYv484Y.

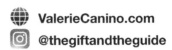

Valerie Canino is an author, intuitive mom, and certified life coach. A born and raised New Yorker, she transformed her life and found her passion when she moved to San Diego. She is a "gifted guide" who serves as the bridge for connection between moms and their teens so they both feel listened to, liberated and loved in their relationship. Over the years through parenting, spiritual exploration, community building, and advocacy, Valerie has developed a heart centered process that heals and transforms relationships. Using her intuitive gifts, she creates a sacred space for both moms and teens to gain clarity to recognize the wisdom in their struggles so they can write a new future story in their own lives.

In 2021, Valerie is launching a transformational book for teen girls. Each chapter is filled with real stories where she shares secret wisdom to empower teens to move beyond survival so they can master their life now. Her book also comes with a bonus parent guide that has tools and information about her heart centered parenting approach that helped her create a close connection with her own teens.

To learn more visit ValerieCanino.com. and Instagram @thegiftandtheguide.

The Mind Sometimes Lies

By Veronica Watkin

This chapter is dedicated to my two children, my step daughter, my son in law, my adopted family, my bio-parents, my grand baby, my children's father, my friends, my love, all the people I love, all adoptees, adoptive parents, the families that took me in, the Schaerer family, and anyone else who needs inspiration. My hope is that everyone knows and understand this is my story and not meant to hurt anyone in anyway.

Before we get into my experiences and story, I would like to share a little about myself. I have two beautiful daughters, a step daughter and a five month old grandbaby that was born during this pandemic! I am so in love. I have a love that I am grateful for, and thankful for the opportunities I have had to learn and grow from him. A couple years ago, my children's father and I parted ways after 18 years. In no way shape or form was it meant to hurt anyone, but of course it did. He taught me a lot. I am thankful for learning and growing through this. I truly wish the best for him.

The world is a challenge at this moment so now I have a lot of time on my hands. I am looking at it like an opportunity to write and share part of my story. I had every excuse why I should not share my experiences. I want to share my story in hopes to inspire you in any way that you need. I hope it touches your heart and you remember that you are worthy of love.

This is my first time writing and sharing a part of my adoption story. I am writing this three weeks before it is due for the press. I have procrastinated a lot due to fear; fear of hurting those I love! Fear can hold us back and get in the way, in many areas of our lives! I have a lot of time on my hands now due to the pandemic and my injury. I am sure many do. In the greater Edmonton area, everyone has to social distance 6ft from each other, unless you live in the same house. If you cannot maintain social distance you have to wear a mask, and some places are mandatory regardless. Our world is adjusting to this new way of life. We are all getting used to our new normal.

I was learning to box and to kickbox from my love. I was on my last round of boxing and kickboxing class. I was kicking with my left leg. Learning how to do it properly. I was eager and maybe being a little sassy because I wanted to make myself proud. I put my all into this kick and BAM...I kicked the pads he was holding, the next moment I hit the back of my leg on something. At that second I had no idea what I hit. The first thought was I am going to get up and kick again, then realized I was in a lot of trouble. I went into a state of shock from the pain. He remained calm and got me to the hospital. The pain was so intense. I realized after what I had kicked, and it was a metal ab roller bar on the floor. There is a reason I am sharing this with you all. I was then told I had to have surgery, no weight bearing, 10 weeks in a boot, and 6-12 months of physio due to my achilles tendon and my calf muscles being damaged. I feel like my freedom and independence has been taken from me. I have moments that I want to give up, but I fight these moments and utilize my time in as constructively as possible. I honor and sit with my feelings of discomfort.

I still remember to this day being around five or six and I was so excited running up to that house with my baby brother holding his hand. I was so happy that we would get to be a part of a family together. When we reached the door, I was thinking to myself "be on your best behavior" in hopes they would pick my brother and I. The first lady was pleasantly smiling at us and another woman walked up, she was not smiling and looked at my brother and I and said "they are too dark!!" GASP! Really! Who says that to a traumatized child? She knew we were up for adoption and I am sure she did not think we were objects?!?! My heart sank.

It was that moment my world fell apart...

I knew I would have to hold on to my brother and take good care of him but I had no idea how because I was so young...I knew it was him and I from that moment on. I did not understand why my bio parents didn't want us at that time. I did not understand things and went through some very painful experiences.

Later on that day, someone very special (my adopted mum) told me that they are keeping us. Our foster mum and dad decided to keep my brother and I. We were legally their children at nine and seven years old. This family is a strict English family with very strong values and ethics. They raise strong women and men.

My life was getting settled and we moved in shortly after I was adopted, to a beautiful acreage. I knew my biological mother and father were not coming back now and I needed to accept it. I tried to understand. I still fantasized that they would come through the door and take me home. I had some challenges and was a bit of a stubborn girl. If I did not get my own way I would scream or pout, and do what lots of kids do at that age. I was a handful. I wanted to be with my brother and I ran away. I knew the rules before I ran away. My mum was very clear and firm. She said "If you run away you will not be coming back." Well, I did it anyways, I didn't care and left anyways being a stubborn teen. The police brought me home, not sure if it was days, hours, or weeks later. My mum answered and told the officer that I was not welcome here anymore. I knew the consequences of my choices. The officer would not have it, he said you can call welfare in the morning.

Off to bed I went, sad that my mum did not want me anymore. I didn't understand. I apologized and I begged but nothing changed her mind. I woke up in the morning and I called child welfare and told them that they needed to get me. From that day on I never went home and went into multiple group homes, institutes and foster homes. I was angry and wondered why someone would adopt a child and give up on them knowing they have already been through this. My heart hurt.

Why did she leave me?
Am I flawed? Maybe I am too dark?
Why did I run away knowing the rules?

I had many questions in my head and I did not understand. I was angry and young and did not understand. It took years and years for that day to come where I understood. I was broken and on self-destruct from then forward in many areas of my life. I did not think I would ever fit in. I wanted more than anything to be loved and accepted for who I was with my mistakes. I never felt that I was good enough all my life and I still struggle with this automatic thought. I felt like making mistakes was forbidden. I still think that even to this day.

As time went by, I started to understand why things went this way. I am still at times hard on myself and hurt by my experience. However, I am thankful that my adopted mum is strong and stuck to her belief and values. Even though this hurt me, I realize now that she did it out of a place of love. She did the best she could with what she knew. She wanted me to understand right from wrong. She wanted to teach me the importance of following through with what you do and say, and many other values. I hope that she understands when she reads this that I love her and I appreciate her and everything she has done for me. I appreciate my adopted dad for all he has done too. I am thankful for the things that happened regardless because my adopted mum and dad gave me the tools they thought were best to help shape the good strong person I am today. I would not be me if I did not have this experience.

The reality is that my brain grew up with trauma and abandonment. It affects me daily if I allow it too. The pain is there and I have learnt to live with what I was given. It is all about how I speak to myself. I am unkind with myself at times. I question if I am every going to be good enough for anyone.

I get into that deep dark place...it sucks me in at times. I get those automatic thoughts and challenge them. It can be a battle. As time progressed and I was out of the house I wanted to have a family and I decided that I wanted a baby, and it happened very quickly and I was young. I don't regret it at all however I do not recommend having children as a teen.

Now that I am a mom, I understand things on a much deeper level. I have made a lot of parenting errors. I can confidently say I have done a great job raising my girls authentically. I am human and did my best to show them that I am. I want my adopted mum and dad to know that I love them and see that everything that was done was from a place of love and was different based on the needs each of their children. I feel like it is our job as parents to teach our children the best we can. I realized that each child has different needs based on their personality. My children are very different, yet the same. I love them both very much. I do my best and yes, I do make mistakes. Like the love languages book, we all love differently and we feel it very differently. So do children. I did have to adjust my parenting based on each one of my children out of love, not out of being unfair.

I want my kids to know that I love them. I want them to love and forgive me for my errors and I want them to celebrate the good with me. So therefore, I need to do this for my bio-parents and my adopted parents. I would not be me if I was not with them. I love them with all my heart and soul and THEY picked me, even though things were tough they still picked me. They are human and it's time for me to let this all go and I am.

I share my story in hopes that you exercise compassion and understanding with yourself and others. Love your inner child and be kind to yourself. Understand that we all have our experiences, our parents do too. I realize that a lot of people were hurt by my adoption. My bio-parents have had to learn to live without my brother and I, to forgive themselves for letting us go. My bio family was without us too, my aunties, uncles, and grandparents. That hurt them too. Now as an adult I understand why they gave us up. That doesn't make the pain go away, it helps me process it and have compassion towards it. My biological parents were unable to provide for me in the ways they wanted and they were not fit or capable at that time to provide a safe loving environment. They wanted us safe and knew that they could not do it. It must have been hard to admit that. I forgive them. I forgive everyone.

You do not have to be "your story." Your story is your experience from your view. You are not your experience. Every person's experiences will be different even if they had the same things happen to them. We each have our own thoughts and worldviews. Take time to reflect and love yourself and be gentle with yourself. Treat yourself and others how you want to be treated. Remember that the pain is okay, sit with it let it pass through your body. You are worth it. Believe in yourself. Exercise self- compassion and treat yourself like you would an important person in your life. Take time to celebrate your successes.

From my heart to yours thank you for reading this and remember your self-worth.

In Health & Wellness,

Check me out on Instagram @foundationscoachingwithvee
Facebook @foundationscoachingwithvee
Website https://foundationswithvee.wixsite.com/coaching

🌐 https://foundationswithvee.wixsite.com/coaching
🔵 @foundationscoachingwithvee
📷 @foundationscoachingwithvee

My name is Veronica, I like to be called Vee. I have my own business life and business coaching. I am working on finalizing my certification as a personal trainer, nutritionist, and CBT coach. I coach individuals and dental clinics. I love what I do and I am passionate about health, wellness, personal development, and leadership. I take as many opportunities to learn and refresh my education. I love the outdoors, snowboarding, being with my loved ones, laughing, learning, and listening to music.

Grieving with Grace: Learning to Grieve Together

By Heidi Dunstan

In April of 2014, I found myself at a crossroads — to take my life or keep on fighting. I knew I didn't want to die but years of undealt with emotions and traumas had literally snowballed and were suffocating me. I chose to fight. With the encouragement of some good friends and family I attended a personal development program called 'Choices Seminars.' This program was pivotal for me to see that I had a life worth leading and that I, indeed, make a difference in this world. I got to know some amazing people, people who saw me, and allowed me to see them. I mean really see them, not the bullshit masks we see in everyday life. I was able to be vulnerable and authentic and, in turn, others were the same with me.

It was there that I met Mike Wilson, a retired fire veteran, and general contractor. He was struggling and needed a friend, and our friendship grew quickly. We became best friends and for many it didn't make sense as he was 24 years my senior, but life doesn't always make sense, we just knew we were able to support each other.

After Mike's marriage ended our friendship transformed into a loving relationship, and with a very strong foundation of being such good friends, our relationship flourished quickly. We explored this world in every way possible; travelling near and far, spending time with people that we loved and cared about, and sharing new experiences together. Many times, I questioned how this could be possible, considering just a couple of years earlier I was ready to give up on living. In many ways it did not make sense, and yet it was the most secure I had felt in as long as I could remember.

Mike moved in with me in 2016. It was an adjustment for both of us, as two very different entrepreneurs faced challenges of our businesses colliding, but we took advantage of the perks of both of us having a mid-week quiet day, sneaking to the mountains for a soak in the hot springs. We worked hard but played harder.

The morning of December 27, 2018, we both woke up still full of too many delicious Christmas dinners and both wondered if we should work today, but we didn't feel like it. I had heard rumblings that he was planning a surprise birthday party for my 40th which was the next day, so I probed as to what the menu would be for this event, and decided that we needed to get some groceries. As we headed to the till at the grocery store Mike mentioned that he wasn't feeling well, and it confirmed that we were going to just relax so he could rest.

When we got home, I brought a load of groceries to the front door and came back to the car to find Mike had collapsed face down and was unresponsive in the driveway. My world spun instantly. I screamed and cried and administered first aid. I called 911 and started CPR, neighbours came to help. Within minutes his fellow firefighters were on our driveway taking over his care, as neighbours stood watching in shock. My world was spinning, yet moving in slow motion, and an hour from the time I dialed 911, the doctor at the hospital announced his time of death. My life in that moment stopped too. A big piece of me died that day.

It's almost two years that I have grieved the loss of Mike, my love, and I have realized that we as a society are not equipped to deal with grief. Many of us have not been taught how to grieve or to be comfortable being uncomfortable with someone who is grieving. The reality is that most of us are walking around grieving the loss of family members, friends, marriages, pets, and jobs. We are all just a bunch of grievers walking around. I have seen that so many of us want to know how to grieve better.

I have realized that grief isn't easy to 'learn' because everyone grieves in their own way. There isn't a manual that says on day 21 you should feel this way, and on day 180 you should be here, and this is when you should take your wedding ring off, and this is when you should date again, and on day 365 you should be done grieving. Those rules simply do not exist, and as much as it would help someone who wants some structure, it doesn't work that way because each of us grieve in our own unique ways.

It is easy to judge someone who is grieving because they do it differently than you. What is hard is to sit with them exactly where they are at and allow them to be where they need to be. Having someone sit with me in a restaurant while I sob cannot be easy, but it allows me to let the armour down and truly be seen. It doesn't matter that it's over a year since Mike died, it doesn't matter that people are watching. There was no story of when they experienced grief, there was no 'I am sorry for your loss', it was just space that allowed me to authentically hurt and be heard by my loved one. To say, "I miss him and want him back, that this isn't what I had planned for my life" and let the tears and snot flow, and love me exactly where my hurting heart was at.

It is also very easy to judge myself during grief. We live in a world that isn't comfortable with pain, and so when pain goes on for what we think is too long, our mind wants it to stop. I spent months wondering why I was still crying, why I couldn't just get it together, why my roommate was always eating crackers...it was because widow brain is real and I would forget that I had bought two boxes the week before, and still hadn't opened them. When I stopped asking 'why does this hurt?' and 'when am I supposed to feel better?' I found that my grief journey got a whole lot easier when I realized there was no time clock on grief. This process is messy because there is no right or wrong. I learned that I must take it as it comes.

Speak to anyone riding the crazy grief train and we all have our stories of good and bad support from people that we care about. The awkward platitudes that people say like 'I know loss, my grandma died' is an attempt to connect with you; sadly, there are comments that miss the mark. I acknowledge that every strange platitude is someone attempting to connect at a time when I felt completely disconnected from the world. Because so many people have no idea what to say when someone is grieving, comments weeks after Mike's funeral like 'don't worry you will find love again', often left me feeling like the safest place for me to grieve was alone, which is furthest from what I really needed.

The world of social media has provided me some beautiful grief support. Setting up a memory page in honour of Mike on Facebook allowed for many friends and family to post how they missed him, their memories of their relationship with them, and how he was important to them. Those first few weeks, I read these posts repeatedly, it gave me glimpses of the man that I loved, and how he was loved by so many others. Mike and I only had a few short years together so some of those stories really helped me to see other aspects of him that I had yet to experience. And looking back and seeing the hundreds of comments and posts in various pages and spaces, I see that this wonderful man has left a lot of holes in hearts down here on earth. These stories and memories really exemplified the beautiful part of grief and are something that I still look back on and re-read.

While riding this crazy grief train, I have been blessed with some graceful grief lessons. The best gift that I was given was the day after he died, it was a Costco-size pack of good Kleenex, which was well used! Some people were amazing at gently leaning in to hold space. A few weeks after losing Mike someone asked, 'how is today?' rather than the typical how are you? This simple change in a typical question allowed me to not have to lie and say I am fine, or okay. It gave me space to say, 'it's been hard,' or 'day by day,' or 'I miss him.' Grief forces you to live in that very moment. There is truth when they say take it day by day, or minute by minute and in those first few months of grief.

A long time ago I heard the parable of the long spoons which many describe as the difference between Heaven and Hell. *'One day a man said to God, "God, I would like to know what Heaven and Hell are like."*

God showed the man two doors. Inside the first one, in the middle of the room, was a large round table with a large pot of vegetable stew. It smelled delicious and made the man's mouth water, but the people sitting around the table were thin and sickly. They appeared to be famished. They were holding spoons with very long handles and each found it possible to reach into the pot of stew and take a spoonful, but because the handle was longer than their arms, they could not get the spoons back into their mouths.

The man shuddered at the sight of their misery and suffering. God said, "You have seen Hell."

Behind the second door, the room appeared exactly the same. There was the large round table with the large pot of wonderful vegetable stew that made the man's mouth water. The people had the same long-handled spoons, but they were well nourished and plump, laughing and talking.

The man said, "I don't understand."

God smiled. It is simple, he said, Love only requires one skill. These people learned early on to share and feed one another. While the greedy only think of themselves...' [Author unknown]

Many grievers say that grieving the loss of a loved one is isolating and compare it to Hell. I can say that during my grief journey with losing my Mike, I have had moments that felt like Hell, where I was starved, felt alone, and sometimes I isolated myself. I can also say that I had moments where others reached out and nourished me. They shared stories of their favourite memories of Mike, or they let me share openly some of the great memories I have, or the hard realities I was facing in the painful journey of grief. I find the parable of the long spoons makes it clear that we are all connected, and when one person is starving, we both benefit when we feed and love each other.

I have been on this crazy grief journey for almost two years and I can say that there are some very hard ugly moments in grief, but there are also some beautiful loving moments too. Grief is love, and it hurts because we have loved. I will love Mike for the rest of my life, which means I will grieve him for the rest of my life too. I am still learning about this crazy grief train ride, but now I am looking forward to lean in and feed others with my long spoon and know that others will raise their spoon to support me. Grief isn't easy, but when we do it together it offers us some grace, and beauty.

www.summitdesignsltd.ca

Heidi Dunstan is an entrepreneur, author and speaker. She has immersed herself in moving through grief after the sudden loss of her spouse in 2018. Heidi has always actively participated in various personal development seminars over the years and has found that she continues to find support and healing through the various courses and training to assist her through her grief. Heidi is excited about her upcoming book to be released in 2021 and hopes that the stories and examples given can help grievers and those supporting them to learn to lean into grief, to support each other and to grieve gracefully.

The Destination

By Miriam Grunhaus

Imagine you are driving on the way to your destination. You know where you are going and when you should be arriving. You are dressed for that occasion, armed with the knowledge that you need to accomplish the goals that have been set up for this trip. You are excited as you have prepared for this day for a long time, and you feel empowered. You know you will succeed, and you will accomplish your goals; you can taste the success that is coming your way! You are excited, motivated, and you are determined! You are feeling good!

But then, you hit a roadblock, and traffic is redirected.

You have no idea where you are going or how you are going to get back to the original destination that you set out to go to. The more you drive, the more your heart starts racing. You are going to be late. That is if you even find your way back.

There are signs with directions, and you have no choice but to keep following them as the other streets are closed off. You hope that the road signs will bring you back, but you notice that you are far away from where you were meant to go. You feel very hot, the AC is no longer cooling enough, and your body temperature is going up. The unknown is creating this heat, this uncertainty.

You reach for your cell phone, but there is no connection. You can't use the GPS, you can't call someone for help or just to calm you down and figure out a plan of action. You can't change your meeting time. You are alone and have no other way but to trust, have faith, and keep going to where the road is leading you.

You decide to put on some music, but your nerves are not letting you focus, and the noise becomes an unwanted distraction from your thoughts, so you shut it off. The palms of your hands are sweating and sliding off the wheel. You dry them on your clothes. You take a peek at the mirror, and you notice your face is red, overheated. You are very worried.

Somewhere in our lives, we will all hit these roadblocks and find ourselves navigating uncharted waters. We don't recognize our environment, ourselves, or how we got there. We are faced with disappointments; we find ourselves vulnerable because we are unprepared. There are so many unknowns. What's next? We may try to reach out for help, we may try to distract ourselves, but we find that the unknown is painful, and we can't focus on anything other than the pain, the agony, and the worry.

But there are no other roads; in that moment, there is only us and the path we are on. And so, we have a choice to make. Do we trust the journey? Do we allow ourselves to be taken to this place where we did not plan on going? Do we look out the window and enjoy the journey, learn from it, live it to the fullest? Do we embrace the change and look forward to the surprising turn of events? Or do we keep forcing our return to what we thought was the right destination?

What can we see from the car's window? The beautiful sky, with birds flying around and singing in unison? Maybe the ocean and waves crashing by the rocks? A large field with so many flowers that the aroma is actually coming through the AC vents? What is outside your window? This new path is not a straight line but a mountainous terrain taking you to a different place, completely different from the one you had planned to go to. There is a tunnel that leads you into the mountain and out on the other side. The view is different once again, the sounds are unique. They are exciting; they are new.

You are now focused on what is outside the window, you are checking out the journey, and you start noticing the beauty in nature, the smells, and the sounds. You roll down the window so you can immerse yourself in all the sensations that are available, and you notice that your heart rate is regular, that your face is no longer red and overheated, and you understand that you are not going to the place you set out to be this morning, the meeting is over. The time has passed, and so, you embrace the journey, and you start enjoying the process because you are looking for the beauty and you are taking notice of what's around you.

Unless you choose to fight it and keep trying to figure out a way back, an explanation for your delay. You keep trying your phone, and you keep turning your eyes to the rearview mirror to see if there are cars behind you so you can stop them and ask them how to get back. It is your choice. It is my choice.

Most likely, your life has faced roadblocks, redirects, and drastic changes of events. I believe that we all face these changes, and it affects each one of us differently. Some will embrace the outside, the newness, and the mystery, and some will fight to go back to a life we dreamt about and expected to have. And there are many different reactions in between.

My life has shown me that there is no way to fight the roadblocks, and the sooner we embrace the redirect, the sooner we will feel good in general. Aren't we all looking to live a fulfilling and joyful life?

My husband and I sat by the island in our kitchen, talking about life, talking about the future, and the past. How life has changed and evolved, how it has been different from what we imagined it would be, in more ways than we can count. We are trying to understand the last year, because more than that would be more than we could chew.

Last year, as we were getting closer to the end of the year, my business was growing, thriving. Things were getting better in many areas of our personal lives. We were working very hard at being more and more resilient and overcoming the many adversities we had experienced until that point. We were hopeful. And then we hit a major private roadblock. My husband suffered a stroke. He was relatively young, thin, and ate healthy, and this came out of left field. There had been no signs of any health issues. But that is not what we found out at the hospital. There had been invisible signs. There had been some bumps on the roads that we dismissed, "drove" over them, and kept going to what we thought was our destination. Thirty days later, I lost my beloved father—another roadblock.

I was in that car, going nowhere I recognized. My palms were sweating, shaking, I was feeling a heat that was like a fire. The rug had been pulled out from under me. I was looking back at the mirror...when can I make a U-turn? Why wasn't there anywhere safe for me to turn around?

I was filled with worry and pain and questions. There were so many questions, and I was reaching out for the phone, but there was no connection, and I was feeling so utterly alone.

I was counting on 2020. I relied on the new year, wanting to believe that things would change for the better and looking for my arrival at my final destination, where everything would make sense, and I would get clarity. I am sure you may have felt these feelings before. I know you understand.

But then the world changed.

I am writing these words when the world map shows red markings everywhere, depicting a pandemic that has torn the world apart. It has broken the economy, it has separated human contact, and it has split humanity into different groups, those who believe, and those who don't, those who are well and those who are ill, those who lost and those who gained. This is a roadblock of massive proportions. We have all experienced private roadblocks, and now we are facing one together, the entire humanity as one.

We are left with a choice to make. Do we try to go back in time to a place where we believed that there was some certainty and fight it because naturally, there is no way to achieve that? Or do we understand that in reality, there has never been any assurances, any scripts, or any certainty at all? Do we realize that our dreams...well they were dreams and wishes, but there have never been any guarantees?

There have been dreams, expectations, and beliefs that we have created in our minds. It is time for us to understand that to achieve Joy, we will have to trust, we will have to have faith, and we will have to look out the window.

We will have to count our blessings by reaching in and reaching out. We will have to look at the small and hidden goodness we experience that we have taken for granted for a long time. You see, we have a car and it has gas in it. We have an AC, and when we start to trust and have faith, we feel our heart rate goes back to normal, then the AC can actually keep us cool and refreshed. The radio is playing and the music is beautiful. The sky is blue and the birds are singing. The ocean is crashing its waves on rocks, creating a natural lullaby.

And for each one of us, a car and the waves and the sky may mean something different, but we are all surrounded by blessings and by miracles and it is up to us to find them, to catalog them, to sing from the rooftops and praise them because when we do, we understand.

We understand that the journey is actually the destination. That there is no there, but rather the way there. That there is no light at the end of the tunnel because we are the light and the tunnel is the journey.

Joy is a choice, and it is hard work. Joy is a commitment that must be made each morning anew. Joy is for me, and it is for you. When we realize that life is working for us and not to spite us, when we recognize that we have to commit to prioritizing the really important things in life, we will see things transform.

As a society, we spend more time at work and on social media than we do with our loved ones. We don't work on our personal bucket lists as we work on our business resumes and qualifications. We forget the window on the car; we forget that there is a beautiful field that we should actually experience by walking in it, picking up the flowers, smelling the fresh air, and blowing on dandelions. We forget that the most beautiful treasures could be on the other side of our beds, or in the room next door.

Computers never get shut down. They are always on. Phones are not turned off or put away; they are connected to our bodies as if they were limbs that we are so attached to and couldn't live without.

It is time to look out the window. It is time to enjoy the journey and to find and count our blessings. It is time to plan, not where we are going, but how we live in the here and now. So we can be better spouses, parents, and employees, but most of all so we can be better humans.

The world was set on time out. We were given time to reflect. Now is the time to stop looking in the rearview mirror and embrace all that is wonderful in the here and now.

www.mikahfashion.com
www.healwithgold.com
www.HealwithGold.com/book

After working for 25 years as a marketer with expertise in Ethics and Compliance, Miriam Grunhaus, native of Brazil, entered the world of Fashion Design and started her brand Mikah Fashion. Miriam's commitment is to the women she serves. After learning about Kintsugi (the Japanese art of mending pottery) and feeling empowered by its message, Miriam decided that her brand will be a source of hope and support for women.

Mikah's mission is to empower women to accept themselves with all of their imperfections and limitations. We want women to "wear their scars" with pride; to understand that each one of us is a unique work in progress. We want women to know that they are beautiful; not despite their circumstances, but because of them. We want to empower women to own their struggles — and in doing so — to own their strength.

In 2020 Miriam launched her first book, Heal with Gold. The book has been endorsed by Tal Ben Shahar, PhD. Dr. Tal ben Shahar is the author of the New York Times Best Seller Happier, and founder of the Happiness Studies Academy. Coming out by the end of 2020 is the extension of the book, a course on healing with a Kintsugi spin.

Fashion
www.mikahfashion.com

Book and Course
www.healwithgold.com
www.HealwithGold.com/book

NOW

By J Wiley

I watched with curiosity and wonderment as you took the dominos and spread them out so we could play. Or the time you set up the chessboard as you handled each piece carefully. I watched, as you would get in position to teach me to dance. Or sat down on the floor with your legs spread apart to roll the ball back and forth with me. Then there was the time you taught me to pick vegetables from the garden or how to frame a building, how to hammer a nail and how to build a shed. All these while you were blind.

Yes, hammering a nail while blind, imagine that.

Before you were blind you took me on the tractor riding and would teach me to drive. Fishing and hunting were a must do. My first fish wasn't even a fish it was a huge turtle that came walking out of the water. I could ride that thing. Of course, I can't remember if we got the hook out of its mouth, I hope we did. The last time you saw me was when I was 6 years old, you would mention that quite often.

All this was possible because you made it so. You spent time with me, you made time for me, you put me first and without even knowing it you taught me so much. Our favorite game to play was dominos, the indentions on the pieces made it possible for you to see them with your hands. Our relationship was based on love, pure love. You didn't want anything from me; you just wanted to spend time with me. As an only child that was critical because otherwise I would have always be playing alone.

I learned not just the obvious lessons: I am important, self-esteem boost, love, kindness, and compassion. But I learned the not so obvious: NOTHING, ABSOLUTEY NOTHING can stand in your way unless you let it. Life is about choices, you can choose to allow things to stop you from living or you can choose to live. Life can be an obstacle if you let it. You can choose to be a victim to your circumstances or you can choose to rise above and live your life. It is all up to YOU!

As I get older I value these lessons and try to teach them to my children. But as I really think about it everyone needs to hear the lessons. So many of us are not doing what our soul came here to do. It is time to step out of the stress and anxiety that we have created for ourselves and live the way we were all meant to live. It is all a matter of choice.

As I write this there is a pandemic gripping the world. Providing people with the perfect opportunities to slow down and reevaluate their lives. While everyone was in lockdown, nature came out from hiding and reestablished itself. People got to spend more time with their families. The world had time to heal. And people showed more compassion and love for each other. Of course, the negatives to this pandemic are showing up. But this is about what you choose to focus on and for this chapter I choose to focus on the positives.

One side effect of life and now - the pandemic is stress and anxiety, which is a projection of us focusing on the future. All the 'what ifs', 'could haves', 'would haves', 'should haves' are what create the stress and anxiety that is prevalent in our society today. We all need to focus on the NOW!

Right now, I am sitting in my chair, with a computer in my lap, writing a chapter for a book, the sun is shining in the window and there is a calm after a storm, the air is humid and the squirrels are playing. My mind goes to what I am going to do after I finish this, but I bring it back to the present and continue writing. I stall out on what to say next and try to refocus on the topic at hand. I hear a crow squawking and wonder what is it saying. I realize that grounding ourselves will help us stay present.

One way to help all of us is to ground ourselves. Too many of us are walking this earth without knowing how to ground ourselves to it. If you ever feel flighty/spaced out, not able to focus, feel fearful, feeling dizzy, forgetfulness, clumsy, feeling aggravation, unable to understand what people are saying, and unable to communicate effectively with others. These are just a few symptoms of being ungrounded.

Everyone does grounding slightly differently but I will teach you a quick way and a longer way to do it. Once you have done it several times the long way will get quicker. A quick way is to put your tongue to the roof of your mouth. This helps ground you instantly.

Longer way is visualizing a rope going from the base of your spine down your legs, through your feet and into the ground. Now visualize the rope going down through the layers of the earth to the center. Envision a rose quartz crystal at the center of the earth, this is sending love to the earth, wrap the rope around the crystal then bring the rope back up through the layers of the earth towards your feet. Bring the rope back through your feet, up your legs, up your spine to your heart and wrap the rope around your heart. This does three things: grounds you, helps you send love to earth and earth sends love back to you.

Can helping with stress and anxiety be as simple as grounding ourselves? I think so. Other techniques can help as well like smudging yourself and your space, balancing your chakras, buying plants, crystals, opening windows for fresh air, going for walks, taking your shoes off and walking in the grass, LAUGH lots, and just a simple smile, especially when you don't want to. These are simple tricks to get you out of your head and into the NOW.

When you're blind, living in the NOW is important. You can't focus on the past or the future and get yourself from point A to point B safely. You have to know with every step where you are at, at that very moment. Funny I didn't really consider LIVING IN THE NOW as one of the lessons I learned from my grandfather, my papa as I called him.

So let me recap the lessons learned from my papa who didn't let blindness stop him. One, only you stand in your way of accomplishing your goals and dreams. Two, life can be an obstacle only if you let be. Life is about choices and how are you going to choose to live it. Three, living in the NOW is what will help alleviate our stress and anxiety, and don't forget to ground yourself.

As Pierre Teihard de Chardin said: "We are not human beings having a spiritual experience; we are spiritual beings having a human experience."

As Prince said: "Dearly beloved, we are gathered here today to get through this thing called life." Let's all step into the NOW especially during these difficult times and help each other navigate this thing called life.

Sending everyone healing and loving vibes and thoughts! <3

 www.intuitivesoul.ca

 www.artzfartzphotography.ca

Hello my name is J Wiley. I have been a photographer for over 30 years and a spiritual advisor and healer for 7 years. Both have been my passion all my life.

I have done many things in my career life from customer service to waitress to bookkeeper to sales to photography developer to mediator to business owner to photographer to spiritual advisor to healer and now author. And it is the later four that I am most proud of. Having a Bachelor of Arts in Cultural Anthropology has provided me with the interest in and knowledge of diverse cultures, spirituality and real relationships.

Photography has changed drastically in last 30 years and I have enjoyed the journey immensely. My work has been seen all over the world. As a photographer I have grown, adapted and changed with the industry. My style is to capture real people, in true situations, with true emotions, having fun. Minutes may go into taking the photo but hours go into creating a work of art.

All my life I have had signs and symbols directing me, I am intuitive, empathic, clairaudience, clairsentience, and claircognizance. Having had this calling towards spiritual teachings and healings for a very long time, my life changed drastically 7 years ago. Ever since the heartache and hardships I have once again followed my heart and my love for spirituality.

This world is in dire need of spiritual teachers and healers right now, and I hope that my knowledge and teachings can help others. By teaching others, I am learning, others are learning, and in turn we all will help heal this world.

When What's Driven You to the Top is Now Driving You Crazy...

By Dr. Avis Attaway

$40,000...

I had just committed myself to paying that lump sum in order to further my business. I had no idea where that money was going to come from. The terror was so intense that my heart was pounding - slamming - in my chest. It felt like a vice grip on my temples. I was experiencing massive anxiety. Is this what a panic attack feels like? There was no way that I was going to sleep that night. I had to figure out how I was going to find that money.

How had I gotten myself into this, you may ask?

The promise had come out of a feeling that I *must* do this thing if I was going to be successful. But why did something as exciting as investing in my success feel so compelling – yet so paralyzingly terrifying? From all my training, I finally understood...this is what fight-flight-freeze feels like in pure form.

This was all because I was trying to grow my business and so had come to an event. I was stimulated by all the stories of success by the people on stage and razzle-dazzled by their reports of monthly incomes that exceeded many people's annual salaries. I wanted that, too, and I knew I had it in me. But I also knew that there was something I was missing that kept me from making that kind of an impact. It looked like these people knew what that was and could tell me. For $40,000.

Now you might wonder why, with a doctorate in psychology and a successful professional practice, that I believed anybody could tell me anything about myself that I didn't already know. But that's the case when you rely on what you believe to be true. And what I believed was that I wasn't one of *those* people.

Despite the fact that I had worked so hard to earn credentials and gather years of experience, I still didn't see what others saw when they looked at me. My expertise and wisdom proved inadequate against the voice of my ego declaring that I wasn't enough. Every effort to overcome that voice only served to strengthen it. *Nope, still not enough.*

This was insane, because in my clinical work I had facilitated tremendous healings. So many of the most wounded individuals had found release, and with it not just relief, but transformational experiences that connected them to their inner essence. Spiritual revelations, physical and relational healings, and most importantly, a new relationship with self. So why couldn't I do this for myself?

I had easily become the epitome of the saying, "You teach what you most need to learn."

Year after year - literally for decades - I had worked on *me*. Therapy, meditation, coaching and studying personal development, even exercise and nutrition, all with the goal of making myself into one of those people. The people who seem to have *it* figured out. The ones with the *Midas Touch.*

I wanted to be the one where people would say, "Anything she touches turns to gold..."

You see, the more I earned, the more I owed. Although at one time I could never have imagined making the kind of money I was making, I was constantly struggling to stay ahead of the game. And as a game, it wasn't very much fun.

It looked to me like there must be something I was missing, and if I just found that then everything would fall into place. I drove myself to find that missing piece. I was going to make it happen - *no matter what*. (More on that story at another time.)

I kept looking outside myself for the answer.

Through all my years, I've experienced this as an underlying core theme for most people. Something we share as a commonality with one another, even though it seems counterintuitive. We've been conditioned across the board to conform to our surrounding society from the moment we open our eyes and become a participant in what can only be summed up as ... life. Every experience we have instructs us in how the world works and how we can get our needs met.

We learn how to survive.

Einstein once said that the first and most fundamental thing a human being learns is whether the world is a friendly or a hostile place. These earliest lessons come from our parents. As an infant, there is no filter in place to interpret experiences. Everything registers as true. What makes some messages more true than others is the frequency of delivery.

It isn't always about what's happened to us, but sometimes more about what has not happened that *should* have - such as protection, nurturing, cherishing or unconditional love. A child in distress without that needed support will learn to fill in the gaps. Instinctively, every child knows what they need. When they can't get it from their caregivers they will blame themselves as unworthy of care and love; as not enough.

This is when decisions get made, ones that last for a lifetime. The little kid whose parents are constantly fighting may believe it's her fault because she didn't clean her room. Instinctively she knows that she is dependent upon these two people for her survival. This instinct will cause her to come up with a solution. One that will get her the attention she needs, to be seen and cared for, to feel secure. She may decide that cleaning the whole house will stop the fighting and it may work for a little while. And when it does, her parents focus on her and this reinforces her plan.

But since the problem was never really about her this solution soon fails. She then recommits to the plan and ups the ante by increasing her caretaking behavior - maybe throwing laundry or cooking into the solution. But again, she can never really fix a problem that was never hers to begin with.

However, this way of being becomes ingrained and a part of the personality that carries through into adulthood and for a lifetime. Trying to do more to fix situations that are out of our control is a classic coping mechanism that most women will recognize. Lots of men will, too. I call it *performing for love.*

If you think that you have to *do something* in order to *be enough* then you most likely have the syndrome. Thousands of hours spent working with hundreds of clients have shown me the many ways in which people perform. Overachieving in academics or sports may be the sign of a gifted child - or the outcome of endless attempts to win the love or earn the parent's blessing. This translates into driven adults who have achieved success but at a price.

The price is a secure sense of self. This is about your relationship with yourself. It comes from a direct experience of unconditional acceptance and love just for being you. This gets internalized and is the foundation of how you feel about you.

In the beginning was the parent. The One who provides for every need and knows everything (at least until you become about 12 years old). This care teaches the child that they are worthwhile, deserving, loveable and that they matter. It teaches belonging and significance.

A parent does not need to be a perfect person to truly love their child. True love is selfless and extends a spiritual experience. To be accepted just as one is. That is the ultimate gift.

Any deficits in feeling acceptable become the seeds of searching and performing to get that love. Ultimately, it's about feeling the love within. Pretty tough to do when you are constantly being reminded by the voice of your ego about of all your shortcomings.

And the ego is brilliant at keeping us from reaching our full potential...

Ego will tell you that you suck. You're not enough. You can't have what you want in this life. Who do you think you are, expecting to get the good stuff? What have you done to earn it? You've never been truly successful before, so why do you think you will be now? Ego is only concerned with survival and will use its only tool: FEAR.

Now I'm not talking about ego in the sense of "Oh, she thinks she's all that." I'm describing the conditioned part of the mind that seeks only to ensure our survival. It relies on memory - both conscious and unconscious - for what has worked in the past. This is then brought forward to deal with current situations, as well as for anticipated situations in the future. This is especially handy to keep us from stepping out in front of a bus and getting mowed down. However, it's less handy if we're trying to live our life according to our dreams.

The fears that come up as we imagine the path to the fulfillment of our dreams are what stop us in our tracks. These obstacles in our path aren't external to us, although sometimes they may appear so. Things may happen and we point to them and say that's why we didn't make our goal. Sometimes these obstacles are undeniably real and big.

But it isn't really what's happening to us that makes the difference. It's what we do with what happens to us. No matter how big it is. We decide. No one else. Only we can decide how we'll interpret it. Maybe it is hopeless. At what point do you throw in the towel on your dreams?

Or maybe the dream wasn't big enough... Maybe your dreams have begun to shrink. You've downsized them to keep from feeling the pain of disappointment. The older we get the more time we have to accumulate disappointments. Have they piled up? The ego will stockpile them for you. Then trot them out to remind you that it's better to be safe than sorry. Just trying to make it safely to death.

So if we all have this constricting ego running its show from the shadows, what chance do we have to overcome its effects? Are we doomed to repeat the patterns of our past and live a life that feels recycled? That was where I was at when I began to question myself. I believed that I was responsible for my own life yet I didn't feel empowered to change it. I knew that my thinking had to be ambushing me despite my positive mental attitude.

Since ego reflects our survival instinct mixed with our conditioning I knew I had to find something more powerful to overcome both. As I looked back at my earliest experiences for the source of my negative thinking, I realized that the feeling of *not enough* was rooted in my own lack of self-love. The deficit had left me sitting in judgment of myself. And the ego fed me a steady stream of reasons why I should continue to judge myself. To not judge myself risked everything - rejection, ridicule, or something worse.

I realized that now I was performing for my own love! I was both judge and jury. Only I could decide if I had made the grade. And with the risk of an existential threat, I had been on a hamster wheel of performing and judging, performing and judging - and I couldn't get off. When would I ever pass the test? Make the grade? I was exhausted from trying to make something happen. Setting a goal, ramping-up my energy, then forcing myself to do the things that I believed would bring me success. Always with the same results. Not enough.

I decided that if I was the final judge then I had to figure out how to find myself as enough. I had to decide to find myself acceptable. Acceptance. Unconditionally (otherwise it wouldn't be real). It was beginning to look a lot like love. I had to love myself despite whatever the ego used to try to scare me.

I'll admit that I needed something bigger than me in order to do this. The cool part is that It wasn't outside me. It had been in me all along. It had never left me although I often couldn't see It or feel It. That's because I had been only listening to the loudest voices in my head. Not the still, small one.

The realization didn't really come like a flash but more over time. But I share it with you now to save you time. Because when you find It inside yourself you can allow It to love you until you're in love with yourSelf. And this is when the creating begins.

Instead of trying to make things happen in your life, you can create your life by allowing It to flow through you. This power will cause things to happen beyond what your conditioned mind could ever imagine. It will cause your dreams to come true - because your dreams come from It. Anything you've ever dreamed is possible if you will allow It.

I know how difficult it can be to see beyond the step you are on now. It was for me. Especially when we've become a natural at putting up blocks that are high enough to block out the sun. The greats before me have a saying. That saying is, *We live in a box - and the directions for getting out of that box is on the outside of the box.*

How true is that?!

Someone had to point me in the direction that was right for me and I was blessed enough to get tools. Without that guidance, I would still be struggling and believing that I'm not good enough, strong enough, smart enough...the list goes on. But because someone gave me a hand-up, I now can do the same for others.

If you're struggling with limiting beliefs and haven't been able to rid yourself of them despite the best efforts of coaches and counselors, give yourself one more chance. Let's have a conversation - one that will give you the hand-up that you need. Talking with someone who knows and who's been there and back makes all the difference. It's the difference between theory and experience. You can read about it and you can hear about it. Or you can experience it yourself. Let me walk you through it. Reach out to me at DrAvisAttaway@gmail.com and we'll walk through it together.

 dravisattaway@gmail.com

www.DrAvisAttaway.com

There's something greater within you... something unawake that's waiting to be awakened, yet you don't know how to fully access what this is.

This is where Dr. Avis Attaway loves to play. In between the unconscious and the conscious, she has helped hundreds of high performing individuals tap into who they truly are, what they are here on this earth for, and the path that they have been denying themselves for one to many decades.

Through her years of experience and education in multiple therapeutic modalities, mixed with her own special intuitive wisdom, Avis guides you to your own inner truth so that you can fulfill your purpose and stop searching for the missing pieces of your life.

Contact Dr. Avis, dravisattaway@ gmail.com for a personal discovery call to finally tap into what has been missing all along - you!

www.DrAvisAttaway.com

Obstacles

By Dawnalyn Webster

At 19 years old I moved to another province approximately 10 hours away from my home, my family and all that I knew, to be with the boy I was in love with despite my mothers protective warnings. More honestly, it was inspite of her warnings. I needed to go explore far, far away and he was intoxicating. He was the tall, dark, handsome dirtbike riding boy of my dreams.

Over the course of the next 4 years our googly eyed love affair faded and progressively turned into a toxic life. We fought all the time, seethed nasty words at one another but smiled outwardly, too ashamed of ourselves to show what our relationship had become.

At the 4 year mark we moved back to our home Province to a city 5 hours from "home". He moved before me. The evening I arrived at our new apartment it was empty, cold, had no electricity turned on and he was at the bar with friends. I felt completely lost and alone. Abandoned even.

Over the next few months my loneliness grew exponentially. This place doesn't feel like home and neither does this relationship. What do I do? I'm stuck, away from home, scared and very young. We had emotionally battered one another to the point that I feel as though I am an inch tall. I need support but I am too proud to ask. One day I went to the library, desperate for an answer. There I found a book on Buddhism. I took it home and read it cover to cover. In that book was a key to what I was missing in my life, meditation.

I began meditating daily. It was incredibly challenging to sit still for even 10 minutes. My feet would tingle and my legs would go numb. Nevertheless I persevered. I needed this. Although I still felt very weak I began to feel my inner strength growing. I knew that I had to remove myself from this relationship somehow. Sitting quietly each day allowed space for this knowing to grow so large within me that I was finally able to tear myself away him and that toxic love. I guess my mom's warnings were valid afterall, I wonder if she was actually coming from a place of love rather than control? Interesting.

I stumbled through my 20's. I was stubborn and the few lessons I learned made me feel some confidence and I plunged ahead. Naturally I landed in another long-term relationship and once again I move far away from home. This is the relationship in which I became a mother. Just before I got pregnant I decided I needed a change of career, retail management was becoming tiresome. My heart wants to help others.

Low and behold, one day at work a lady walks in the store promoting her new business just around the corner. She had the most gentle energy I've ever felt, yet so self-assured. Her business was a massage therapy clinic and school. That was it! I was drawn not only to this woman's beautiful energy but also to a health centered career option. I called her shortly after and began my training. Meeting this woman was a major turning point in my life.

When my training was completed and motherhood had begun it was very clear I was on a new path. I learned as much as possible. I took additional massage trainings, became an instructor, taught yoga classes, gave and received treatments of all kinds. I felt happier more often than I had in a very long time. Through growing my practical skills and learning many lessons along the way I moved more deeply within myself. I still don't always listen to my knowing but I am much more in touch with myself that I once was. My work life was amazing; my home life was not.

I grew and evolved at a different rate and in different ways than my partner. We hurt each other a lot and often! We had a child, so what am I to do break up a family for my own happiness? What about my baby? I cannot leave, I don't know how to be a parent on my own. I need his financial support and I'm afraid. Paralyzed. I've lost myself in him/ us/ my baby and all of the self-development I have achieved, isn't enough.

Fast forward a few years, we have since moved back to our home province, closer to family supports. I learned to mountain bike and have an amazing group of friends. I learn that a community of support is soul food in a way I had not fully recognized in the past. I have a great job with wonderful people and I'm feeling more self-assured than ever.

With elevated and growing self-esteem, I open a Yoga Studio. My friends come and support me, my daughters class comes to play, my parents cheer me on. My partner does not. The stress of running the business, on top of a strained relationship, parenting and continuing to work another job is the breaking point.

Just days after my daughter's birthday I break down. The relationship is over, after 6 months of endless requests for counselling, rejected solutions and fights in attempt to salvage our family they instead lead us further away from one another. I'm pissed that he didn't try harder to save what we have built over the last 8 years. I can't understand why he is willing to lose me. I moved out. I was crushed. I just made the decision to alter life not only for the 3 of us, but to force change upon all the relationships in our lives. The phone would ring and I would cringe. I couldn't stomach another conversation explaining myself, and defend my choices to family members who think it's better to suffer in silence than to screw up your child with a separation. I cried every day, mostly in the bathroom or in bed, so my daughter wouldn't see. I couldn't always hide from her or myself, some days she watched me pick mysefl up off the kitchen floor after yet another fight. How is this being a good mom? The guilt came pouring in like scorching hot lava scalding every inch of me.

Shortly after the break up, I had to close my yoga business. I was more than crushed, I was devastated. I was drowning in emotions, in pressure, in life, in the continuous fights. The embarrassment and shame that came next was overwhelming to say the least. It took every ounce of pride I had to get out of bed and face the world. I felt ill daily. I just wanted it all to stop so I could pick myself up off the floor for good. But that's not how the Universe works.

There was a sense of relief, from being out from under the pressures of relationship and business. My parents told me they were proud of me; this was a first from my dad. And still there was an overshadowing sense of defeat. I failed at partnership. I failed at parenting (I was the one to cause a broken home). I failed at business. I constantly fell down biking. I'm 30, this is when you're supposed to be an adult, have it all together, a family/ career/ goals... and my life is in pieces on the floor- all by choice.

Here is where the opportunity lies, if only I can see it. I have the chance to rebuild myself and my life. I begin asking myself some serious questions:

Do I still want to be who I have been working to become? Yes! Does this relationship fit? No.

Can I be a good parent on my own? Of course!

What can this sense of failure and defeat teach me?

Confusion sets in, this is all so overwhelming not to mention exhausting. How did I survive ego bruising heartbreak in the past? That's right. I need to slow down. To get quiet. Listen to my heart. Open myself to the Universe again.

That's just what I did. I rode my mountain bike like I had something to prove. I spent my childless days with friends and family who love and support me. In the deafeningly quiet of the evenings I got quiet and still. I bought a truck and went on adventures. I cried and grieved. I reflected on my values, morals and goals. I stood firm in the choices I was making from my heart. I adjusted the ones that were causing me embarrassment or shame. I returned to my motives often to hold myself accountable. I called on the Universe for guidance. I felt all the pain, over and over. Until it started to ease and some relief started to filter into my life.

Opening and closing a yoga studio all within 6 months was devastating to my practice. I haven't done yoga in 3 long years until a friend calls on me. She wants me to join a Retreat she is hosting and requests that I teach a yoga class each morning. Without hesitation I say yes. I have the utmost respect and admiration for this friend so I am happy to support her in any way possible. It isn't until I arrive at the retreat that I realize I haven't taught a class in 3 years. Holy shit, what have I gotten myself into?! My friend tells me I'll be fine. Mild panic and stress set in, I have trouble sleeping the night before my debut and wake up early. Laying in the dark I slow my breathing, become still and silent. Very soon a confidence washes over me like a gentle wave followed by excitement. The class not only went great, they all did and I felt a renewed appreciation for yoga and the gift of guiding practices.

I have continued to listen inwardly for guidance and less outwardly for well intended advice about my life. The relationship I have with myself has deepened, I trust me. I love me and I value my opinion of myself far greater than that of others.

So, when I decided to add Life Coaching to my career on top of being a Nurse; people asked me questions like: "What does a Life Coach even do?" "So, people pay you money to fix

their problems?" "What is an Intuitive Life Coach anyhow?" "Why are you doing this?" it didn't throw me off course. If a question, text or sideways glance shook me I turned inward. I return to my WHY, my purpose. I know why I am doing this and I know how to listen with a trusting heart to the words of my inner wisdom.

That being said, I don't have it all figured out. Intimate relationships still confuse and scare the hell out of me, as do many other situations that come up for me. Now when I get scared or confused I know what to do. I understand that the answers I need are all within the silent stillness in the quiet depths of myself. Call it listening to your heart, following your gut, trusting your intuition, or having faith. Regardless of what you title this as, trusted knowing it is just that, knowing.

In addition to holding space for this knowing to emerge it is essential, to have supports in place. For me, this is not only places I go to rejuvenate or allowing myself time alone to reset and integrate. But also the community of people who always cheer me on like my parents; people who hold me up like the life-long friend I found by accident the day she walked into my workplace so many years ago; like my friends who inspire me to keep working towards expanded versions of myself; like my daughter who evokes so much laughter and joy; like my intimate relationship that motivates me to explore and dive more deeply within. For all of you, for myself and the Universe I am forever grateful.

 dbruincoaching@gmail.com

🌐 **www.dawnalynbruincoaching.com**

Dawnalyn Webster is an Intuitive Life Coach, passionate about speaking with and supporting empowered, motivated women to elevate through self-doubt and limiting fears into powerful, guilt free self-actualization.

Her purpose is to support, empower, inspire, motivate and donate.

By focusing on self-exploration, inquiry and discovery to overcome blocks and challenges she assists women in reclaiming their personal power and to connect more deeply to their strengths, whether that be professional, personal, relationships, etc.

Dawnalyn's methods are rooted in both personal experiences with self discovery and healing and, her professional experience in therapeutic relationship building, yogic philosophy, skills in alternative health care, teaching, leadership and mentorship

Your Business Is Not Your Identity

By Alyssa Schmidt

Someone close to me once said: "always start with why." So that's exactly what I'm going to do. I'll be honest, being an entrepreneur never crossed my mind when I was asked what I wanted to do for a living. According to my parents, I wanted to be a doctor by grade 5, and not just any doctor, an anesthesiologist. Clearly, I watched too much ER as a child. I stuck to this path moving into University. Within pre-med, I fell in love with the brain and decided to switch to the honours psychology program with the intention of going for a PhD in neuro-clinical psychology. Then life happened.

I left University after writing a thesis focusing on developmental child psychology, vowing to never work with children again; I had spent 7-8 years with children with developmental disorders by that point. Naturally, I did exactly what I said I wouldn't do and ended up at an intensive trauma treatment home for children. Okay universe, what are you doing? The truth is, I was good at it, BUT, I was a workaholic who also invests a little too much emotionally. I became attached to some of the kids I worked with and started my first lessons with boundaries the hard way. As I was suffering burn out, I started seeing an acupuncturist and doing yoga to try and help balance me out. Funny thing about working with trauma, usually at some point your own s**t comes up and that can be a major slap by reality. Acupuncture and yoga brought me into my body for the first time and unleashed a whole new world I was unaware of. I fell apart completely, as the life I thought I knew seemed to be stripped away from me. My perfect childhood that was all rainbows and unicorns? Gone. At least, that's how it felt. My repressed traumas surfaced along with all the emotions I never allowed myself to feel. I am quite close with my parents, so trying to navigate this part of my childhood was confusing. I had moments thinking I was clinically insane and needed to check myself into an institute. I became depressed hitting my first rock bottom. What does that look like for me? To the person who was always happy, positive, energetic, health/fitness fanatic, perfectionist, it was devastating. I spent hours every day before work lying in bed lost, ruminating about the best way to end my life. I felt completely alone and unimportant. Working out became a chore. When I came home from work, I made a cocktail consisting of a variety of pills and maybe some wine to chase it down, just so I could turn off my mind and escape everything I was feeling emotionally to get a few hours of sleep. In my sleep, I was haunted by past memories.

Me being me, I thought I would figure this out myself. I was already doing this for a living, how hard could it be to apply it to myself? I bought books about trauma in the body and navigating the process of healing. I'm sure those of you reading this now are already predicting how this went. It didn't f**king work! Surprise, right? The mind that created negative coping strategies to deal with the trauma, is concurrently overwhelmed, and is self destructive was suppose to fix it? I can laugh at this now.

With the help of my roommate, I began to reach out for help. She helped me find a therapist and even walked with me to my first appointment to ensure I went. At first, I went downhill with therapy; I didn't feel better at all. My anxiety and depression worsened, but I continued to go twice a week at this point. I bumped into an old friend walking in the river valley, and we went for coffee. She referred me to a Craniosacral Therapist. At this point I was working out 5-6 days a week, attending yin yoga classes (which by the way, I absolutely hated at first), seeing a therapist, Craniosacral Therapy, and my chiropractor. I was desperate to get better. I joined the Centre for

Spiritual Living to be with a community of people who expressed love and didn't know me. Who was this person? Anyone who knew me before this point, knew me as someone who was scientifically driven, emotionally disconnected, and did not believe in any god or spirituality. Little did I know, this wasn't me losing my mind. It was me waking the f**k up! I was becoming conscious for the first time in my life, and man was it a painful experience. But I was healing and becoming the truer version of myself.

This experience led me to my true purpose and opened the doors for me to help people with their health, but in a different way. I realized that the medical model of the West has its limitations and science is not the end all be all. Some things cannot be explained through numbers and experiments. Moreover, many of us often look at our health through a narrow lens that does not truly encompass wholeness. When it comes to trauma, we become such fragmented beings and we need to put the pieces back together. It's going to take more than one approach to get there. I had a vision to create a safe place to help others heal, as everyone has some sort of trauma and all of us need some form of healing. It was tough for me to go from practitioner to practitioner, always starting from scratch and having to tell my story of why I was sitting in their office. If you don't know, people trying to open up and get help for the first time typically struggle hard and feel a lot of shame.

My intention behind 4 Points Health and Wellness was to offer people a team of like-minded practitioners who share similar values around health and wellbeing. I did not want people to have to go from place to place, hunting down various practitioners, paying more money, and retelling their story over and over. More importantly, I wanted the person to walk through the doors and feel like they were part of a community; a community that they mattered within. After all, one of the most healing aspects of my journey, and in my life currently, was the connection I felt in the yoga community, group fitness and Centre for Spiritual Living. Without those, I don't know where I would be today. As Brene Brown says, "we are neurobiologically wired for connection." Intrinsically, we heal by connecting with our self with others.

Fast forward to today. 4 Points is 5 years old, and I have grown more being an entrepreneur than any other stage of my life. There have been some tough lessons, and many breakdowns. So how does one keep a "4 Points life" of balance and health while growing a business from ground zero? I would be lying if I told you I had it all figured out. I have learned what not to do and hope to point you in a better direction. As mentioned earlier, I reached a burn out point before my rock bottom breakdown. Since then, I have hit burnout more than once running 4 Points. This past year I did it again, but this time, I shifted my perspective after an unexpected event. At the end of last year, I lost someone closest to me, whom I considered a rock in my life. The one I went to every time s**t hit the fan, another relationship failed, or I needed guidance. And my first thought? I wish I made more time.

Maintaining relationships, self care and boundaries are vital to survive this long-term. Time is the most valuable thing we can give. Starting a business means you need to work a ridiculous number of hours to keep it alive and get it off the ground; with no initial pay-out I might add. It is your life and you have to be available most hours of the day. You don't get to "leave your work at work," the same way a typical 9-5 career does. This is reality, and necessary to achieve the end goal. However, you need to make the time for the people most important to you in your life, no matter what. Mahin Daniel says, "in the end, it's not the years in your life that count. It's all about the memories you made when life gave you a chance to make one." Sharing our best moments with people we love and care about is what matters most. Your business can fail at any time, that is the truth and reality of anyone taking the risk of starting a business, and if you neglect your important relationships, what is left when the one thing you have given all your attention to is gone? Do I have great memories with the people I work with and building this business? Absolutely! And I'm damn proud! But, in the end, we need a life outside our business. It's too easy for your business to become your identity. People in your life will understand you need to work more than the average person, but don't forget to value the people who are supporting you and will be there in the end. Boundaries between your work and personal life are imperative.

Boundaries are often misunderstood and seen as synonymous with being mean, unaccommodating, putting up walls, etc. The truth is boundaries are created with love and respect. Boundaries allow all parties involved to preserve their self-worth and create a mutual love and respect. Boundaries enable us to teach others what we will and will not accept, growing a deeper connection in the relationship. This is quite different from walls which keep everyone out. Boundaries can be applied in all aspects of life including our business relationships. In business, one learns quick that this is non-negotiable. When making new partnerships or negotiating in business, you must remember the person sitting across from you is not your friend; they are an entrepreneur as well looking out for their own best interest. If they can get a better deal at your expense, they will take advantage of your naivety or lack of "back bone." Fight for your worth, and do not negotiate anything less. Learn to say no and embrace the discomfort you will initially feel. If it does not serve you, let it go. Something that fits your vision and values will show up; keep the door open. This applies to your romantic life too! When first starting out, we often feel desperate to make connections and bring people into our business so we can pay the bills. This usually results in getting walked over, taken advantage of and burnt out faster. Say No! If it is your day off, only tend to what's necessary. There are often minor necessary engagements, and that's okay, it's part of your role as an owner. Use this time to connect and maintain your relationships and do your self-care.

Self-care? The last thing on my mind was self-care when I was just starting out. I STILL need to be reminded by my business partner and team to do this, but if we don't take care of ourselves to maintain our sanity and physical health, we eventually begin to pour from and empty cup. At this point, we risk making needless mistakes that may cost the business money, or worse, our clients will suffer. This will have a chain effect and begin to impact all other areas of our lives including those previously mentioned relationships.

We want to be the best version of our self and live a quality of life that makes us happy. Isn't that what everyone wants? So, my advice to you, even if you're not an entrepreneur: Be vulnerable and take chances to do what you're passionate about. Remember to prioritize your loved ones, embrace boundaries, and do your self-care so you can live a more balanced life while on the journey you choose to walk, and always lead with why.

4pointshealthandwellness@gmail.com

4pointshealth.com

Alyssa was born and raised in Edmonton, and grew up passionate about sports. She always had an interest in health, seeking a University education in psychology. Working in an intensive trauma treatment home for children, Alyssa began to see the value of integrating health modalities to help individuals resolve trauma related issues. Through her own personal health journey, she began to envision a different approach to healing. She founded 4 Points Health and Wellness in 2014 and began to build a team of practitioners whose values were in line with her vision. Alyssa continues to build upon her passion with health and sharing her knowledge to help others along their journey to wellness.

Afterword

There you have it. The latest edition of the bLU Talks book series. My hope is that you leave this book feeling inspired, motivated, educated, and entertained. I know I am.

I also hope this book gives you a distraction from everything that is going on in the world as we wrote it.

The co-authors here have bared their souls for you. I myself, in reading this edition, was close to tears and past laughter at many points.

I am as proud of the authors in this edition, as if I was sitting there writing their stories with them.

I believe many people spend a lot of focus on feeding their body, and yet far too little focus on feeding their mind.

I hope this book helps to solve that problem at least to some degree, and at the same time, you may acquire methods for taking care of your health just the same.

This edition is also far from the last edition, and so with great excitement, I say, To Be Continued... (and thank you for joining us on this journey)

Corey Poirier

Dec. 2020

Source: *12 Businesses that started During a Recession,*
by Annisha on Looka, April 14, 2020

Made in the USA
Columbia, SC
15 January 2021